The Bakhtin Circle

The Bakhtin Circle
Philosophy, Culture and Politics

Craig Brandist

Pluto Press
LONDON • STERLING, VIRGINIA

First published 2002 by Pluto Press
345 Archway Road, London N6 5AA
and 22883 Quicksilver Drive,
Sterling, VA 20166–2012, USA

www.plutobooks.com

British Library Cataloguing in Publication Data
A catalogue record for this book is available from the British Library

ISBN 0 7453 1811 8 hardback
ISBN 0 7453 1810 X paperback

Library of Congress Cataloging in Publication Data
A catalogue record for this book is available

Reprints: 10 9 8 7 6 5 4 3 2 1 0

Designed and produced for Pluto Press by
Chase Publishing Services, Fortescue, Sidmouth EX10 9QG
Typeset from disk by Stanford DTP Services, Towcester
Printed in the European Union by Antony Rowe, Chippenham, England

Contents

Preface

The present work began its life as a project commissioned by a different publisher to write a historically grounded introduction to the work of the Bakhtin Circle. In the course of composition and negotiation it turned out that what was required was rather more of an introductory text than I was prepared to compose. After spending several years researching the intellectual sources of the work of the Circle in the Bakhtin Centre at Sheffield University as part of the project 'The Russian and European Contexts of the Works of Mikhail Bakhtin and the Bakhtin Circle', funded by the British Arts and Humanities Research Board (AHRB), I was keen to make sure that new research on the work of the Circle formed the basis of the study. The 'primer' format excluded such a possibility. The work was thereafter completely redesigned critically to survey the work of the Circle in the light of the considerable amount of research into the sources of their ideas carried out by a number of Russian and Western scholars in recent years. As well as bringing together the insights of others, I was naturally concerned to foreground my own research. This is most apparent in analyses of the Circle's debts to Hegelianism and Marxism, the Brentanian tradition exemplified by such figures as Karl Bühler and Anton Marty, Oskar Walzel and the mediation of the ideas of such figures as Lucien Lévy-Bruhl and Ernst Cassirer through the work of Nikolai Marr and his followers, particularly Ol´ga Freidenberg.

In highlighting the sources of the ideas of the Circle I do not want to suggest that they had little original to say. Rather, I am concerned to show that while Bakhtin himself was a less revolutionary thinker than was often argued in the 1980s, and is still often argued in Russia, members of *the Bakhtin Circle* were nevertheless talented and significant thinkers who responded to the ideas around them in extremely productive ways. In understanding the work of the Circle as an ongoing engagement with several intellectual traditions, we also need to be aware of the specific social and political circumstances that conditioned that engagement. While the coherence of the ideas of the members of the Circle and their individual contributions might appear to be lessened by such an approach, the historical significance of their engagement and the importance of the ideas with which they grappled are heightened. Intellectual history is not a gallery of great individual thinkers, but a history of ideas in their socio-historical becoming, enmeshed in institutional forms and ideological battles. The Circle lived through some of the most significant transformations of the twentieth century, and they necessarily rethought their ideas in relation not only to new publications but also to the wider conflicts of the world around them. We can thus learn as much, if not more, from their revisions, contradictions and limitations as we can from their greatest successes and systematic expositions.

In writing this study I have accumulated debts to several scholars, to whom I have turned for information and advice or with whom I have debated, clashed, polemicised or simply chatted over the last few years. Among these I must highlight Galin Tihanov, whose formidable knowledge of debates in several languages, good humour, helpfulness and encouragement have been unfailing supports; David Shepherd, whose constant intellectual and practical support has been a precondition of much of the work done here; Iurii and Dar´ia Medvedev and Dmitri Iunov, whose hospitality, good will, knowledge and intellectual stimulation have helped to make my frequent visits to St Petersburg so valuable; Nikolai Nikolaev, Nikolai Pan´kov, Vladimir Alpatov and Vitalii Makhlin for their good-natured support, hospitality and/or assistance in Russia and abroad; and Mika Lähteenmäki for many valuable discussions about the philosophy of language and for facilitating opportunities to present my research in Finland. I have also benefited from discussions with, among many others, Brian Poole, Michael Gardiner, Ken Hirschkop, Erik Dop, Jonathan Hall and my many other interlocutors on the conference circuit: the present book would certainly be poorer without them all.

The text itself has benefited considerably from the critical responses of David Shepherd, Galin Tihanov, Mika Lähteenmäki and Karine Zbinden, who read parts or the whole manuscript at various stages, pointing out my many misconceptions, exaggerations, flawed expressions and confusions. While the text has certainly been improved by their interventions, any remaining flaws are, of course, my own responsibility.

The following text makes no pretensions to be an exhaustive account of the sources of the works of the Bakhtin Circle; while archival access remains severely restricted this will be deferred.

However, an account of some of the main contours of the Circle's engagements with the ideas around them and an indication of how I think this should inform our reading and application of their work are presented below. Furthermore, I have attempted to consider some of the many problems and limitations of the work of the Circle and some possible revisions that may overcome these difficulties. If the book stimulates and facilitates further non-reverential, historically grounded and constructive engagements with the work of the Circle it will have succeeded in its aim.

1 Introduction

The problems of Bakhtin studies

The work of Mikhail Bakhtin and what is now known as the Bakhtin Circle has, in recent years, aroused enormous interest and exerted a significant influence on a variety of areas within the humanities and social sciences. The Circle's work on the philosophy of language, the study of Russian Formalism, and the theory and history of the novel have become firmly established as very important developments in all these fields. Although the Circle's initial impact was within literary and cultural studies, it has now begun to establish a presence within philosophy, social science, history and cultural studies. Bakhtin's key notions of dialogism and carnival have been adopted as analytical tools for examining such varied phenomena as the novels of Jane Austen, popular uprisings in the Middle Ages, the Blackpool Pleasure Beach, Brazilian cinema and the car boot sale. The bewildering variety of applications is mirrored by an equally bewildering variety of comparisons with the ideas of other thinkers, including Marxist theorists such as Walter Benjamin and Theodor Adorno, phenomenological philosophers like Edmund Husserl and Maurice Merleau-Ponty, American pragmatists, Jewish mystics and Russian Orthodox theologians. In such circumstances it is hardly surprising that the newcomer to Bakhtin often finds him- or herself confronted by an implausible variety of perspectives on a single figure. In the last 30 years there has been a slowly increasing torrent of Russian and English publications about Bakhtin. Ten large international conferences and numerous smaller events dedicated to the Bakhtin Circle have been staged, and there is little sign of interest waning. Bakhtin, it seems, offers something to everyone. He is invoked in the cause of liberal humanist criticism, idealist philosophy, Russian nationalism, Marxism, anti-Marxism, postcolonial theory and many more positions besides. Indeed, it often seems there are as many 'Bakhtins' as there are interpreters.

It is important to understand why this situation has arisen. The terminology of the Bakhtin Circle, and especially that of Bakhtin himself, is rather particular and has a plurality of connotations. Terms such as 'monologue' and 'dialogue', for example, may seem

1

innocuous enough, but the sociological and philosophical loads that Bakhtin forces the concepts to bear is quite unusual. During the Stalin years, when censorship was particularly tight, this strategy was employed to discuss social questions that would otherwise have been out of bounds. Terms such as 'poetry' and 'the novel' and words derived from them were endowed with a significance that extended far beyond their normal aesthetic meanings so that they gained an ethical and even a socio-political character. At the same time words that had an established socio-political resonance were employed in a more broadly philosophical fashion. The borders between ethics, aesthetics and politics therefore became unclear, as one layer of meaning was deposited on another, leading to the formation of subtexts. This left the way open to, and indeed encouraged, a wide range of interpretations, but this was not the whole story.

As we shall see later, the majority of the philosophical ideas with which the Circle were working did not originate in Russia, and the rendering of key terms in the Russian language was fraught with difficulties. German philosophical terms were imported into a language without an established philosophical discourse and in the absence of ready-made alternatives the great morphological flexibility of the Russian language was employed. Words with an everyday meaning had prefixes and suffixes grafted on to them and were used in new ways, leading the final product to acquire additional connotations. Sometimes two Russian words were employed to render a single German word, or one Russian for two German, with the result that the connection between a term and the tradition from which it derived was obscured. This obscurity was, on occasion, deliberately utilised to conceal sources unacceptable to those in authority who decided upon publication. Then there are problems that derive from Bakhtin's own compositional practice. While in the late 1920s two major members of the Circle, Voloshinov and Medvedev, were consistent and relatively open about providing footnote references to the works upon which they were drawing, Bakhtin was notoriously cavalier about such matters even before censorship was a serious problem. Bakhtin's rather condescending attitude was signalled in an essay of 1924:

> We have also freed our work from the superfluous ballast of citations and references, which generally have no directly methodological significance in non-historical research, and in a compressed work of a systematic character they are absolutely

superfluous: they are unnecessary for the competent reader and useless for the incompetent. (PCMF 257; PSMF 259)

This has led some scholars in the area to base their interpretations on the very terminological resemblances with the work of other thinkers that, we have seen, is deeply problematic. Bakhtin's archive remained firmly closed until very recently, with the effect that the sources upon which he drew could only be guessed at and were sometimes ignored totally. The peculiarity of terminology, the absence of any obvious intellectual parallels and of any reference to sources led some to see Bakhtin as a totally original thinker of truly monumental genius who anticipated whole schools of thought. If this were not enough, the history of publication and translation further complicated matters.

Problems of publication and translation

Apart from a few scattered minor articles in periodicals only the two editions of Bakhtin's now famous studies of the works of Dostoevsky (PTD (1929) and PPD (1963)) and Rabelais (TFR/RW (1965)) were published in his name in his own lifetime. Since his death, however, several collections of his work have appeared in Russian, in which works from several different periods in Bakhtin's career, often written up to 50 years apart, are gathered together. This has rendered the task of seeing Bakhtin's work as a developing whole extremely problematic. The earlier works have been read through the prism of the later work, giving the impression that his ideas did not fundamentally change. Furthermore, much of this work had not been prepared for publication by Bakhtin himself and so it is uncertain if these texts constitute anything like definitive editions of the works in question. A paucity of information about the manuscripts, and of informative editorial notes by competent scholars with archival access, meant that the material was often presented in a rather baffling, raw form.

The translation of these works into Western European languages has often added an additional layer of confusion for readers without access to the originals. English-language translations have been appearing since 1968, although the quality of translation and editorial work has been extremely uneven. Up to ten different translators have published work by a writer whose terminology is very specific, often rendering key concepts in a variety of different ways. To take just one example: the word *stanovlenie*, which we now know derives from the German *das Werden*, and which is usually rendered in English translations of Hegel as *becoming,* is rendered in no fewer than ten different ways in the English translations, including 'emergence' and 'development'. It even appears in four different and unacknowledged variants within a single text. Such translations further obscure the philosophical resonance of such central terms and thus of the work in general. It is not only a question of consistency, however, for some translations include serious mistakes and omissions that have further compounded the problems inherent in the Russian texts. These problems to various degrees also plague translations into French, Italian and German. It is for these reasons that the quotations of the work of the Circle given in this book will be my own translations, and reference will be given both to the currently available English translation and to the Russian original.

Finally, there is the problem of authorship of the works published in the names of Voloshinov and Medvedev, and of the extent to which the Marxist vocabulary found therein should be taken at face value. Although these works are rather less problematic in terms of establishing some of their philosophical sources, the water has been muddied by an argument over the very character of the works. Those, for example, who argue for Bakhtin's sole authorship also tend to argue that the specifically Marxist vocabulary that appears here is mere 'window dressing' to facilitate publication, while those who support the authenticity of the original publications also tend to take the Marxist arguments seriously. Moreover, those who deny that these works are the work of their signatories downplay the general significance of these figures, and the distinct perspectives presented in the texts are thereby minimised. The current study seeks to highlight the original character of these works.[1] As a result of this, and of the other problems mentioned above, commentators on Bakhtin have tended to choose one period of Bakhtin's career and treat it as definitive, a practice which has produced a variety of divergent versions of 'Bakhtinian' thought. The recent appearance of the first volumes of a collected works in Russian and the planned publication of a harmonised English translation should help to overcome some of these problems, while recent archival work has uncovered some of Bakhtin's notebooks, which point to the sources of his ideas.

The current book aims to help the reader find his or her way through this maze of appropriations and some of the problems inherent in the primary texts that gave rise to it by investigating some of the foundations of the Circle's ideas. In the 1980s Bakhtin was often presented as a single isolated individual writing on a wide range of material in his own name and in that of his friends and developing a totally original and unitary philosophical method. This has begun to change significantly, even though Bakhtin's manuscripts are still carefully guarded by the custodians of his estate. It is surely a strange situation when even the editors of the new complete edition of his works in Russian have not all had access to the entire archive. It seems that as this material becomes available we shall uncover further influences on his work not discussed here; but an important start has been made. As we will see, the work of the Circle needs to be understood within the European intellectual context of its time, and seen as a particular ongoing synthesis of mainly German philosophical currents in peculiarly Soviet contexts. Only this can really explain the similarities and differences between the work of the Bakhtin Circle and that of mainstream cultural theorists, sociologists and philosophers, and facilitate a meaningful engagement with their ideas.

A historically and philosophically grounded study of the work of the Circle is a precondition for any assessment of the strengths and limitations of its ideas and thus for well-rooted applications. Where certain categories turn out to have been based on philosophical principles that have been seriously undermined in subsequent work, it is likely that the categories themselves need to be reconsidered. Similarly, knowledge of the philosophical resonance of certain ideas will often make those who attempt to combine them with ideas from other traditions more aware of what is at stake in such an enterprise. This book therefore aims to encourage the reader to engage critically with the work of the Circle rather than simply adopt any of their specific formulations. It will provide little comfort for those who wish simply to apply the work of the Circle as a completed whole, but should help to facilitate more substantial engagements, and the development of more adequate critical perspectives.

Biographical sketch

The Bakhtin Circle, which at various times included Mikhail Mikhailovich Bakhtin (1895–1975), Mariia Veniaminovna Iudina (1899–1970), Matvei Isaevich Kagan (1889–1937), Ivan Ivanovich Kanaev (1893–1984), Pavel Nikolaevich Medvedev (1891–1938), Lev Vasilievich Pumpianskii (1891–1940), Ivan Ivanovich Sollertinskii

(1902–1944), Konstantin Konstantinovich Vaginov (1899–1934) and Valentin Nikolaevich Voloshinov (1895–1936), began meeting in the provincial town of Nevel and the major Belorussian town of Vitebsk in 1918, before moving to Leningrad in 1924. Their group meetings were terminated following the arrest of some of the group in 1929. From this time until his death in 1975, Bakhtin continued to work on the topics which had occupied the group, living in internal exile first in Kustanai (Kazakhstan, 1930–36), Savelovo (about 100 km from Moscow, 1937–45), Saransk (Mordvinia, 1936–37, 1945–69), and finally moving in 1969 to Moscow, where he died at the age of 80. In Saransk, Bakhtin worked at the Mordvinia Pedagogical Institute (now University) until retirement in 1961.

The Bakhtin Circle is reputed to have been initiated by Kagan on his return from Germany, where he had studied philosophy in Leipzig, Berlin and Marburg. He had been a pupil of the founder of Marburg Neo-Kantianism, Hermann Cohen, and had attended lectures by Ernst Cassirer, a philosopher who was to figure significantly in Bakhtin's later work. Kagan established a 'Kantian Seminar' at which various philosophical, religious and cultural issues were discussed. Kagan was a Jewish intellectual who had been a member of the Social Democratic Party (the precursor of the Bolsheviks and Mensheviks) but was attracted by the ethical socialism of the Marburg School (Cohen regarded his ethical philosophy as completely compatible with that implicit in Marx's works). The Circle did not restrict itself to academic philosophy but became closely involved in the radical cultural activities of the time, activities that became more intense with the relocation of the group to Vitebsk, where many important avant-garde artists such as Malevich and Chagall had settled to escape the privations of the Civil War. One of the group, Pavel Medvedev, a graduate in law from Petrograd University, was before joining the group already an established literary scholar, with publications dating back to 1912. Medvedev became rector of the Vitebsk Proletarian University, for a time served as the equivalent of Vitebsk's mayor, and edited the town's cultural journal *Iskusstvo* (Art) to which he and Voloshinov contributed articles. Medvedev's established position within Soviet society was later to facilitate the publication of some of the Circle's works, but his high profile also made him a target of Stalin's purges. While in Vitebsk, Bakhtin and Pumpianskii both gave public lectures on a variety of philosophical and cultural topics, some notes from which have now been published (LVB).

It is known that neither Bakhtin nor Pumpianskii, the future literary scholar, ever finished their studies at Petrograd University, despite the former's repeated claims, now disproven, to have graduated in 1918. It seems that Bakhtin attempted to gain acceptance in academic circles by adopting aspects of his older brother's biography. Nikolai Bakhtin had indeed graduated from Petrograd University, where he had been a pupil of the renowned classicist F.F. Zelinskii, and the Bakhtin brothers discussed philosophical ideas from their youth. Nikolai was compelled to leave Russia after the rout of the White Army, into which he had enlisted (Bachtin 1963: 45–61), and contacts between the two brothers seem from then on to have been severely limited. When Mikhail moved to Nevel, it seems that Kagan took the place of his brother as unofficial mentor, exerting an important influence on Bakhtin's philosophy in a new and exciting cultural environment, although the two friends went their separate ways in 1921, the year Bakhtin married.

Kagan moved to take up a teaching position at the newly established provincial university in Orel in 1921. While there he wrote, in 1922, the only sustained piece of philosophy to be published by a member of the group before the late 1920s, entitled 'Kak vozmozhna istoriia?' (How is History Possible?). The same year he produced an obituary of Hermann Cohen, in which he stressed the historical and sociological aspects of Cohen's philosophy, and wrote other unpublished works. 1922 also saw the publication of Pumpianskii's paper 'Dostoevskii i antichnost' (Dostoevsky and Antiquity), a theme that was to recur in Bakhtin's work for many years. While Bakhtin himself did not publish any substantial work until 1929, he was clearly working on matters related to neo-Kantian philosophy and the problem of authorship at this time. Bakhtin's earliest published work is the two-page 'Iskusstvo i otvetstvennost' (Art and Responsibility) from 1919, but a larger project on moral philosophy written in the early 1920s, now usually referred to as *K filosofii postupka* (Toward a Philosophy of the Act), remained unpublished until surviving fragments were published in the 1980s.

Most of the group's significant work was produced after its move to Leningrad in 1924, where new members joined the Circle, such as the biologist and later historian of science Ivan I. Kanaev and the specialist in Eastern philosophy and religion, Mikhail I. Tubianskii. It seems that the group soon became acutely aware of the challenge posed by Saussurean linguistics and its development in the work of the Formalists, both of which will be discussed later. Thus, there emerges a new awareness of the importance of the philosophy of language in psychology, philosophy and poetics. Voloshinov enrolled as a postgraduate at the Institute for the Comparative History of the Literatures and Languages of the West and East (ILIaZV) in 1925, where he was supervised by the Marxist literary critic V.A. Desnitskii and advised by the linguist and specialist on dialogue Lev Iakubinskii. Until 1933 he also wrote abstracts of new foreign works on literature and philology for the institute, information which was subsequently provided to the Circle.[2] It is therefore not surprising that the most significant work on the philosophy of language published in the period 1926–30 was composed by Voloshinov: a series of articles and a book entitled *Marksizm i filosofiia iazyka* (Marxism and the Philosophy of Language, 1929). Medvedev, who obtained access to the archive of the symbolist poet Aleksandr Blok, participated in the vigorous discussions between Marxist and Formalist literary theorists with a series of articles and a book, *Formal'nyi metod v literaturovedenii* (The Formal Method in Literary Scholarship, 1928), and one of the first serious book-length studies of Blok's work. Voloshinov also published an article and a book (PTSS (1925); FKO and FMC (1927)) on the debate that raged around Freudianism at the time. In 1929 Bakhtin produced the first edition of his now famous monograph *Problemy tvorchestva Dostoevskogo* (Problems of Dostoevsky's Work, 1929), but other works dating from 1924–29 remained unpublished and usually unfinished. Among these was a (completed) critical essay on Formalism entitled 'Problema soderzheniia, materiala i formy v slovesnom khudozhestvennom tvorchestve' (The Problem of Content, Material and Form in Verbal Artistic Creation) (1924) and the unfinished book-length *Avtor i geroi v esteticheskoi deiatel'nosti* (Author and Hero in Aesthetic Activity) (mid 1920s).

Since the 1970s the works published under the names of Voloshinov and Medvedev have often been ascribed to Bakhtin, who neither consented nor objected unambiguously to this ascription, at least in writing. A voluminous, ideologically motivated, often bad-tempered and largely futile body of literature has grown up to debate the issue. Since there is no concrete evidence to suggest that the authors whose names appear on the publications were not at least largely responsible for the texts that bear their names, however, there seems no real case to answer. The verbal testimony usually adduced to support Bakhtin's authorship cannot be objectively confirmed, and most derives from sources who are certainly not neutral with regard to the debate in ideological or, indeed, in financial terms. Furthermore, archival evidence (LDV, Medvedev 1998) shows that Voloshinov and Medvedev were indeed specialists in the areas in which they published, at a time when Bakhtin was primarily concerned with other matters. It seems much more likely that the materials were written as a result of lively group discussions around these issues, in which group members presented papers for discussion based on their own research and then amended them in the light of the comments of their colleagues. There are clearly many philosophical, ideological and stylistic discrepancies which, despite the presence of certain parallels and points of agreement, suggest that these very different works were largely the work of different authors. In accordance with Bakhtin's own philosophy, it seems reasonable to treat them as rejoinders in ongoing dialogues between group members on the one hand and between the group and other contemporary thinkers on the other.[3]

The sharp downturn in the fortunes of unorthodox intellectuals in the Soviet Union at the end of 1928 effectively broke the Bakhtin Circle up. Bakhtin, whose health had already begun to deteriorate, was arrested, presumably because of his connection with the religious-philosophical and quasi-masonic group *Voskresenie* (Resurrection), and was sentenced to ten years on the Solovki Islands. After vigorous intercession by Bakhtin's friends, a favourable review of his Dostoevsky book by the Commissar of Enlightenment Anatolii Lunacharskii, and a personal appeal by the major writer Maksim Gor'kii, this was commuted to six years' exile in Kazakhstan. With the tightening of censorship at the time, very little more by Voloshinov appeared in print, while Medvedev published a book on theories of authorship, *V laboratorii pisatelia* (In the Laboratory of the Writer) in 1933 and a new version of the Formalism study, revised to fit in more closely with the ideological requirements of the time, in 1934. Medvedev was appointed full professor at the Leningrad Historico-Philological Institute, but was arrested and disappeared during the terror of 1938. Voloshinov worked at the Herzen Pedagogical Institute in Leningrad until 1934, when he contracted tuberculosis. He died in a sanitorium two years later, leaving unfinished a translation of the first volume of Ernst Cassirer's *The Philosophy of Symbolic Forms*, a book that is of considerable importance to the work of the Circle. Kagan died of angina in 1937 after working as editor of an encyclopedic atlas of energy resources in the Soviet Union for many years. Pumpianskii pursued a successful career as Professor of Literature at Leningrad University, but published only articles and introductions to works of classical Russian authors. Sollertinskii joined the Leningrad Philharmonic in 1927 as a lecturer, but soon established himself as one of the leading Soviet musicologists, producing over 200 articles, books and reviews. He died of a heart attack, probably resulting from the privations of the Leningrad blockade, in 1944. Kanaev worked as a highly successful and respected experimental geneticist in Leningrad, but in 1951 took up a post at the Leningrad branch of the Institute of the History of the Natural Sciences and Technology, under the auspices of the USSR Academy of Sciences. From this time Kanaev produced many works on the history of science, with particular reference to Goethe.

While in Kazakhstan, Bakhtin began work on his now famous theory of the novel, which resulted in the articles *Slovo v romane* (Discourse in the Novel) (1934–35), *Iz predystorii romannogo slovo* (From the Prehistory of Novelistic Discourse) (1940), *Epos i roman* (Epic and Novel) (1941), *Formy vremeni i khronotopa v romane* (Forms of Time and Chronotope in the Novel) (1937–38). Between 1936 and 1938 he completed a book on the *Bildungsroman* (novel of education) and its significance in the history of realism; this was allegedly lost when the publishing house at which the manuscript was awaiting publication was destroyed in the early days of the German invasion of the Soviet Union in 1941. Voluminous preparatory material still exists, although part is lost according to one, possibly spurious, story because Bakhtin used it for cigarette papers during the wartime paper shortage. Bakhtin's exceptional productiveness at this time is even more remarkable when one considers that one of his legs was amputated in February 1938. He had suffered from inflammation of the bone marrow, osteomyelitis, for many years, which gave him a lot of pain, high temperatures, and often confined him to bed for weeks on end. This had been a factor in the appeals of his friends and acquaintances for clemency when he was internally exiled, a factor that may well have saved his life. It did not, however, prevent him from presenting his doctoral thesis on the great French novelist Rabelais to the Gor´kii Institute of World Literature in 1940. The work proved extremely controversial in the hostile ideological climate of the time, and it was not until 1951 that Bakhtin was eventually granted the qualification of *kandidat*.[4] His thesis was published (in amended form) in 1965.

The period between the completion of the Rabelais study and the second edition of the Dostoevsky study in 1963 is perhaps the least well known of Bakhtin's life in terms of work produced. This has recently (1996) been rectified with the publication of archival materials from this period, when Bakhtin was working as a lecturer at the Mordvinia Pedagogical Institute. The most substantial work dating from this period is *Problema rechevykh zhanrov* (The Problem of Discursive Genres), which was most likely produced in response to the reorganisation of Soviet linguistics in the wake of Stalin's article *Marksizm i voprosy iazykoznaniia* (Marxism and Questions of Linguistics) of 1950. Many other fragments exist from this time, including notes for a planned article about the Futurist poet and dramatist Maiakovskii and more methodological comments on the study of the novel.

In the more liberal atmosphere of the so-called 'thaw' following Khrushchev's accession to power, Bakhtin's work on Dostoevsky came to the attention of a group of younger scholars led by Vadim Kozhinov who, upon finding out that Bakhtin was still alive, contacted him and tried to persuade him to republish the 1929 Dostoevsky book. After some initial hesitation, Bakhtin responded by significantly expanding and fundamentally altering the overall project. It was accepted for publication in September 1963 and had a generally favourable reception. Publication of the Rabelais study, newly edited for purposes of acceptability (mainly the toning down of scatology and the removal of an analysis of a speech by Lenin) followed soon afterwards. As Bakhtin's health continued to decline, he was taken to hospital in Moscow in 1969, and in May 1970 he and his wife, who died a year later, were moved into an old people's home just outside Moscow. Bakhtin continued to work until just before his death in 1975, producing work of a mainly methodological character.

The phenomenon of the Circle

The Bakhtin Circle as an institutional phenomenon in some ways inherited the tradition of discussion circles (*krug*) that had been a major form of intellectual life in Russia since the 1830s. The economic and political backwardness of Tsarist Russia, coupled with the ruling class's hesitant and sporadic attempts to Westernise the state in the face of European imperial expansion created a democratically minded intelligentsia without firm institutional foundations (Raeff 1966). Faced with severe censorship, the disaffected intelligentsia formed secret discussion circles in which their enlightenment ideals could be given expression. The critiques they developed of the Russian social structure could not lead to open political movements in the Russian Empire, and so they often took the guise of literary criticism. Ultimately, such groups became the basis of the revolutionary political parties that came to the fore as the state structure proved incapable of controlling the forces it had unleashed in the drive to industrialisation that followed defeat in the Crimean War (1854–56) (Venturi 1960).

In the immediate post-revolutionary and post–Civil War period a more open form of intellectual life was a real possibility, for those at least not hostile toward the current direction of social and political change (Kagarlitsky 1989), and it was in these circumstances that the Bakhtin Circle was formed. The topics with which the Circle was to engage were those shaped by the concerns of the pre-revolutionary intelligentsia, but updated according to the new social, political and intellectual context. As we shall see, this is particularly important in understanding the relationship between ethics and literature. During the so-called 'cultural revolution' that was part of Stalin's 'revolution from above' (1928–32) the ability of such circles to maintain a formal existence was abruptly ended. However, the concerns of the pre-revolutionary intelligentsia remained, in amended forms, in the work of Bakhtin throughout his career. In this sense the experience of the Circle was a formative one for Bakhtin.

Periods of work

Although it is impossible to draw firm boundaries, we can provisionally state that the work of the Bakhtin Circle falls into the following periods:

(1) Early philosophical work on ethics and aesthetics (1919–26)
(2) Works dealing with the philosophy of language and of signification in general, with particular reference to literary material (1927–29)
(3) Bakhtin's writings on the novel as a genre, and on its history (1934–41)
(4) Works on literature and popular culture, with particular reference to Rabelais, Goethe, Gogol´ and Dostoevsky (1940–63)
(5) Writings of a methodological character (1963–75).

This scheme masks some significant developments. (1) and (2) constitute the works of the Bakhtin Circle, when Bakhtin's own work represents only a distinct contribution to the work of a group, while (3) onward refers to the work of Bakhtin outside a group context. (3) and (4) represent Bakhtin's own work on literature proper, and may be understood as a single subdivided category, but this does not include the first study of Dostoevsky, which is an aspect of (2), or his general aesthetic writings, which are featured in (1). I have devoted a separate chapter to the Dostoevsky study, since it marks an important transitional work. The works mentioned in (3) and (4) are quite distinct from the first Dostoevsky study for they are concerned with literary and cultural *history*, rather than presenting a static phenomenological account of Dostoevsky's method. The period covered by (4) also includes some work of a generally methodological character, most notably the long 1953 essay 'The Problem of Discursive Genres', whose subject matter is much more in keeping with the works considered in (5).

My periodisation avoids the strict dating of the early philosophical texts to the period ending in 1924 which one finds, for example, in Clark and Holquist (1984a) and Morson and Emerson (1990), since the dating of these incomplete texts is problematic. It seems that rather than finishing the texts once and for all, Bakhtin eventually abandoned the projects, probably after a gradual disillusionment with their direction. Furthermore, as Poole (2001b) has argued, they display bibliographic influences that post-date the 1924 threshold. I have also resisted Ken Hirschkop's (1999) characterisation of 1924–29 as a time for Bakhtin's 'turn to science' (linguistics, psychology and sociology) since it appears that while Voloshinov, for example, was working on psychology and the philosophy of language Bakhtin was still predominantly wedded to his earlier philosophical orientations. Bakhtin's transition is apparent only at the end of the 1920s, with the publication of the 1929 Dostoevsky book. Even so, my periodisation remains close to that in all these earlier texts, suggesting that, whatever the substantive disagreements over the interpretations of these works, a significant degree of consensus remains over the shape of Bakhtin's career.

The character of the works in each category and period among other things reflects the influence of particular philosophers and schools of thought. The works in (1) reflect the dominant influence of the neo-Kantian philosophy of the Marburg School, the so-called life-philosophy (*Lebensphilosophie*) of Georg Simmel (1858–1918) and

the phenomenology of Edmund Husserl (1859–1938) and Max
Scheler (1874–1928). Those in (2) constitute the response of the
Circle to, *inter alia*, the challenge of Saussurean linguistics and
Russian Formalism. In addition to the previous influences, that of
the last major Marburg neo-Kantian, Ernst Cassirer (1874–1945),
becomes apparent at this time, particularly in the work of
Voloshinov, but this is tempered by the influence of the anti-
Kantian psychologists and philosophers of language Anton Marty
and Karl Bühler. This crucial influence has been largely ignored in
Bakhtin Circle scholarship and will consequently be given special
attention here. The works of Voloshinov and Medvedev also begin
to take on a Marxist vocabulary and to demonstrate the influence
of Nikolai Bukharin, whose standing within the Soviet Communist
Party was at its height, and of the linguist Nikolai Marr (1864–1934).
The result is a general concern with language and a shift toward a
more sociological vocabulary among all members of the Circle. In
the 1930s Bakhtin's work begins to show the profound and
systematic influence of the work of Cassirer. This is especially clear
in the way that genres are treated as what Cassirer had called
'symbolic forms' which unfold in historical time and enter into
conflicts with each other. Not only had Cassirer been deeply
influenced by the Marburg School and Simmel, but also incorporated significant elements of Hegelian philosophy, the traces of
which can also be seen in Bakhtin's work. For the first time a
systematic historicism appears in these central essays, a feature that
signals not only the influence of Cassirer but also that of the
Hungarian Marxist thinker Georg Lukács, who maintained a high
profile in this period. The dominance of Marrism in the humanities
is also detectable in these works. In the 1940s and 1950s the dual
neo-Kantian and Hegelian aspects of Bakhtin's thought are in uneasy
coexistence, which leads to work of a highly ambivalent character.
An inclination to historicise competes with an attempt to uncover
the eternal elements of culture. Socio-historical conflicts within
culture are now sometimes treated in a fashion reminiscent of
Simmel's notion of an eternal conflict between life and form, an
ambivalence that is most apparent in Bakhtin's study of Rabelais.
Bakhtin's work in this period bears the marks of his isolation: he was
working at a provincial pedagogical institute with little access to
books and was writing at a time when dogmatism reigned in Soviet
scholarship. The only thing that was permitted was the renarration
and application of a set of ideas that were pronounced to be true.

One window of opportunity did, however, open up in June 1950 when Stalin published *Marxism and Questions of Linguistics*, in which the reign of the ideas of the dogmatist linguist Marr was decisively terminated, and linguistics was effectively pronounced to be akin to the natural sciences and thus immune from political considerations. Bakhtin seized the opportunity to return to the areas that had concerned Voloshinov in the late 1920s, but with some significant differences. Fresh from his literary work, Bakhtin seeks to examine the question of genre in language use and thus introduces a new aspect into the Circle's study of language: the distinction between the sentence and the utterance.

The end of the Stalin period led to the opening of a significant space for intellectual debate. It was in this period that Bakhtin published his revised Dostoevsky study (PPD (1963)) and the book on Rabelais (TFR/RW (1965)). The first of these is an excellent illustration of Bakhtin's intellectual ambivalence in the period. The original Dostoevsky study was a static phenomenological analysis of the Russian novelist's artistic design. Except for some minor amendments to terminology this is presented once more in the 1963 version. However, a new 80-page chapter on the history of genre, including a discussion of the concept of carnival, which had been developed in the Rabelais study, has been added. The new chapter bears the marks of the influence of neo-Hegelian philosophy, while the earlier text, into which it was inserted, is a much more neo-Kantian work. In many ways this stands as an index of Bakhtin's intellectual development in the intervening period. Bakhtin's final work is of a methodological character. He returned to many of the concerns of his early years and to a more straightforwardly neo-Kantian attempt to delineate the domains of the individual sciences.

Philosophical trends

The work of the Bakhtin Circle can only be properly understood if one has a general understanding of the philosophical traditions with which it intersected and out of which it developed. The following are merely thumbnail sketches of the main trends (Hegelianism will be dealt with in Chapter 5), with certain features highlighted. The reader is directed to the bibliography for more substantial overviews of the philosophical contexts of the Circle.

Neo-Kantianism

Neo-Kantianism was a particularly abstract and abstruse philosophy that developed out of a widespread urge in German philosophy to return to and develop the teachings of Kant. As neo-Kantianism developed, however, it proposed a very different philosophy. Kant had argued that knowledge was possible through the application of a priori categories to sensory data acquired when we encounter objects existing independently of our minds. The neo-Kantians of the Marburg School, Hermann Cohen (1842–1918) and Paul Natorp (1854–1924), however, argued that the object of cognition was actually *produced* by the subject according to a priori categories dwelling in 'consciousness in general' and that the mind could only know what the mind itself produces. Kant argued that the objective validity (*objektive Gültigkeit*) of concepts is established in their application to sense impressions, that is, ideas must be checked against the empirical world. The neo-Kantians, however, argued that the validity (*Geltung*) of concepts is independent of any potential application in the world. Instead, knowledge is based on the 'factual validity' of mathematical principles that underlie the individual sciences. The validity of those sciences was simply assumed, and in the case of the human sciences, which were the Bakhtin Circle's focus of attention, the 'mathematics' was provided by jurisprudence, the science of legal concepts. Logical validity is now considered a separate realm, somewhat akin to Plato's realm of Ideas, and all knowledge of the empirical world is denied. Science is now transformed into a methodology for the *creation* of the objects of perception: objectivisation.

Bakhtin adopted from the Marburg School the notion that the object of the human sciences is the person as understood by the German tradition of jurisprudence. German Civil Law, as codified in the *Bundesgesetzbuch* (§§ 1–89), defines legal subjects (*Rechtssubjekte*) as natural persons (*natürliche Personen = Menschen*, that is, humans) or juristic persons (*juristische Personen*), the latter being subdivided into associations (*Vereine*) and foundations (*Stiftungen*). Only the legal subject is capable of bearing rights and obligations and is defined solely as such a bearer. All questions of the physical nature of human beings, their openness to economic pressures and the like, were ruled to be beyond the concerns of the human sciences by the Marburg philosophers, and so it remains in Bakhtin's own philosophy. Social interaction was reduced to the interaction of legal persons, the principles of which were treated as 'a sort of "mathematics" obeying only the logical necessity of abstract concepts' (Zweigert and Kötz 1987: I, 146). While Bakhtin moves away from the formalism of the neo-Kantian model, he retains the legal person as the object of the human sciences throughout his career, and this has some important ramifications that will become apparent later.

The rationalism and extreme idealism of this philosophical trend is clear to see, as is the absolute faith in the validity of scientific disciplines. However, there were variations in neo-Kantianism that should not be ignored. The Marburg School was challenged by a rival, the so-called Baden (or Freiburg) School led by Wilhelm Windelband (1848–1915) and Heinrich Rickert (1863–1936), who gave *values* precedence over validity, arguing that these form an absolute 'Ought' based on truth, beauty, goodness and holiness. They also argued that the methodology of the 'cultural sciences' was different from that of the 'natural sciences', since the former deal with individualities and the latter with generalities. Each branch of science has its own distinct structure of a priori categories. Although less directly influential on the Bakhtin Circle, the Baden School were very important in the formation of classical German sociology, such as the work of Max Weber (1864–1920) and Georg Simmel. The latter was particularly influential on Bakhtin and his colleagues. The Marburg School was of decisive importance in the development of Husserl's phenomenology from a fundamentally realist philosophy based on anti-Kantian principles into a type of idealism also based on object constitution.

One of the key features of neo-Kantianism passed on to the Bakhtin Circle was the view that the 'production' of objects according to either the 'factual validity' of science (the Marburg School) or universally valid values (the Baden School) means that the world is not something that is given to the senses but something that is 'conceived'. Thus, for the Marburg School, the production of the object is a 'never-ending task', while for the Baden School it is a 'prescription' (*Sollen*). The dominance of neo-Kantianism in German philosophy was in serious decline by 1910 and soon after the First World War the schools fragmented and the coherence of the philosophical trend was lost. The last generation of neo-Kantians of the respective schools, Ernst Cassirer and Emil Lask, began systematically to revise important tenets of neo-Kantianism to bring about a convergence with *Lebensphilosophie* (Cassirer) and phenomenology (Cassirer and especially Lask). These revisions, which are discussed below, are of crucial importance for the Bakhtin Circle's attempts to overcome the theoretical abstractness of neo-Kantianism while maintaining some of its key features.

Lebensphilosophie

By the outbreak of the First World War neo-Kantian philosophy was in deep crisis. It was widely regarded as stratospherically abstract and irrelevant to a world poised on the edge of an abyss (this feeling also permeates Bakhtin's early work). Some thinkers were led to develop a new variety of neo-Kantian thinking, arguing that the realm of validities and values that made up culture had a precondition: *life*. This move had already been anticipated in the work of philosophers such as Arthur Schopenhauer, Friedrich Nietzsche, Henri Bergson and Wilhelm Dilthey, but Georg Simmel developed an account of the relationship between life and culture that was particularly influential for the Bakhtin Circle.

Apart from the Baden School, Dilthey (1833–1911) was the person chiefly associated with the claim that the natural and human sciences are heterogeneous domains, requiring different problematics and methodologies. The natural sciences explain material entities, but the human sciences provide an understanding of non-material entities that are endowed with meaning. The human sciences need to be a 'science of the whole man' rather than just the intellect, to be grounded in 'lived experience' (*Erleben*), 'expression' (*Ausdruck*) and 'understanding' (*Verstehen*). In lived experience the willing, feeling and representing capacities of the person are involved, in addition to rationality, and these make up the 'expressive' qualities of experience. Understanding is the understanding of these expressions by 'putting oneself in the place of', 'reproducing' or 'reliving' them as objectifications of life. This was accepted by Simmel, but for him there is a crucial difference between understanding what is expressed and understanding the person who expresses, for 'life' is 'a homogeneous and undifferentiated process' that cannot become an object of experience or knowledge. It is for this reason that forms are necessary for any knowledge. The shifting 'manifold of life' is, claims Simmel, 'in a state of perpetual flux. It is constantly creating, increasing, and intensifying its own potentialities and energies.' It is this self-renewing or reproducing factor that leads Simmel to define life as 'more-life' (Oakes 1980: 13–14). Life is also able to 'go out beyond itself, to set its limits by reaching out beyond them, that is, beyond itself', to create new entities, forms or 'objectifications of life' that are 'more than life'. These become detached from the flux of life and acquire independence as 'objective culture'. As objective culture becomes more complex, an 'unreconcilable' and indeed tragic 'opposition between life and form, or, in other words, between continuity and individuality' develops. This appears as 'the unceasing, usually unnoticed (but also often revolutionary) battle of ongoing life against the historical pattern and formal inflexibility of any given cultural content, thereby becoming the innermost impulse toward social change' (Simmel 1971: 364–7).[5]

Simmel presented form as the realm of validities/values (for which he borrowed the Hegelian term 'objective spirit'), which are created in historical time but which attain an increasingly remote independence. The creation of objective spirit is a process of objectivisation not unlike Cohen and Natorp's 'production' of the object. Each individual subject stands at a unique point between historical actuality and the independent realm of forms, with the task of making them a unique unity. This forging of a unity between life and culture Simmel calls 'subjective culture', which is achieved in the process of social interaction, or what he calls 'forms of sociation'. The 'tragedy of culture', according to Simmel, is that subjective culture cannot keep up with the development of objective culture, on which it is dependent, with the result that the latter becomes something alien and restricting for the development of personality.

The relation between life and culture is a recurrent theme in the work of the Bakhtin Circle, and cannot be restricted to a single period.

Phenomenology

Phenomenology undoubtedly represents one of the major philosophical trends of the twentieth century. The slogan of the movement, 'to the things themselves!', undoubtedly underlies the Bakhtin Circle's preoccupation with 'concreteness'. Although the founder of phenomenology, Husserl, was to move close to neo-Kantianism in the 1910s and 1920s, the Circle was chiefly influenced by the so-called Munich phenomenologists who gathered around Johannes Daubert and Adolf Reinach and refused to follow Husserl in this direction (Schuhmann and Smith 1985). These philosophers remained close to Franz Brentano's Aristotelian theory of knowledge, in which the individual mind 'feeds' on encountered objects, deriving formal categories from this encounter, rather than applying formal categories a priori. This was fundamentally incompatible with the Kantian and neo-Kantian accounts, and the Circle was often trapped in a difficult position between these two trends.

It is, of course, impossible to give a full account of something as rich and complex as phenomenology here, but some important points should be made. According to Brentano and his heirs, consciousness is always consciousness *of* something, with the object of cognition (real or otherwise) presented to the mind in intentional acts. There is nothing akin to the neo-Kantian 'consciousness in general' in the Brentanian universe, only empirical consciousnesses which intend (existent or non-existent) objects, and it seems that the Bakhtin Circle followed this component of phenomenology closely. The intentional object is fundamentally different from the putative object beyond consciousness. The former is 'given' to consciousness in a particular way and is always the object of a cognitive act. However, this did not stop the Munich phenomenologists from regarding themselves as realists and defending a correspondence theory of truth in which the truth of a proposition depends on the state of the world. In this argument, it is the 'being red of this rose' which *makes* the proposition 'this rose is red' a true proposition. In the phenomenological casting, the individual views, or rather *intuits*, certain essential features of the world that are located in objects and 'states of affairs' (*Sachverhalte*), the structured 'hanging together' of objects. A priori connections are now not, as Kant thought, formal 'forms of thinking', but forms of states of affairs subsisting independently of the mind's activity. Reinach made this anti-Kantian point in a 1913 lecture at Marburg University, the citadel of neo-Kantianism, and this in some ways represents a milestone in the ascendance of phenomenology over neo-Kantianism:

> All objects have their 'what', their 'essence'; and for all essences there hold essence-laws. All restriction, and all reason for restriction, of the *a priori* to the, in some sense, 'formal' is lacking. A *priori* laws also hold true of the material – in fact, of the sensible, of tones and colours. With that there opens up an area so large and rich that yet today we cannot see its boundaries. (Reinach 1969: 215–16)

While not accepting the realism of the Munich phenomenologists, Bakhtin seems to have adopted their idea that the a priori is not limited to formal principles, but can be intuited in connection with objects of consciousness. Voloshinov's relationship to this type of philosophical realism is, however, rather more problematic, as we shall see.

One of the Munich phenomenlogists, Max Scheler, had achieved great fame in Germany and beyond partly thanks to his bellicose pro-war articles during the First World War (Kusch 1995: 212–19 *passim*). By the 1920s he was perhaps the most famous German philosopher in the world, and he exerted an important influence on the Bakhtin Circle. Scheler argued that the intuition of essences (*Wesensschau*) and thus of the material a priori also extended to *values*. According to Scheler, *value essences* can be intuited in the process of interaction between subjects in which 'intentional horizons' meet without merging. Scheler argued against then popular theories of empathy in which the self merges with the other to experience what the other experiences. Instead, he argued that it was necessary to maintain a 'phenomenological distance' between the self and the other in the development of spirit (culture). According to Scheler, it is only by resisting being swept along in the flow of *life* that the realm of *spirit* can be attained. Moral consciousness and thus individual responsibility is achieved through the development of personality, and this is dependent upon the attainment of spirit through a consciousness of one's uniqueness with regard to that of others. An unconditional merging with the other is thus counterproductive and indeed dangerous. We will see that this position was particularly influential on the early Bakhtin's account of aesthetic activity.

Among its many effects, phenomenology had important implications for theories of the use of language. In intentional acts of a discursive type the speaker infuses the linguistic structure with meaning according to his or her perspective or 'intentional horizon'. This view went through several developments in the work of two key thinkers for our purposes, Anton Marty and Karl Bühler, resulting in a theory of speech acts (*Sprechakt*) which are rooted in specific communicative situations. The significance of this will become clear when we examine Voloshinov's work on language.

Gestalt theory

Gestalt theory was another development from the philosophy of Brentano, initially delineated by Christian von Ehrenfels (1859–1932), but developing in many directions. The chief claim of

Gestalt theory is that humans do not perceive atomic sensations (of colour, and so on) which they then piece together to form a whole, but that they perceive the object as a whole, picking out its essential features against a background of other objects. The example Ehrenfels used to great effect was that of a melody, which can be recognised in two or more different keys even though none of the individual notes remains identical. The melody was said to have a *Gestaltqualität*, a specific quality of wholeness. Gestalten have two key features: the whole predominates over the parts and the structure of the whole is transposable (as in the case of a melody to another key). The fact that music was an important application for Gestalt theory probably led Voloshinov to encounter the theory in the early 1920s, when he was writing on 'the philosophy and history of music and verse' (Vasil´ev 1995: 9).

The notion of Gestalt was developed in a number of ways, especially in the area of psychology, where two trends of thought predominated. In the work of the so-called Graz School (Alexius Meinong, Stephan Witasek, Vittorio Benussi), the percipient intellectually *produces* a Gestalt quality from the given stimulus complex. The Gestalt is an 'object of a higher order' whose production is based on lower-order objects. For the Berlin School (Max Wertheimer, Kurt Koffka, Wolfgang Köhler, Kurt Lewin), on the other hand, the complex already *is* a Gestalt, and this complex is encountered as such. In each case, however, the Gestalt is dependent upon an autonomous formation *and* a percipient. Gestalt psychology was extremely influential in Russian psychology (Scheerer 1980; van der Veer and Valsiner 1991: 155–82) and literary studies (Erlich 1969: 199ff.) until 1931, when Ivan Pavlov's (1849–1936) reflex theory was granted a monopoly in Soviet psychology (Windholz 1984). Gestalt theory was also brought into the study of art and literature by the Austrian philosopher Stephan Witasek and the German literary scholar Oskar Walzel.

Gestalt theory was particularly important in Voloshinov's work on psychology and language and Medvedev's book on Formalism.

The crisis of neo-Kantianism

Faced with challenges from all directions, the last generation of the two schools of neo-Kantianism sought to rescue their philosophy by making it more concrete, and this brought about certain key revisions which threatened to destroy the philosophy from within as well as without (Motzkin 1989). The key developments pursued by Cassirer, the last major Marburg neo-Kantian, will be discussed in Chapter 5, but those of Emil Lask, his Baden School counterpart, are also important, even if there is no direct evidence of Bakhtin's familiarity with Lask's work.[6] This is because Lask was the neo-Kantian who moved closest toward phenomenology and his conclusions were often remarkably similar to those of Bakhtin. Of key importance was the central role given to the Brentanian notion of intentionality, which shifted attention to individual consciousnesses rather than the abstract neo-Kantian 'consciousness in general'. The result was that neither thinker any longer treated the realms of being and validity as separate realms; and they both also abandoned the neo-Kantian insistence that *nothing* was given to consciousness. Instead, the experienced world consists of a given but undefined (meaningless and shapeless) substratum (brute content or a bearer of properties) and the objectively valid categories of logic. These are not separate realms but incomplete elements that are united in specific acts of cognition. The empirical world *as given* is therefore still unknowable, for what can be known is only a 'produced' compound of content and form.

It is important to note that unlike early phenomenology and Gestalt theory, this theory makes no distinction between the structures of perceived things and the structures of thought. Where for phenomenology and Gestalt theory the percipient detects already structured phenomena prior to any reorganisation that might take place in thought, for Lask (and for Bakhtin) what is perceived appears to be already formed only because, since the time of the 'mythical Adam', no-one is ever the first to define an object (SR 92; DN 279; Schuhmann and Smith 1993; Crowell 1996).

Religion

Bakhtin, it is known, was a religious man. His work undoubtedly contains Christian overtones, but it would be misleading to regard him as a *theological* thinker. While his work includes terminology with a theological history, there is little evidence to suggest that he actually drew directly on theological sources. The extent of religious influences on his work is difficult to assess because the versions of German idealist philosophy on which he drew all had their own religious dimensions (this is especially true of Simmel, Cohen and Natorp, and also of Scheler). In the main, however, religion was treated 'within the bounds of humanity', as Natorp put it. There are important distinctions between religion, religious philosophy and a philosophy of religion, and religious overtones detected in a basically secular philosophy are a different matter again. In addition to this, the terminology of German idealism did not find simple equivalents in Russian, where there was no established philosophical discourse at the beginning of the century. Terms with religious connotations were thus often adopted for general philosophical discussions. I will not be addressing the question of religion in this book except to the extent that it impinges directly on the philosophical concerns that will be discussed. Two monographs which deal with this question should be singled out as presenting valuable material on this matter (Mihailovic 1997; Coates 1998), but their conclusions need to be balanced with a consideration of the Circle's saturation in general European philosophy.

Patterns of appropriation

As we will see, neo-Kantianism, life-philosophy and phenomenology are all-important ingredients of the work of the Bakhtin Circle. However, their influence should not be understood mechanically. The influences are *cumulative* rather than serial, with the result that the periods of the Circle's work do not neatly coincide with the influence of a single trend, but combine aspects of each in a rather original fashion. In Bakhtin's work of the 1930s new, Hegelian, influences appear, although they do not simply replace the earlier influences. We will examine these influences later, but it is worth saying here that neo-Kantianism itself developed in a fashion that brought it closer to Hegel's philosophy. This was already quite evident in the later work of Paul Natorp, but took on a much more systematic form in the work of Ernst Cassirer from the 1920s onward.

However, it is crucial to stress that the development of this trend within the Bakhtin Circle does have distinctly Soviet features. These philosophies were employed in debates that were set within Soviet scholarship: the reception of the works of Dostoevsky; the disputes between the Russian Formalists and their Marxist critics; the debates about the way forward in the Marxist 'reform' of psychology; the discussion around the nature of realism and the novel in the 1930s in which Lukács took a leading role; and the attempts to develop a Marxist theory of language that were made between the 1920s and 1950, when Stalin effectively ended the debate. No consideration of the work of the Circle can avoid these issues without presenting a distorted picture. The influence, and indeed dominance, of the ideas of the linguist and archaeologist Nikolai Iakovlevich Marr (1865–1934) in Soviet scholarship in the humanities between 1930 and 1950 (Alpatov 1991; Thomas 1957) is especially important in understanding the shape of Bakhtin's work in that period.[7]

From 1929 until Bakhtin's death Soviet scholarship was to a greater or lesser extent isolated from the main currents within European culture. While many thinkers writing in the West during this time often echo some of the concerns of the Circle there is little likelihood of direct influence. Resemblances usually derive from the fact that Western thinkers often share the same roots as the Circle in German philosophy of the early twentieth century. One of the most interesting facets of the work of the Circle is the distinct way this was developed in Soviet conditions, and this tells us much more about the peculiarites of the Circle.

One of the most significant and contentious issues surrounding the work of the Circle has to do with its attitude toward Marxism in general and the specific types of Marxism developed in the Soviet Union. There are important points to be made at the outset: the members of the Bakhtin Circle did not share a monolithic attitude towards Marxism, and the types of Marxism that were dominant in the 1920s are quite different from the narrow dogmatism of the 1930s and 1940s. Furthermore, the opportunity to publish works which sought to present a dialogue between Marxism and other philosophical trends diminished sharply at the end of the 1920s, when the Bakhtin Circle as such ceased to be. Voloshinov and Medvedev were, by the mid-1920s, sincere if not 'orthodox' Marxists, and their works of the late 1920s reflect an attempt to integrate Marxism into a perspective framed by neo-Kantianism, life-philosophy and phenomenology. Bakhtin's own work was, however, somewhat different, being much more firmly rooted in philosophical idealism and engaging with Marxism in a much more oblique fashion. Even here, however, the relationship should not be neglected or oversimplified.

One final point that should be made is that while the works published by the various members of the Circle shared many influences and were broadly sympathetic towards a particular orientation in science, they do not represent a fully unified project or approach. There are significant differences of emphasis and theory in these works, ranging from Bakhtin's close adherence to the fundamental contours of neo-Kantianism, even while he adopted certain ideas from phenomenology, to Voloshinov's appropriation of fundamentally anti-Kantian ideas from Gestalt theory. Within this range there are several types of theory that can potentially be developed in various directions, and this book will highlight some of the distinct strands within the work of the Circle which need not be developed in the way that Bakhtin chose.

2 The Early Ethical and Aesthetic Philosophy of the Circle (1919–26)

Bakhtin's early works are among the most difficult works by the Circle for the modern reader to engage with. This is partly due to the fragmentary nature of what has survived, but more specifically due to its close relationship to the debates in German philosophy of the time. Many of Bakhtin's early sources are now seldom read even if, as we have seen, they continue to exert an influence on social science and cultural studies. The unusual terminology that Bakhtin develops at this time does not help matters, and only some of this terminology continues to be used in the later work. Yet an understanding of these works adds a great deal to our appreciation of the later ones. A successful engagement with these works requires an appreciation of the specific historical conditions in which they were written.

Philosophy, culture and politics

In the aftermath of the First World War, two revolutions and then a devastating civil war, the need for a constructive philosophy for the emergent new order was felt by many Russian intellectuals, who generally accepted the changed conditions at the beginning of the 1920s. The Bakhtin Circle was no exception, and the group as a whole sought to play a constructive role in the new post-revolutionary conditions. The members of the Circle were not Marxists, at least at this time, but nor were they supporters of the old regime or Western-style liberals. It is important to note that many of the German idealist philosophers to whom they were attracted regarded themselves as socialists of one type or another. Hermann Cohen and Paul Natorp, for example, both considered themselves to be forging a socialist philosophy that could bridge the gap between the liberal middle classes and the labour movement by replacing the Hegelian dialectics of history that had become part and parcel of Marxism with Kant's ethical philosophy. In the Russian context this idealist socialism offered the prospect of an ethical philosophy that could bridge the gap between the traditional intelligentsia and the people, allowing the former to achieve its long-sought-after role as the cultural leadership of society. Cohen regarded his philosophy as in complete agreement with the ethics implicit in Marx's work, and in 1920 Natorp even wrote a book on idealist socialism called *Sozial-Idealismus* (Social Idealism), which Kagan began to translate into Russian the following year (Natorp 1995). Simmel described his *Philosophie des Geldes* (The Philosophy of Money, 1900) and his work on objective and subjective culture as developments and generalisations of Marx's work on the cultural consequences of capitalism and repeatedly described his work as socialist. His work was consequently extremely influential on many Marxists of the time including Georg Lukács and Walter Benjamin. Whatever one's opinion of these philosophies, they were all works which were considered to be of political significance and to be generally socialist in character (Willey 1978). This was undoubtedly an important aspect of their influence on the so-called Western Marxist thinkers of the inter-war period, and to a large extent explains the numerous parallels between these thinkers and the Bakhtin Circle.

There is certainly no case for describing the work derived from these ideas as indifferent to politics or even conservative in character (as some have argued, usually pointing toward Bakhtin's early works). Rather, the Circle is in this period relating to politics from an *ethical* perspective typical of the pre-revolutionary Russian intelligentsia, but through the ideas of contemporary German philosophy. Three Christian members of the Circle, Bakhtin, Pumpianskii and Iudina, were at this time members of a left-leaning, quasi-Masonic sect called *Voskresenie*, which was led by the mystic and philosopher Aleksandr Meier. The group sought to support the Bolsheviks' economic policy but oppose their atheistic cultural policy, and in so doing to 'renew humanity and the construction of communism'. According to Meier, 'religion cannot be indifferent to humanity's historical path. In principle the Christian religion supports the transcendence of individualism, and in this the main path is the union [*smychka*] of Christianity and the social revolution' (Brachev 2000: 183). It is therefore clear that the Circle at this time was composed of what Trotsky called 'fellow-travellers', intellectuals who critically accepted the regime, but who also wanted actively to influence the direction of historical development. To do so meant to overcome all traces of academic aloofness and abstractness, but the neo-Kantianism in which these intellectuals were steeped was notoriously wedded to both of these vices. To become socially effective, neo-Kantianism would need to be transformed into something relevant to the concrete issues of life. This was the problem that appears to have motivated the Circle's earliest work.[1]

The terms of the Circle's attempts to concretise its ideas often seem to be quite far from political discourse, but this may be a misleading impression. Drawing on Jürgen Habermas's ideas about the 'public sphere' within which Western bourgeois intellectuals defined their ideas about freedom and democracy during the time of the absolute monarchies of the eighteenth century, Ken Hirschkop (1999: 157–60) suggests that the terms of the Circle's engagement were closely related to sociological conditions. In the absence of a well-established layer of middle-class intellectuals with their own economic means of subsistence in Russia, the Circle had only a vague idea of whom they were addressing. This led to some cryptic formulations about ethics when dealing with issues that were actually related to the nature of political democracy. Hirschkop argues that the lack of a civil society in both Tsarist and Soviet Russia that could have more clearly defined the specific intellectual circles to which its work was addressed led the Circle to speak in terms of abstract categories such as 'the people' and the 'superaddressee', to which we shall return. This may well have been an important factor underlying Bakhtin's vague formulations and his pervasive tendency to transform all political questions into ethical ones. This is a tendency that is constitutive of neo-Kantian socialism.

Taking Hirschkop's analysis one stage further, it is difficult not to think that in shifting such considerations not only from politics to ethics but, further, from ethics to aesthetics, the Circle was indulging in what Terry Eagleton characterises as the 'ideology of the aesthetic', that is, a 'dream of reconciliation' typical of an emergent middle class 'newly defining itself as a universal subject but wedded in its robust individualism to the concrete and the particular'. In this dream individuals are to be 'woven into intimate unity with no detriment to their specificity' while an 'abstract totality' can be 'suffused with all the flesh-and-blood reality of individual being' (Eagleton 1990: 25). One can certainly sense this agenda in the work of the Marburg School and others who, caught between an autocratic German state and an increasingly insurgent proletariat, tried and failed to build a bridge of *Kultur* between the liberal middle class and the labour movement through social democracy. In pre-revolutionary Russia this 'dream of reconciliation' was articulated most powerfully by Vissarion Belinskii, who argued that 'our literature has created the morals of our society, has already educated several generations of widely divergent character, has paved the way for the inner rapprochement of the estates' (1962a: 6). In post-revolutionary Russia the situation was even more difficult for social-democratic intellectuals like the members of the Bakhtin Circle. They lacked a firm social base and operated among a largely illiterate population in the context of a backward economy further decimated by world war and civil war. All this was presided over by an isolated revolutionary regime that was going through bureaucratic distortions in an effort simply to survive and which ruled in the name of a class that scarcely existed any longer. The aesthetic 'dream of reconciliation' was certainly attractive in these circumstances, but questions central to social and political life continually invaded the cultural realm.

The aestheticisation of social and political change is the grain of truth in talk about the Circle's early indifference to politics. As Nikolai Bakhtin noted in retrospect, attempts by traditional intellectuals to avoid politics were doomed to failure: 'I observed the events [of 1917] with intense, but quite detached and even somewhat ironical curiosity.' This reaction

> ... was fairly typical of a representative selection of the Russian intelligentsia at that time, especially all those too-damned-clever young intellectuals who lived in the pleasant illusion that they were above politics and had better things to do – poetry, philosophy, art, pure science. As a matter of fact, they were not above politics but *below* politics, as later events showed, when most of us, in our romantic ignorance, became the blind tools of militant reaction – and had finally to realise to our cost that we had backed the wrong horse. But then it was too late. (Bachtin 1963: 45)

While the members of the Circle did not make Nikolai Bakhtin's mistake of joining the Whites, some at first partook of the illusion that they could stand above politics. Bakhtin and Pumpianskii were both drawn into the Hellenistic cult among the intelligentsia at the time and were, at first, adherents of the idea of the 'Third Renaissance' in the early 1920s. First formulated by F.F. Zelinskii in 1899 and refracted through the views of the symbolists I.F. Annenskii and V.I. Ivanov, this idea was based on a cyclical account of history in which the growth, decline and rebirth of culture was repeated. It became a new form of slavophilism, with advocates arguing that where the first Renaissance had been Italian and the second German, the third would be Slavonic (Zelinskii 1995; Khoruzhii 1994: 52–6). At the time of the October Revolution, Nikolai Bakhtin had been a member of Zelinskii's so-called 'Union of the Third Renaissance', when he spoke of 'the coming dark age', which would lead to the rebirth of classical culture in Russia (Bachtin 1963: 43–4). This undoubtedly permeated the early thinking of the Bakhtin Circle. Kornei Chukovsii (1989), who knew some of the Circle personally, argues that in his novel *Kozlinaia pesn´* (KP; TT) Vaginov constructed such a mythology, in which the Revolution was seen as but a destructive phase.[2] Vaginov allegedly considered the writer to be like the isolated monk of the Dark Ages: a preserver of cultural artefacts in order to facilitate the ultimate rebirth of culture. Vaginov's parodic portrayals of Bakhtin, Medvedev and (especially) Pumpianskii in this novel were depictions of a group engaged in just such an enterprise among an increasingly philistine population. Whatever the truth of this interpretation, there is no doubt that the idea that the classical tradition would be reborn in Russian culture of the time was a preoccupation of Bakhtin and Pumpianskii in the early 1920s (Nikolaev 1997). This was one of the main themes of Pumpianskii's 1922 pamphlet *Dostoevskii i antichnost´* (DA), and the idea of bringing about a Third Renaissance to combat Simmel's 'crisis of culture' was a recurrent theme throughout the Circle's work of the time.

The treatment of the Renaissance in this way reflects the position of Bakhtin and Pumpianskii as what Gramsci called 'traditional' as opposed to 'organic' intellectuals. As Benedetto Croce noted:

The movement of the Renaissance remained an aristocratic movement and one of élite circles, and even in Italy, which was both mother and nurse to the movement, it did not escape from courtly circles, it did not penetrate to the people or become custom and 'prejudice', in other words collective persuasion or faith.

To this Croce, and Gramsci following him, counterposed the 'Lutheran Reformation and Calvinism' which 'created a vast national-popular movement through which their influence spread: only in later periods did they create a higher culture' (Gramsci 1971: 293–4). It is significant that on returning to Leningrad in 1924 Bakhtin and Pumpianskii already felt the need to attach themselves to a quasi-masonic organisation that sought to revolutionise popular consciousness, and by the time of Bakhtin's later work the democ-ratisation of popular culture emerges as a precondition for renaissance. We already have evidence of this reorientation even in Bakhtin's early philosophical work. Meanwhile Pumpianskii joined Medvedev and Voloshinov when he made a sudden and unexpected conversion to Marxism in 1927.

Matvei Kagan

The notional leader of the Circle in its earliest years was Matvei Kagan, whose early work grew out of that of the Marburg School, of which he had first-hand experience. In an obituary of Hermann Cohen (published in 1922 but written earlier) Kagan stressed the political aspects of Cohen's work on ethics and its kinship with the work of the Russian populists (GK 118), who were the first to engage in a productive and friendly dialogue with Marx and Engels in Russia (Walicki 1969). Kagan, it seems, had an equivocal attitude towards Marxism. In 'The Sociology of the Individual', an article written on his return from Germany, Kagan argued that Marx is 'far more idealistic than is generally accepted':

> Marx's assertion that social labour fundamentally defines social use value is profoundly social in its sociological truth. It is symp-tomatic that, despite his expressed disdain for idealism and ethics, in his foundation of history Marx defines value not by labour understood generally as work, not by the work of a machine or a neutral element, or even of any living creature other than man. In Marx, value is defined by human labour. Surplus value too is calculated only in terms of human labour. This is not to reproach Marx, but to note a positive aspect of his thinking.

He goes on, however, to argue that Marx was mistaken to include culture in the economic sphere, preferring to ground the 'human sciences' in a neo-Kantian ethics (Kagan 1998: 12). Bakhtin adopted a similar position towards Marxism in his early work, praising Marxism because 'a striving and act-performing consciousness can orient itself within the world of historical materialism'. He then goes on to criticise Marxism for committing the 'methodological sin' of failing to distinguish between 'what is and what ought to be' (TPA 19–20; KFP 25–6). Marxism thus becomes an ally in the struggle against abstractly rationalistic and positivistic conceptions in philosophy and cultural theory, but the connections it establishes between cultural and economic phenomena are to be replaced with connections between culture and ethical philosophy. Although this complex issue is especially significant when considering the works of Voloshinov and Medvedev, it is also important for understanding the sociological nature of Bakhtin's early work.

The early Bakhtin repeatedly refers to 'the open event of being,' the idea that human existence is a goal-directed, and not determined, condition in which individuals live their lives. History is an open process, a process of becoming, whose goal is eternally anticipated in each act. But in all cases the world is open and incomplete. In a 1922 article on art Kagan noted:

> The sphere of art is open like all other spheres of being. It is unfinished as all of being is unfinished. The whole world is not finished, all of being is not ready. The world of art is not ready. The identity of all spheres of being is the identity of process, the open process of becoming. (DUI 48)

But art, and art alone, brings about completion in relation to a given moment:

> The work of art is ready and identical once and for all. There can be no talk of corrections, changes, of improvements, revisions and developments of the work of art as such. Otherwise it would not be a work of art. It would otherwise be an illegitimate pretence at art or at best, a fact of science, of nature or technology, industry, a fact of the world in general, but not of the world of art. (DUI 48)

This dichotomy between the openness of the world and the closure of the work of art becomes of crucial importance in Bakhtin's early aesthetics.

Kagan was clearly an important conduit between Bakhtin and German idealist philosophy, in some ways shaping Bakhtin's understanding of that philosophy. Furthermore, as a Jew who shared the broad objectives of the *Voskresenie* group, he helped to ensure that the Circle did not become a Christian sect. Rather, all religions were treated equally. For Kagan,

> it is when paganism, Christianity, Judaism all stand together for the new Renaissance of the creative culture of meaningful history

that history will have meaning. It is quite certain that such an organically creative, fraternal life will not come immediately and all at once, but it is only this path of history that does not lead to crisis. (EKK 235)

Kagan also bequeathed to Bakhtin the monotheistic notion that history as a whole has meaning only when viewed from without; this is perhaps the origin of the ideas of the 'superaddressee' in Bakhtin's last work. However, Kagan's own publications are few in number, and until the planned volume of his works appears in Russian we are limited to some puzzling and often turgid articles which are often little more than pale derivatives of the German idealist philosophy in which he was steeped.

Ethics and aesthetics

The short essay 'Iskusstvo i otvetstvennost´' (1919), Bakhtin's earliest published work, is usually translated into English as 'Art and Answerability', suggesting a strong link with the later notion of dialogism. However, in common with all Bakhtin's early work, this essay lacks any systematic treatment of language, and the term *otvetstvennost´*, although it may be translated as 'answerability', is the usual Russian word for 'responsibility'. The title neatly summarises Bakhtin's main concern in his early work: the relationship and boundaries between aesthetics and ethics as dimensions of life and culture. The theme was one that occupied several neo-Kantian philosophers at the time, but most important for Bakhtin was the examination of the problem in two of Cohen's central works (1904; 1923). Here Cohen argued that harmony and *humanity* together form the bridge between the two distinct realms of spirit (Poma 1997b). Bakhtin argues that responsibility must provide a bridge between the two realms: 'Art and life are not one but must become one in myself – in the unity of my responsibility' (AAn 2; IO 8). The notion that responsibility has ethical and aesthetic moments is elaborated in the works we know as *Toward a Philosophy of the Act* and *Author and Hero in Aesthetic Activity*, neither of which has survived in its complete form, and in the essay 'The Problem of Content, Material and Form in Verbal Art'.

The first of these is a piece of ethical philosophy that is fundamentally, some would say obsessively, concerned with finding a way to make neo-Kantianism in general, and its ethics in particular, concrete and relevant to 'life'. Bakhtin highlights the problematic dichotomy between the abstract, formal categories of science discussed by neo-Kantians and the 'event-character' of being as experienced.[3] He argues that this gulf must be overcome and that this is possible only by a concentration on the intentional act, in which the objectively valid categories of science are brought into the practical world. Any doctrine that fails to relate these factors falls into a theoretical abstractness or an uncritical dogmatic attitude, which is fatal to both science and life. Bakhtin's analysis of this division, and his proposed solution for overcoming it, is explored most systematically with reference to ethics.

Like Franz Brentano (1969) in his pathbreaking *Vom Ursprung sittlicher Erkenntnis* (*The Origin of Ethical Knowledge*, 1889), Bakhtin sets the intentional act at the centre of his ethical theory. Also like Brentano, Bakhtin seeks to negotiate a way between what he sees as the excessively formalistic ethics of Kant's 'categorical imperative' and what he calls 'content ethics', that is, the type of ethics that stipulates a universally valid moral end. A representative of this latter trend would be utilitarianism, the doctrine that pleasure or the satisfaction of desires is the sole element of what is humanly good. Bakhtin sees Kant's formalism being continued in contemporary neo-Kantian ideas about a 'theoretical ought' in accordance with which the individual must act. So-called 'content ethics', on the other hand, is fundamentally flawed in being unable to establish any specifically ethical norms. Both trends are criticised for being cases of 'theoretism', that is, doctrines in which 'the deed is split into an objective semantic content and a subjective process of achievement', leaving no room for the 'actual, responsible deed-performance' (TPA 22–9; KFP 27–33). Ideas have become disembodied and treated as abstract principles, rendering them aloof from life and irrelevant to people acting in the practical world. In ethics this means that what 'ought to be' ultimately becomes impotent in life. As Ken Hirschkop puts it:

> The essential point is that one cannot derive such an 'ethically obligating position', the sense of oughtness which turns a norm or value into something compelling, from a demonstration or proof that something is right, for a proof can only justify something that is objectively right, and objective norms – laws, we might call them – always provide escape hatches for subjects

because they apply to people in general and to no-one in particular. (Hirschkop 1998: 585)

Like Simmel, Brentano and Scheler, Bakhtin criticises the 'prejudice of rationalism', that 'only the logical is clear and rational'. For Bakhtin the contrary is true, logic 'is elemental and dark outside the responsible consciousness' (TPA 29; KFP 33). Brentano's 'intentional' ethics were attractive to Bakhtin because here the strengths of both types of ethics were combined while their weaknesses were apparently avoided. To achieve this combination Brentano divided mental phenomena into presentations, judgements and emotive phenomena, and foregrounded the act itself rather than the object of that act. Truth and falsity, for example, pertain to the judging *act* and not to the object that is judged. Good and evil similarly pertain to 'feeling *acts*' rather than to the object that is 'felt'. However, while distinct, Brentano maintained that both acts share an intentional relation to an object that is presented to consciousness. As in 'content ethics' the knowledge of right and wrong is linked to emotional experience, but as with the Kantian position, the judgement made is *analogous* to rational judgement. Ethical and logical principles are not to be (con)fused, but they are nevertheless parallel and kindred (McAlister 1982).

While Bakhtin readily adopts the centrality accorded to the act by Brentano, unlike Brentano he retains, in modified form, the neo-Kantian dichotomy between being and validity, fact and value. Like Simmel and Lask, however, he finds the normal neo-Kantian bisection of the experienced world extremely problematic. When the world is divided in such a way

> ... two worlds stand opposed to each other, having no communication and impervious to each other: the world of culture and the world of life, the one world in which we create, cognise, contemplate, live and die; the world in which the acts of our activity are objectified, and the world in which these acts actually proceed and are accomplished only once. (TPA 2; KFP 11–12)

In a situation where culture is no longer accessible to the subject in life, where ethical principles are deemed irrelevant when deciding how to act, the 'ideal moments' of the ethical deed give way to 'elementary biological and economic motivation'. This Bakhtin presumably saw manifested in the wars and revolutions that had

gripped Russia and much of Europe in the years before the composition of his essay. Bakhtin argues that the split between objective
culture and life must be rectified by 'participative' rather than
abstract thinking. Thinking must take place within the ethical deed
itself, since the deed is like the Roman spirit Janus, double-faced and
looking towards both 'worlds' simultaneously. The experienced
world is constantly being created as the incomplete elements of
being and validity are fused together in every unique and unrepeatable intentional act. Following Brentano, he says that the ethical
deed is but one species of intentional act, but unlike Brentano, and
like the neo-Kantians, Bakhtin sees this as a contribution to the
ongoing *co-creation* of the experienced world.

Bakhtin forges his thesis by combining the Brentanian insight
with three other ideas: (1) Simmel's contention that the subject has
an inner relation to the quasi-autonomous 'realm' of validity
(culture); (2) Scheler's claim that it is through intersubjective interaction that consciousness itself is defined and the realm of values
can be intuited; and (3) the Marburg School ideas of the production
of the object and their juridical model of the person. We will deal
with these in turn.

(1) In his book *Einleitung in die Moralwissenschaft* (Introduction to
Moral Science, 1892–93) and then in *Lebensanschauung* (Life-view,
1919), Simmel had transformed the Kantian concept of duty (as
embodied in the categorical imperative) into the structure of
individual experience. Rationally discerned obligation was now
replaced by the *sentiment*, or feeling of obligation. This allowed
Simmel to argue that what one is morally obliged to do is dependent
on historical circumstances and that the 'sentiment of obligation',
conscience, is the internalised promptings of social discipline.
Certain practical requirements, ethical life, crystallise in the social
and individual consciousness through tradition and the synthesising
processes of the mind to form principles of conduct. These principles
arise in a neo-Kantian process of objectification: although formed in
historical time (life), forms crystallise into principles of conduct that
are gradually displaced by new principles.

(2) Developing Brentano's idea about the relation of feelings to
judgements, Scheler argued that the subject is structured in such a
way that he or she has access to 'value essences' through feelings –
what, following Pascal, he called the 'order of the heart'. For Scheler,
these feelings are involved in the 'participation' of the 'I' in the
'world' of the 'other' and vice versa. Each encounter forms a sort of

intermediate realm of Spirit (*Geist*) in which certain essential principles of conduct can be gleaned by resisting the unreflective flow of Life (*Leben*). These principles are universal and a priori, but they are not formal principles of reason like Kant's a priori. Instead, they are what Scheler calls a 'material a priori', being fundamental and irreducible but always given to us in connection with something. Ethical value-essences are given through feelings, but these essences can only be intuited under certain conditions, when certain forms of intersubjective interaction take place. Thus, different types of social organisation realise different values, and this Scheler was to schematise with a hierarchy of forms of society ranging from a basic herd existence governed by the values of the senses to a 'love-community' (*Liebesgemeinschaft*) governed by religious values (Scheler 1973).

(3) While Scheler provided an important methodological under-pinning for Bakhtin's writing on intersubjectivity, the latter's ideas were still rooted in those of Cohen, for whom the other is the 'logical springboard' for positing the I. In other words, consciousness of the other is a neo-Kantian precondition for consciousness of the self. Despite Bakhtin's apparent hostility to legalistic ethics, this principle is built upon legal foundations (Brandist 2001b), especially Cohen's contention that a moral act should be defined as a legal act that is based on a contract. The contract is a 'unification of the will' (*die Willenvereinigung*) of the persons involved, and the unity of will is the foundation of the person as a legal person (*Rechtsperson*). The legal person is exclusively the bearer of a unified will, with rights and responsibilities consequent upon this; all other factors are excluded from consideration. Thus, consciousness of the self and that of the other form a 'correlative unity' and this is inherent in the founding of the self in the contract: self and other are simultan-eously united and separate. Furthermore, knowledge of the other is not a matter of perception but is a priori: since the model of social interaction is the (social) contract, and since jurisprudence is the 'mathematics' of ethics, the self and the other are akin to math-ematical principles. However, the self and other are able to make a claim on each other in accordance with the contract, transforming strangers into an I and a Thou by addressing each other. This addressing is realising objective validity in life in the infinite task of self-consciousness: the generation of the state in which the correl-ation of the I and the Thou results in 'plurality in the unity of the allness'. In his final work on religion the *contract* on Earth which

Cohen outlines here has its counterpart in man's *covenant* with God (Munk 1997).[4]

From these sources Bakhtin develops the idea of 'emotional-volitional acts' in which two or more subjects co-experience (*soperezhivat´*) an instant of being. The act is a unique moment of co-being (*sobytie*, a Russian word which also means an event), in which obligation becomes manifest.

One of the distinctive features of Bakhtin's reworking of Scheler's intersubjective ethics is an insistence that there is an aesthetic moment involved in co-experience. To act ethically towards the other does not mean that the 'I' must fully and unconditionally empathise with the other. Rather, the 'I' projects him- or herself on to the other and empathises actively, but then withdraws to the original position outside the other and brings the experience to consciousness. This return to one's own unique position in being, from which the other can be objectified, constitutes 'aesthetic activity', to which we will return later. Here, however, we are dealing with only the 'aesthetic moment' of intersubjective ethics. The maintenance of one's unique position in being, what Bakhtin obtusely calls the 'non-alibi-in-being', is essential for individual responsibility: to give this position up is also to lose one's own individuality as an ethical being. This aesthetic moment allows the 'generally obligating', the 'ought', to be intuited in a phenomenological sense, without entailing theoretical abstractions from the 'event' within which the deed is performed. What is ethically obligating is now given to the subject as *conscience*. Aesthetic 'vision' (*vídenie*) becomes a version of what Husserl called the intuition of essences but, following Scheler, it is now applied to values (TPA 14–16; KFP 21–2).

The fragment of *Toward a Philosophy of the Act* that has survived is of interest chiefly for what it tells us about Bakhtin's later work. With a knowledge of the sources of the ideas, which are nowhere overtly signalled, we can now see that it represents little more than a (rather too) self-conscious combination of themes from contemporary German and Austrian philosophy. Furthermore, the labyrinthine argument, tortuous style and peculiarity of terminology make the text a particularly difficult one with which to engage. The work is full of the themes that recur in various ways throughout Bakhtin's later work: the hostility to rationalism and positivism; the need to overcome neo-Kantian abstractness by adopting intentional consciousness in place of 'consciousness in general'; a concern to overcome the split between objective culture and life; the place of feeling in experience and expression; a concern for non-formal ethics and the centrality of intersubjectivity. The themes have, however, yet to be woven together into a distinctly Bakhtinian fabric. Studying this work can be very productive for showing some of the ingredients present at the outset of Bakhtin's work and his initial, faltering steps to move beyond his sources, but it is not a major work in itself. It was not until Bakhtin transgressed the bounds of ethical philosophy that he really began to add something unique to the German ideas. He did this through the *application* of the ethical philosophy with which he had already been concerned to the question of art in general and of authorship in particular.

From ethics to literature

The move from ethics to literature was a natural one for a member of the traditional Russian intelligentsia like Bakhtin. As Nikolai Bakhtin noted some years later, the Russian intelligentsia shared a peculiarly ethical approach to art:

> With varying degrees of consciousness, in different ways and by different means all art strives ... to pervade our being; to affect our deepest impulses and our most intimate reactions; to shape our sensibility; to transform and organise our vision – and thus to affect our whole behaviour; 'to teach us how to live', in short. (Bachtin 1963: 26)

This ethical role for art in general and literature in particular had been delineated in its classical form by Belinskii in the 1830s and had dominated Russian criticism ever since. Belinskii had drawn upon German aesthetics, especially those of Kant, Herder, Schiller, Schelling and Hegel, and adapted them to the cause of the democratisation of Russian culture and society (Terras 1974). He thus argued that 'all our moral interests, all our spiritual life have hitherto been and will, still for a long time to come, be concentrated in literature: it is the vital spring from which all human sentiments percolate into society' (Belinskii 1962a: 9). For all his philosophical differences from his predecessor, the intimate connection between ethics and aesthetics that Bakhtin advocates in his earliest work places him at least partially in the critical tradition established by Belinskii. This also explains how the same ethical concerns could later be subsumed into work on the novel, a genre that Belinskii himself had championed as the 'widest and most universal genre of poetry' (Belinskii 1962b: 33ff.).

Production of the 'aesthetic object'

Bakhtin's turn towards literary theory is clear in the 1924 essay 'The Problem of Content, Material and Form in Verbal Art' and the major work *Author and Hero in Aesthetic Activity* written but never completed over several years during the mid-1920s. The first of these is an essay Bakhtin completed and submitted for publication in the journal *Russkii sovremennik*, but the journal ceased publication before the article could appear. Like *Author and Hero*, to which we will turn below, this article is much inspired by the rise of phenomenological aesthetics. As Viktor Zhirmunskii noted, phenomenological critics maintained that the issue of the artwork's 'genesis as a historical phenomenon has too long hidden the study of its "essence"'. Instead they seek 'the ideational [*ideinyi*] "essence" of the work of a given poet, or the "essence" of a given literary trend'. They also 'promote the problem of a phenomenological analysis of the "spirit of the epoch"' in which questions of form and content are combined (Zhirmunskii 1927: 9). Not for the last time, Bakhtin here leans heavily on a single but unacknowledged source, Broder Christiansen's *Philosophie der Kunst* (*The Philosophy of Art*, 1909) (Matejka 1996). Christiansen had defined the 'aesthetic object' as a combination of content, material and form, but Bakhtin develops his source in a new direction.[5] Christiansen's book had been translated into Russian in 1911 and was very influential on many Russian thinkers of the time, including Boris Engel´gardt, Viktor Vinogradov and the Russian Formalists Boris Eikhenbaum and Iurii Tynianov (Muratov 1996; Erlich 1969).

Here Bakhtin is again concerned about the split between the formation of culture as an activity within life and cultural artefacts as manifestations of objective culture. This concern recalls the earlier 'philosophy of the act', but in this form it is also quite similar to the ideas of certain Russian avant-garde writers and artists of the time, who saw art as a vital activity, in contrast to culture as the dead incrustations on creativity.[6] Where Bakhtin wished to integrate the 'worlds' of life and culture, the avant-gardists aimed to reintegrate art into life. An urge to return to a vital, oral culture unencumbered by the weight of books held in stuffy libraries, and attempts to transcend the division between high and popular culture, were constitutive features of Futurism and other radical trends of the time, and in their wake a school of criticism emerged which valued formal experimentation highly. This school, the Russian Formalists, specialised in the study of the artistic devices that were employed to achieve certain effects, particularly the 'defamiliarisation' of the world of everyday cognition. Through art the world could be perceived anew and social consciousness could be renewed in what Mayakovsky and others called the 'revolution of the spirit'.

Unlike the Formalists, Bakhtin interprets the split between art as a vital, living process and the artefacts of 'objective culture' in terms characteristic of life-philosophy. Shifting his attention from the ethical deed to 'aesthetic activity', Bakhtin develops the neo-Kantian argument that aesthetic activity is the 'production' of the 'aesthetic object' in contemplation. Like Lask, however, Bakhtin combines the neo-Kantian paradigm with the notion of intentionality to argue that aesthetic activity is an *intentional act* directed towards a work. However, the finished work of art, the artefact, has an inferior status to this intentional object, for it is just *'the realisation of the aesthetic object, as a technical apparatus of aesthetic achievement'*. The creation of a work of art is divided into two distinct moments: 'aesthetic activity', or the 'architectonic form' in which the aesthetic object is 'produced', and 'composition', in which the 'apparatus of aesthetic achievement' is constructed. These are the elements of the work of art as a 'goal-directed whole' (PCMF 267–8; PSMF 269–70). The 'content' of art consists of 'objects of cognition' that are established according to the individual sciences:

> Of course aesthetic form transfers this cognised and evaluated actuality to another evaluative plane, subordinates it to a new unity and orders it in a new way: it individualises, concretises, isolates and completes, but this does not change its already cognised and evaluated nature; it is precisely at this cognised and evaluated quality that completing aesthetic form is directed. (PCMF 278; PSMF 280)

Aesthetic activity 'removes' these contents from the 'open event of being' (life) and subordinates them to a new unity: the unity of form. Previously *ethical* content thus acquires an *aesthetic* validity. Here Bakhtin is close to an idea developed by Simmel, and before him by Schopenhauer: aesthetic experience suspends the practical viewpoint of everyday life, that is, perception enmeshed in the *flow* of life, and momentarily overcomes the split between subject and object in a timeless intuition of essence. Aesthetic activity is thus a timeless moment of phenomenological intuition in which the aesthetic object is produced. The 'material' of the work of verbal art is not, as the Formalists thought, the language of the work as understood by linguistics, but language as transformed by aesthetic creation into a 'physico-mathematical space' within which the aesthetic object is realised (PCMF 295; PSMF 296). Form is the 'form of content' as realised in the material and has two moments: architectonic form (the form of the intentional act of producing the aesthetic object) and compositional form (technique), that is, the form of the material whole of the artefact. Thus, an analysis of form should not simply be an analysis of compositional technique, as the Formalists and others had argued, but also an analysis of the way in which the content (ethical, scientific, and so on) is aesthetically reprocessed to become an aesthetic object.

This critique of Russian Formalism, which is termed 'material aesthetics', anticipates many of the features of Medvedev's later and more celebrated critique, but here the neo-Kantian and phenomenological terminology is still uncompromised. Formalism is accused of confusing architectonic and compositional forms, that is, the intentional production of the aesthetic object and the composition of the work as a material entity. The result is an undervaluing of the former and an overvaluing of the latter. The moment of intentionally recasting content of an ethical, scientific or other type according to aesthetic principles by lifting it out of the 'stream of life' is downplayed in favour of a 'reification' of compositional technique. Thus, for Bakhtin, in Formalism we have another manifestation of 'theoretism': the meaning of the work of art as a composed whole is split off from the moment of intentional engagement with the 'already cognised' aspects of reality in life in which the aesthetic object is 'achieved'. The work of art thus loses its connection with life and is transformed into a dead object of culture.

Bakhtin argues that from within life, the artist bestows form on the contents of life as a 'gift'. Life then, as Simmel had argued, transcends itself, it becomes 'more than life', it becomes art. The artist bestows form as an aesthetic *boundary*, and it thus becomes a part of culture. Culture is now treated not as a 'spatial whole', but as a realm of boundaries:

It is completely distributed along boundaries, boundaries run through it everywhere, through each of its moments, the systematic unity of culture leads into the atoms of cultural life, and like the sun is reflected in every droplet of it. Every cultural act lives essentially on boundaries: here is its seriousness and significance; abstracted from boundaries it loses its soil, it becomes empty, it degenerates and dies. (PCMF 274; PSMF 276)

In this early essay we can see how ethical philosophy becomes transformed into an analysis of aesthetic form. What Bakhtin calls 'aesthetic activity' becomes a point of transition between life and art that will reappear in various forms throughout the work of the Circle in the coming years. However, there is another distinctive feature of Bakhtin's analysis that underlies his later and better-known work on dialogue and the novel: his concern with various types of relationship between author and hero in narrative literature.

'Outsideness'

Author and Hero in Aesthetic Activity is perhaps the most important of Bakhtin's early works. It is a phenomenological analysis of the various types of relation between author and hero in narrative literature based to a large extent on an adaption of Scheler's subtle typology of intersubjective relations to the realm of aesthetics (Poole 2001b). We now have evidence of which parts of Scheler's book on sympathy Bakhtin made extensive notes on and this has made the assessment of his debt to Scheler quite straightforward (OK 654–734). However, the work is more than simply an application of Scheler, for Bakhtin draws on a number of sources and combines them in an inventive way. In *Author and Hero* Bakhtin also expounds the philosophical principles that would underlie his famous 1929 book on Dostoevsky.

When describing the nature of 'aesthetic activity' itself, Bakhtin combines Simmel's notion of culture as boundaries (Tihanov 2000a: 63–4) with Cohen's idea that in art love embraces ugliness and transforms it into beauty (Poma 1997a: 146) to argue that the drawing of aesthetic boundaries is an act of *love*. Bakhtin is here following Kagan's earlier adoption of Cohen in arguing that 'the work of art lives inwardly by love' (Kagan 1998: 13), but Bakhtin's imagery is especially problematic for its gender stereotyping. The artist is an active, masculine subject who shapes the passive, 'feminine' manifold of life by bestowing form: 'in this act the feminine passivity and *naïveté* of available being becomes beautiful' (AH 136; AG 197). There is no doubt that some religious significance is bestowed on authorial activity in this essay (Coates 1998), and this may be the source of this sexist imagery. It is, however, certainly an undesirable element of Bakhtin's phenomenology. The loving activity of the artist, working from a unique and unrepeatable position in being, is a responsible deed, with the result that the aesthetic standpoint of the author towards the heroes of a work has an *ethical* significance. Aesthetic activity proper is possible only when the artist takes up a position in being that is no-one else's; the artist has a unique and unrepeatable perspective on being that allows him or her to take up an evaluative attitude towards the heroes as images of aspects of life.

Scheler had been especially keen to oppose then fashionable ideas that ethical action involved the merging of the self and the other in an act of empathy. To this end he adopted from Husserl's 1907 *Ding und Raum* (*Thing and Space*, Husserl 1997) a distinction between the (living) body as experienced from within (*Leib*) and the (physical) body perceived from without (*Korper*), noting that the individual's experience of the latter is possible only through the eyes of another. Each person thus has a certain perceptual 'surplus'. This reciprocity of seer and seen is then generalised into a theory of the mutual dependence of subjects in society for a sense of their individual unity. Bakhtin adopts the principle of this reciprocity, but turns the argument in an aesthetic direction based on an idea presented in Paul Natorp's *Sozialpädagogik* that 'there is no understanding of the self without the understanding of others as its basis' (Natorp 1974: 95). As Bakhtin puts it, 'my body can become aesthetically valid (*znachimyi*) only in life perceived in the category of the *other*' (AH 59; AG135). The image of a living person can only become part of culture through the perception of the other and this constitutes 'aesthetic activity': the production of an aesthetic object. However, it is not only the body that becomes an aesthetic object in such activity, but also the individual psyche: a coherent individual personality is dependent upon the perception of the other from without. Thus, Bakhtin notes that 'the soul is a gift that my spirit gives to the *other*' (AH 132: AG 194). For this quality of being located outside the other, Bakhtin coins the word 'outsideness' (*vnenakhodimost'*), and for the various types of intersubjective, personal existence he uses the terms 'I-for-myself', 'I-for-another' and 'the other-for-me'.

Outsideness is central to Bakhtin's aesthetics and its importance is asserted, in various forms, throughout his work. As we have seen, Scheler and Bakhtin both argued that intersubjective relations are characterised by the co-experiencing of an 'event of being'. However, this co-experiencing is not in itself an ethical or aesthetic activity. In his book on sympathy, Scheler outlines various and distinct modes of co-feeling which range from mere emotional infection in a crowd to the co-suffering of two parents before the corpse of their beloved child and the sympathy of a family friend on hearing of the death of that child. Although often confused, these modes are quite distinct: the two parents feel pain *with* one another while for the family friend the suffering of the parents is an object for the friend's 'co-suffering' or 'sym-pathy'. Thus, the suffering of the parents and the sympathy of the friend are qualitatively different things. In each case, the act of co-feeling only has ethical significance if the unique position of the percipient is maintained and the *value* of the experience is thus recognised: an abandonment of the self in shared grief or joy has no ethical value. Consequently, the emotional infection that runs through a crowd of people who lose themselves in an intoxicating collective experience is not an ethically valuable experience (Scheler 1954: 12–18).

Bakhtin adopts Scheler's argument that the percipient must not simply empathise, that is, feel and perceive what the other feels and perceives, but must subsequently return to his or her own position outside the other and give shape and wholeness to the one perceived; however, he applies this to narrative technique in artistic literature.[7] He argues that relations between author and hero are open to an analysis based on intersubjective relations between the 'I' and the other, with the *aesthetic* significance of the relations replacing the *ethical* dimensions discussed by Scheler. The authorial consciousness encloses the hero from all sides, allowing the latter to achieve wholeness, but does not merge with the hero's consciousness. Bakhtin's study deals with the spatial qualities of author–hero relations, that is, the types of 'outsideness' through which the author bestows completion on the hero while allowing the latter to maintain autonomy as a unique orientation in being rather than as just an object.

Outsideness also describes a central aspect of the author's relation to the situations narrated in the work of art. The 'participation' of the author in the narrative event is not a direct one, while for the hero it is precisely that. The author's participation is that of a 'disinterested' (unbiased), though not indifferent, observer with an understanding of the ethical meaning of what is happening. The authorial evaluation is a type of 'co-experience' from outside, which allows the event to be given unity and completion in a way that is impossible from within. Outsideness is thus what makes the event productive: the author's so-called 'surplus of vision' (*izbytok vídeniia*) is a precondition for creativity. Thus, the world in which the hero lives is viewed in a fundamentally different way by the hero and by the author. For the hero, the parameters of the world are viewed as a *horizon* (Peursen 1977), with objects encountered appearing as that which stands over and against the hero in the cognitive-ethical and thus intentional openness of living a life. For the author, however, the objects of the world are viewed as the hero's surroundings, his environment. The hero is seen amid other objects. Similarly, the hero does not experience his own life as a whole: his birth and death, for example, do not exist for the hero but only for other heroes and for the author. The hero exists for him- or herself not as a complete life within certain surroundings plotted out against a story line, but as a purposeful and free unity within the open event of being. Aesthetic completion is therefore possible only from the point of view of the author. Only from this perspective does the portrayed life become something that is *determined*, that is, 'liberated' from the open 'yet-to-be' of the future, and thereby become open to any final evaluation. This remains a crucial element of Bakhtin's later work on the novel.

Lived experience, argues Bakhtin, is 'a trace of meaning [*smysl*] in being', it is a trace of culture in life, of validity in existence, which becomes 'aesthetically consolidated' by being cleansed of all that gives it meaning as a yet-to-be-achieved task. It is 'individualised' by being concentrated and combined in an individual unity, a soul, that is an aesthetically valid and completed hero. Meaning becomes embodied in the determinate, and indeed determined, life of the hero by virtue of the enclosing view of the author (AH 115–16; AG 180–1). What is an ethical problem for the hero depends on his or her freedom to act in the 'open event of being'. For the author, however, who views the hero in his or her environment, as determined and enclosed in a strictly circumscribed event whose outcome is known in advance, the hero engages in an *aesthetic* act. The hero acts ethically in his or her own world, experiencing all boundaries as impediments and striving to overcome those boundaries. The author, however, is able to achieve aesthetic judgement by bestowing boundaries, and it is this aesthetic judgement that the reader as external spectator co-creates. But the author's relation to the hero is not like that to any other aesthetic object, since it is a relation that is from both within and without: it is a sympathetic relation in Scheler's sense. The author's and reader's roles are simultaneously 'passive' and 'active': passive in identifying with the hero by a certain conditional erasure of the boundaries between 'us' and the hero, and active when 'we' withdraw and redraw the boundaries to achieve aesthetic closure. In this 'we' achieve a sense of the hero as an ethical being and 'we' also achieve the 'surplus of vision' that produces aesthetic value. In this way, the 'trace of meaning' in the hero's lived experience achieves an aesthetic validity (AH 90–1; AG 160).

Crises of 'outsideness'

In addition to his critique of philosophies of empathy, Scheler argues that there are definite types of pathology that may arise in inter-subjective relations (Scheler 1954: 18–26). These, too, have considerable significance for Bakhtin's argument. At one extreme, what Scheler calls the 'idiopathic' type, the 'I' may project his own unique place in being on to the other and in so doing erase the unique position of the other from the perspective of the 'I'. The 'I' in such cases denies the other his or her own right to a unique position. At the other extreme, the 'I' may become so besotted with the other that the unique position of the 'I' is in danger of being lost. This Scheler terms the 'heteropathic' pathology: the 'I' is so hypnotised that he or she 'lives entirely in' or 'through' the other. This type of identification Scheler finds in totemism and in the mystery cults of the ancient world. Then there is the ecstatic fusion of sexual partners in a 'single stream of life' or the Bacchic revel. The 'I' must raise him- or herself above this merging into a 'vital con-sciousness' and the bodily concerns of life rather than simply give vent to passions and irrationality. By so doing one can attain the realm of 'spirit'. This requires the maintenance of *both* one's own unique place in existence *and* a capacity to co-experience. Absorption into either of these extremes is an ethically bankrupt pathology, and Scheler argues that it is only through a creative, indeed, *loving* tension between the 'I' and the other in intentional acts in which the feelings of the other are considered that ethical virtue lies. In such a relationship the person is not transformed into an object, but a distance necessary for understanding is maintained. Sympathy allows us to see that the other is of equal value to the 'I', existing as genuinely and as truly as the 'I'. Through sympathy, the value of other people as such is given.

Transforming this into an aesthetic argument, Bakhtin argues that there are occasions when the author loses or compromises his or her outsideness and in doing so loses a stable and unified evaluative position vis-à-vis the characters of the work, and thus the events related. As Poole (2001b) has shown, this position is developed in a variety of ways that relate quite closely to Scheler's analysis. At one extreme, the author's relationship to the hero is transformed into the author's relationship to him or herself, with the result that the hero becomes self-determining. This may mean that (a) the hero becomes autobiographical and thus uncompletable, eternally finding new forms that transcend the image others have of him, or (b) his attitude to life becomes the image that the author has of his or her own attitude to life and as such becomes unconvincing. Both (a) and (b) produce unconvincing heroes, but in the first case the form of the whole is also rendered unconvincing. There is, however, a third type of problematic outsideness: the hero is his or her own author and treats life as if it were art. He plays a role.

Conversely, the author might become totally captivated by a hero, accepting his 'emotional-volitional' attitude towards objects and his 'cognitive-ethical' position in the world as authoritative. The author thus perceives and experiences everything from the point of view of the character. In this case the authorial project is thrown into crisis because although some features of completion are necessary for the work to remain an artistic work at all, those features become very shaky indeed, having no stable evaluative position from which a consistent outsideness can be maintained.[8] The centre of value shifts to the problems discussed in the work, which is therefore placed on the verge of being transformed into a philosophical dispute. The boundaries that constitute aesthetic culture are mistrusted as life, and thus creative energy, recoils from them. It is significant that in *Author and Hero* Bakhtin notes that almost all of Dostoevsky's heroes are of the second type and that such a novel represents a crisis of authorship. 'Life becomes intelligible and obtains the weight of an event only from within itself, only where I experience it as an *I*' argues Bakhtin, and for this reason the aesthetic relation becomes *ethicised*, in Dostoevsky 'painfully' so (AH 203–5; AG 251–3). The evaluation of this phenomenon changes significantly in the 1929 Dostoevsky study, as we shall see.

The sociology of interaction

Simmel and Scheler developed a type of sociology that stressed what Simmel called 'forms of sociation'. This notion refers to a concern with forms of social interaction on quite a small scale rather than with larger questions of the institutional structure of society. As we shall see, this concern is present in Bakhtin's work throughout his career, even though he turns toward more general questions in the 1930s. Scheler, it should also be noted, was one of the founders of the so-called 'sociology of knowledge', which Kenneth Stikkers characterises as seeking 'insights into the concrete experiences of persons living with one another in groups, into their co-feelings and co-thinking. It examines ... the inner subjective, psychic bonds which unite persons in sympathy and love' (Stikkers 1980: 12–13). Bakhtin's early work is sociological in the same sense: forms of authorship are symptomatic of certain forms of social interaction, including the degree and type of individual differentiation.

This kind of sociology presents the world exclusively as a collection of overlapping fields of vision, what Scheler called 'milieus' and Bakhtin called purviews (*krugozory*). In essence, the argument is that each milieu is a separate world. Thus, Scheler argues that the objects encountered in a milieu do not have 'the slightest thing' to do either with 'Kant's "thing in itself"' or with the objects conceived by science' (1973: 139). If Scheler's formulation is accepted an important problem arises: how do people (let alone animals of different species) engage in these various forms of interaction in the first place? What is their common environment? There are two possible answers. Agents may be situated within a given, if transformable, common environment (as understood by physics) within which their acts, perceptual or otherwise take place. This realist solution was most systematically pursued by J.J. Gibson (1986), who argued that what Scheler calls a milieu is a sort of 'niche' within a world that is shared by and common to all species. This is incompatible with Scheler's interpretation of milieu. Alternatively, the extradiscursive world can be declared unknowable. In such a case it is through the interaction of minds, which occurs according to universally valid logical principles, that the larger, social and empirical world is forever being constituted. This is a neo-Kantian solution that would be equally foreign to Scheler. Bakhtin, like Kagan before him, follows the latter course while, as we shall see, his collaborators Voloshinov and Medvedev equivocated between the two.

It is now possible to see why narrative literature, and ultimately the novel, was to prove such a potentially fertile area for Bakhtin. In the ethical sphere the final significance of the mutual constitution of the world can only be discerned by an external God, the 'author' of the world. This is consistent with the Marburg tradition, where religion is dissolved into ethics, and the ideal state stands in for the deity as an incarnation of the 'idea of God'. Meanwhile, Bakhtin argues that the aesthetic significance of the world constituted in the novel through the intersecting purviews of the heroes can be discerned only by the author. The author, like the Judaic God is, however, absent and we, as readers stand in, maintaining the 'idea' of an author.

Yet a problem remains. If the world is something that exists in thought, but thought is no longer something that is restricted to the bounds of a single, individual, consciousness, there must be a common medium through which minds are connected. This, many contemporary philosophers found in language, the very stuff of which literature is made. Voloshinov was working on language and literature at the time, and it is perhaps at least partly due to his influence that Bakhtin was to abandon his *Author and Hero* study and embark on a detailed phenomenological examination of discourse in the novels of Dostoevsky.

There is one other important ramification from the solution that Bakhtin adopts. The person in society and the hero in narrative literature is permanently on trial as it were, attempting to justify his or her deeds before a judge who is always just over the horizon but who sees all. We will meet this feature again in the Dostoevsky book and in various new forms in the later work on the novel. In *Author and Hero* this quasi-juridical feature is clearest in the implied aesthetic laws stipulating the rights and obligations governing author–hero relations with each role-player having a certain 'legal' personality. Thus, the author has a duty to engage in a conditional merging of perspectives with the hero before a 'return' to his or her own unique position to bestow wholeness. Failure to observe this results in either a violation of the hero's 'rights' as a 'free' person or an abdication of authorial responsibility, which results in the hero violating the 'rights' of the author. Violation of this aesthetic code would be the equivalent of the state abusing its role as the 'source of law' and engaging in the tyrannical violation of individual rights or a withdrawal from that role, which results in society's moral degeneration.

Bakhtin's early work is thus of both philosophical and sociological significance. The neo-Kantian ideas with which he engaged formed the philosophical foundations of classical sociology and the various schools of phenomenology and life-philosophy spawned their own versions of sociological theory. The emphasis on aesthetics does, however, mean that Bakhtin's focus of attention is predominantly philosophical. But this was to change. From the mid-1920s, other members of the Bakhtin Circle were drawing out the wider sociological implications of Bakhtin's intersubjective phenomenology and linking it to a particular version of Marxism. In addition, the question of language came to occupy a central position in the work of the Circle, demanding a closer consideration of the social nature of human consciousness. It is to these developments that we will now turn.

3 Marxism, Semiotics and Sociology (1926–29)

We have seen that, although Bakhtin is perhaps best known for his various works on language and literature, the question of language is not central to his early work. Bakhtin's discussion of narrative literature is firmly within the bounds of philosophical aesthetics. Even when he deals with those contemporary critics who made the study of poetic language the focal points of their work, namely, the Formalists, Bakhtin was only concerned to distinguish between language as understood by positivist linguistics and by poetics. Beginning with the 1929 Dostoevsky book, however, language assumes a central place in his analysis. This chapter deals with the intervening period, during which Bakhtin finally abandoned *Author and Hero* and worked on his Dostoevsky study. As noted earlier, the works with which we will be concerned in this chapter are of disputed authorship, and Bakhtin's participation in their production cannot be excluded. However, I will discuss them as predominantly the work of their signatories, but also as products of the meetings and discussions of the Circle at the time. We will see that Voloshinov and Medvedev brought to the Circle expertise in contemporary psychology, philosophy of language and German art history that ultimately transformed 'Bakhtinian' theory into what we know today.

Marxism and contemporary philosophy

Apart from the very different tone and language of the works published in the names of Voloshinov and Medvedev, one is immediately struck by the quality and quantity of footnote references found there. Together, these factors signal a very different authorial practice, one seeking to familiarise a perhaps not entirely specialist readership with the field under examination and to make connections between quite varied areas of study. The issue of Marxism in these works is connected with this practice, since in each case we are presented with arguments about the relevance of the topics under consideration to Marxism and the contribution that Marxism has to make to them. In this sense the authors are trying to form a bridge between idealist philosophies of culture and Marxism and, as an extension of this, a bridge between the political leadership and the more traditional intelligentsia to which they belonged. This is in keeping with Voloshinov's and Medvedev's association with the Institute for the Comparative Study of Literatures and Languages of the West and East (ILIaZV), one of the main centres of 'fellow travelling, leftist (including Marxist and Bolshevik) scholarship' in Leningrad at the time (Clark 1995: 206–7). ILIaZV was also one of the institutional bases of the linguist and archaeologist Nikolai Marr, whose significance for the Circle will be discussed in subsequent chapters.

It is significant that Voloshinov and Medvedev both term their works exercises in sociology: Voloshinov's 1926 'Discourse in Life and Discourse in Poetry' is subtitled 'questions of sociological poetics'; his 1929 *Marxism and the Philosophy of Language* 'basic problems of sociological method in the study of language'; and Medvedev's 1928 *Formal Method in Literary Scholarship* 'a critical introduction to sociological poetics'. We have already seen that neo-Kantian philosophy and its various offshoots provided the philosophical basis of classical sociology, and it was for this reason that Lenin had rejected that discipline as such, but it had also been claimed for Marxism in a 1921 book by the extremely influential Bolshevik Nikolai Bukharin. Bukharin's *Historical Materialism: A Popular Manual of Marxist Sociology* purported to be a general exposition of Marxist theory and it had become the basic text for the theoretical education of Party cadres by the mid-1920s. With this in mind it is easy to see how sociology was regarded as the ground on which Marxism and neo-Kantianism could meet. It is also notable that other attempts to create a neo-Kantian Marxism had been pursued throughout the 1920s by, among others, the so-called Austro-Marxists Max Adler and Otto Bauer, with Adler claiming that 'Marxism and sociology are the same thing' (Bottomore and Goode 1978: 64–5). Although there were a number of sharp criticisms of the attempt to convert Marxism into a sociology, and of Bukharin's book in particular, by several prominent Marxist intellectuals, the prestige of Bukharin at the end of the 1920s was such that his work had an authoritative status in Russia.

Bukharin's work did not include any systematic exposition of dialectics, the very core of Marxist philosophical theory; dialectics was replaced by a theory of the shifting equilibrium of social elements driven by a single external cause, technological development. This led the German Communist and theorist Karl Korsch to complain that here 'the fluid methodology of Marx's dialectic freezes into a number of causal interconnections of historical phenomena in different areas of society – in other words it became something that could best be described as a general systematic sociology' (Korsch 1970: 56). Bukharin's brand of Marxism was therefore quite conducive to being combined with classical sociology. One other point about Bukharin's book needs to be mentioned before we proceed: it argues that 'ideology' denotes 'certain unified *systems* of forms, thoughts, rules of conduct etc.' such as 'science and art, law and morality, etc.' (Bukharin 1926: 208). Such an understanding of the term quite easily converges with a more general notion of culture, and with the neo-Kantian idea of a realm of validity divided into particular sciences (ethics, aesthetics, and so on) which are underlain by mathematics.

In addition to their move into sociology, the 'disputed texts' are also particularly interesting for their adoption of ideas from Brentanian philosophy, particularly as developed in the work of the philosopher of language Anton Marty (1847–1914), the psychologist and philosopher of language Karl Bühler (1879–1963) and the Gestalt theory which originated with Christian von Ehrenfels (1859–1932). Close attention to the footnotes of the works of Voloshinov and Medvedev and recently published archival materials from Voloshinov's time at ILIaZV (LDV) make this influence quite clear. Significantly, these philosophies were fundamentally hostile to Kantianism (especially in its neo-Kantian reformulation) and maintained a realist commitment to the existence of a world independent of our consciousness of it. From these thinkers Voloshinov and Medvedev derived a model of discursive interaction that could render Bakhtin's notion of aesthetic intersubjectivity in discursive terms and lead to a conception of genre.

Voloshinov and contemporary psychology

The earliest 'disputed texts' show that contemporary psychology was a crucial influence on the shape of developing 'Bakhtinian' theory. Voloshinov's first major article, 'On the far side of the social: On Freudianism' (1925), was a critique of contemporary Soviet psychologists' attempts to appropriate the work of Freud into a 'Marxist' science of the mind. This was followed by a more detailed critique, *Freudianism: A Critical Sketch* (1927).

These texts were directly related to the debates that followed K.N. Kornilov's[1] article in *Pravda* in 1923 calling for the Marxist reconstruction of psychology (Joravsky 1989). Some young psychologists, such as L.R. Luria, responded by trying to combine Marx and Freud. Kornilov himself was an eclectic thinker who considered Marxist psychology to be a specific type of 'objective psychology'. As such, he argued, Marxism is fundamentally opposed to such 'subjective' theories as those of Wundt and the previous head of the Moscow Psychology Institute, G.I. Chelpanov. Voloshinov explicitly refers to Kornilov (FKO 98; FMC 18), who advocated that organism–environment interaction was the primary focus of objective psychology. Kornilov played a leading role in Soviet psychology until the final victory of Pavlov's reflex theory in the early 1930s. The ideas of Kornilov were open to many different interpretations, perhaps including the dialogic perspective that Voloshinov was to develop. Certainly Vygotsky, who developed what is in some ways a strikingly similar approach to dialogue, felt able to combine many of the same philosophical sources as were used by Voloshinov with the ideas of Kornilov (van der Veer and Valsiner 1991: 112–40).

Voloshinov's interventions aimed to show Freudianism to be an unsound doctrine and one fundamentally incompatible with Marxism. Following Kornilov, Voloshinov positions Freud within 'two trends of contemporary psychology' (FKO 97; FMC 17), which he terms objective and subjective, a strategy he was later to apply to the philosophy of language. Freud is branded a subjective psychologist, and Marxism hostile to Freudianism. Since subjectivism was pronounced the chief defect of Freudianism, selective borrowing from other 'objectivist' schools such as the *Gestalt* philosophers,[2] Kornilov's 'reactology' and American behaviourism were legitimised.

Voloshinov begins his studies by noting how the biological terminology of organic processes became dominant in bourgeois philosophy from the time of Schopenhauer and Nietzsche, and how their influence could still be seen in the work of Bergson, Simmel and even Scheler. Freudianism was the next stage in this progression (or retrogression) notwithstanding its claim to neutral, scientific status (PTSS 26–7). The features that united all these varieties of bourgeois philosophy were characterised as follows:

(1) *A biological understanding of life stands at the centre of the philo-sophical system.* The isolated organic unity is declared to be the highest value and criterion of philosophy.

(2) *A mistrust of consciousness.* An attempt to reduce its role to a minimum in cultural creativity. The critique of Kantianism as a philosophy of consciousness derives from this.

(3) *An attempt to replace all objective socio-economic categories with subjective-psychological or biological ones.* An attempt to understand history and culture directly from nature, disregard-ing economics. (FMC 12; FKO 93)

Voloshinov is thus drawing a strong connection between Freudian-ism and vitalistic life-philosophy in this work, and he refers the reader to the critical article 'Contemporary vitalism' (1926) published in the name of the biologist and member of the Bakhtin Circle I.I. Kanaev, but which Bakhtin is thought to have had a hand in writing. Fashionable vitalist biologists like Hans Dreich, who had a significant influence on such philosophers as Bergson, strove to create an anti-Darwinian theory of evolution based on the idea of a vital life-force that created a space for free will.[3] In response to these theories, Voloshinov makes the following assertion justifying a Marxist-sociological approach:

> The abstract biological personality, the biological individuum, which has become the alpha and omega of contemporary ideology, does not exist at all. There is no person outside society and, therefore, outside objective socio-economic conditions. It [biological personality] is a bad abstraction. Only as part of a social whole, in class and through class, does a human personal-ity become historically real and culturally productive. (FMC 15; FKO 96)

With the exception of the centrality given to the question of class, such a position would meet no objection from the thoroughly sociological Simmel and Scheler, and it is highly questionable whether it would conflict with the work of Freud himself. Indeed, Voloshinov is opposed as much to 'psychologism' as to biological reductionism.

The neo-Kantians and the phenomenologists had all been part of the 'anti-psychologism' movement in philosophy that also included early analytical philosophers such as Frege (1848–1925). This movement is often referred to as the 'linguistic turn' in philosophy, for it resulted in a shift from the notion that thoughts are internal to the psyche to the notion that thoughts are sign-borne and therefore able to be communicated from one to another. The neo-Kantians before Cassirer did not develop any detailed philosophy of language, but they had argued that the a priori elements of thought are objectively valid for all subjects. The question remained, however, as to how thoughts are communicated. Husserl, like Frege, argued that thoughts are external to the mind, external to the world of what happens or is the case, are objective in not depending on our apprehensions of them and play no role in causal relations (Frege called this the 'non-actuality' of thoughts). This all necessitated that a central role be given to language in all considerations of intersubjective interaction.

We will return to this in more detail below. However, it is important to note that these developments underlay Voloshinov's critique of Freud. Voloshinov argues that Freudianism 'transferred into its system all the fundamental defects of the subjective psychology contemporary with it' by arguing that the 'spiritual life' of a person consisted of 'sensations, notions, desires and feelings'. These were now, however, reworked into the domain of the unconscious. The psychological operations that Freud described as 'natural' Voloshinov argued were actually 'ideological' (in the terms of anti-psychologism, 'thoughts'), and that since they were supposedly perceptible in introspection, they could only be perceived by consciousness. The desires identified by Freud were therefore no more objective than the spurious 'life-force' of the vitalists (FMC 69–70; FKO 146–7). Although Freud had recast the previously calm picture of desires characteristic of traditional psychology, turning the individual psyche into a battleground of biological desires, his 'talking cure' method relied on the ability to communicate these desires. As Voloshinov puts it, 'Freud's whole psychological construction is fundamentally based on the person's verbal utterances, it is only a special interpretation of them. Of course all these utterances are constructed in the conscious sphere of the psyche' (FMC 76; FKO 154). Freud presented the interaction of the conscious and unconscious in a way that was quite unlike that between two material forces, since they are described in terms of mutual hostility, incomprehension and a mutual urge to deceive one another. 'Such interrelations are surely only possible between two ideas, two ideological directions, two hostile persons.' What Freud had miscast as a struggle between material forces was actually a projection of a complex intersubjective, discursive exchange between doctor and patient in the psychoanalytical session:

> The patient wants to hide certain experiences and life-events from the doctor, to foist on the doctor his own point of view on the reasons for the illness and on the character of his experiences. The doctor in turn strives to uphold his authority as a doctor, to procure acknowledgements from the patient, to compel the patient to adopt the correct point of view on the illness and its symptoms. With all this there intersect other moments: there may be differences in sex, in age, in social position, finally, differences of profession between doctor and patient – all this complicates their interrelations and struggle. (FMC 78: FKO 156–7)

Voloshinov was here drawing on a model of communicative psychology that had been pioneered by the Würzburg School in the early part of the century, and which had particularly been developed by Karl Bühler in his critique of the main trends in psychology, including Freud (Kusch 1999: 118ff.; Bühler 1926). Bühler's critique had been published in abridged form the year before Voloshinov's study, and it was to prove highly influential both for the Circle and for Vygotsky.[4] Voloshinov's application of this model is certainly no mere recapitulation of the Würzburg arguments, however. To use the terminology of Scheler and the early Bakhtin, the struggle between the conscious and the unconscious is presented here as a struggle between the 'I' and the other. The patient wants the doctor to accept his 'I-for-myself' and the doctor wants the patient to accept the position of I-for-another, but this is complicated by the issue of the 'other-for-me'. Now, however, consideration of issues of social differences assumes a prominent position, and the intersubjective exchange begins to be treated as a form of dialogue.

In place of Freud's model of the conscious and unconscious mind, Voloshinov posits a distinction between inner and outer discourse, which he correlates with 'life-ideology' (*zhiteiskaia ideologiia*) and 'official ideology'. These concepts figure quite prominently in his later philosophy of language and so need to be addressed here. The notion of inner discourse or 'inner speech' can be traced back to von Humboldt, but became especially topical in turn-of-the-century German neurology, psychologistic philosophy of language (Vossler), and some neo-Kantian writings. For example, in a footnote to an article of 1925, which Voloshinov cites, Vygotsky (1997: 377) adduces Paul Natorp (1974 [1899]) as saying, 'Even in solitude, when we silently think to ourselves, we constantly use the words of language and, consequently, retain at least the fiction of communication.' Vygotsky regards this insight as a crucial step toward the 'socialising of all consciousness' (1997: 77), something that Voloshinov also pursues.

The concept of inner speech had been further developed in studies into aphasia, the loss or impairment of the power to use or comprehend words, usually as a result of brain damage. Although studies of aphasia had been developed in the last part of the nineteenth century by writers such as Benno Erdmann, with whose work Voloshinov was familiar (LDV 89), they had remained wedded to associative psychology. During the First World War, especially in the work of the neurologist and psychologist 'fellow-traveller' of the Gestalt psychologists Kurt Goldstein, the study of aphasia took a new, holistic turn with the study of brain-damaged soldiers.[5] The material that resulted from Goldstein's research became 'the main source of information regarding the total activity of the human brain' (Murphy and Kovach 1994: 261), and this provided a wealth of material for those, like Voloshinov, who were keen to oppose the physiological reductionism of the Pavlov School in Russia in the 1920s (FKO 162, 186–7; FMC 83, 129–30). Goldstein's theory of inner speech was developed in several publications from 1912 onwards, and these became the basis of the theory of inner speech developed by Vygotsky in the 1930s (van der Veer and Valsiner 1991: 179).[6] Like the Würzburg School, with whom he overtly allied himself, Goldstein rejected the notion that thinking is the association of images.[7] Instead, he argued that 'inner speech is the totality of processes and experiences which occur when we are going to express our thoughts, etc., in external speech and when we perceive heard sounds as language'. In some key features Goldstein's account is very close to Voloshinov's own characterisation in 1926, making mere coincidence an unlikely explanation (Goldstein 1948: 94; SZSP 83–4; DLDP 26–7). It is quite likely that Voloshinov encountered Goldstein's work on aphasia, which had a high profile among holistic psychologists and philosophers at the time,[8] while researching contemporary psychology in the mid-1920s, and this may actually predate Vygotsky's engagement. For Goldstein 'inner speech' is linked to the fact that the brain is 'set-up to synthesise the chaos of experience into organised wholes' or Gestalten (Harrington

1996: 147). Inner speech is thus governed by an 'inner speechform', that is a 'system of forms' that constitutes the 'special attitude with which the group or individual looks at the facts of life, the special interest and communicative behaviour in general, finds expression in peculiarities in the structure of their means of communication, in their language'. The inner speechform is thus a mental 'set' on intentional objects:

> This is expressed in a special organisation of the forms, by which general communication with other people takes place (the special way how tenses, flexions, articles, are used, the preference which is given to words of general character or words for concrete experience, the difference in rhythm, sentence formation, etc.). (Goldstein 1948: 92)

We are here only a step away from Voloshinov's later notion that style embodies a socially specific refraction of being, and his notion of discursive genres.

Voloshinov makes an important move when he correlates 'inner speech' with 'life ideology'. The English translation of Voloshinov's term '*zhiteiskaia ideologiia*' (life-ideology) as 'behavioural ideology' is a good example of the problems uninformed translations have brought about in understanding the work of the Bakhtin Circle. This completely obscures the connection with life-philosophy and makes its place within the work of the Circle as a whole unclear (Tihanov 1998a: 605). Both types of ideology for Voloshinov have a verbal embodiment, but life-ideology is 'in some respects more sensitive, responsive, nervous and mobile' than 'official' ideology. These differences of degree notwithstanding, the same methods are suitable for studying both kinds of ideology (FMC 88; FKO 166). As Tihanov (1998a) has shown, we here see Voloshinov following Bukharin in dividing the 'superstructure' into a relatively unsystematic 'social psychology' and a more systematised ideology proper. As Bukharin puts it at one point, 'social psychology is a sort of supply-chamber for ideology ... *ideologies are a coagulated social psychology*'. With reference to Simmel, Bukharin argued that social psychology arises in socio-economic life and is an energetic phenomenon that exerts an influence on ideology proper. Using the term life-ideology, Voloshinov is reworking one of the key features of life-philosophy in Marxist terms (Bukharin 1926: 212–17). Life-ideology is present in the relatively unsystematic, fluid and unuttered 'inner speech' that makes up the psyche, while 'official' ideology is uttered and more systematic. Both phenomena, however, assume immersion in a social environment, assume intersubjective interaction. Yet the labelling of the two forms of consciousness as 'official' and 'unofficial' sets them within a socio-political framework: the distinction becomes a politicised Simmelian dichotomy between life and objective culture, with the incrustations of the latter becoming a censoring influence on the former:

> The wider and deeper the chasm between official and unofficial consciousness, the more difficult it is for the motifs of inner discourse to cross into outer discourse (oral, written, printed; in a narrow or wide social circle) in order to be formulated, clarified, become established. All such motifs turn sickly, lose their verbal countenance and little by little actually become a 'foreign body' in the psyche. (FMC 89; FKO 168)

If, however, an element that is in contradiction with the 'official ideology' is rooted in a well-established social group that arises on the socio-economic structure it has the potential to find verbal expression therein and develop into a revolutionary ideology.

The book closes with an attack on those who sought to marry Marxism and Freudianism, with particular attention given to the incompatibility of Marxism and psychologism. With this in mind it is not surprising that attention was next to shift to a full-blown philosophical engagement with language in which an attempt was made to unify Marxist sociology and neo-Kantianism.

The main significance of Voloshinov's work on Freud is that it provides evidence of his engagement with contemporary psychology, and indicates that some of his better known and most productive ideas derive from this engagement. Voloshinov's work on Freud does, however, suffer from a one-sided concentration on the early Freud and thereby overlooks most of the latter's later writings on culture. Nevertheless, Voloshinov brought to the Circle a significant knowledge of trends in contemporary psychology, and this becomes an important element of the Circle's subsequent work.

Voloshinov on discourse in life and art

Two of the Circle's main works written in the late 1920s focused on the relationship between art and social life: Voloshinov's 'Discourse in Life and Discourse in Poetry' (DLDP/SZSP (1926)) and Medvedev's *Formal Method in Literary Scholarship* (FMLS/FML (1928)). Both purport to be exercises in a Marxist sociology of art and take as their point of departure a critique of the positivist treatment of the work of art as a thing. Voloshinov's article, which is our focus here, marks a significant step forward in the work of the Circle. The critique of Formalism and positivism is for the first time transformed into an analysis of the varying functions of language in practical and artistic spheres.

Voloshinov argues that every work actually has three dimensions in a particular configuration: creator, artefact and perceiver. 'It is a particular form of interrelationship between creator and percipient, fixed in a work of art ... To understand this particular form of social intercourse ... is the task of sociological poetics.' Aesthetic interaction is quite different from that in other areas of ideological interaction (political, legal, moral, and so on) for, as Kagan and Bakhtin observed in their early works, the degree of completion is much greater: 'The characteristic feature of aesthetic intercourse is that it is completely finished in the creation of the work of art and its continual recreations in co-creative perception and requires no other objectivisations' (DLDP 9; SZSP 63–4). While this is familiar enough from Bakhtin's early aesthetics the concentration on discourse is quite new.

Voloshinov develops an account of language use that draws heavily on the theory of language that emerged from the psychology of Karl Bühler, whose own intellectual background was in the Aristotelian tradition of Brentano and the early Husserl. Particularly important is what Bühler later termed the 'organon model' of the utterance (Bühler 1990, originally published 1934). Voloshinov had translated Bühler's (1922) article on syntax into Russian in the mid-1920s (LDV 75), and the account of language on which Voloshinov draws was presented there and in another article published a few years earlier (Bühler 1919). Bühler's originality lay in his contention that the utterance, 'speech event' or 'speech act' (*Sprechakt* – Bühler was the first to use this term) is an indivisible unity (a *Gestalt*) with three moments or constituents that can be separated only abstractly. Each utterance has three functions: intimation or notification (*Kundgabe*); representation (*Darstellung*); and 'triggering' (*Auslösung*). To these are correlated three foundational points: the speaker (who expresses him- or herself); the state of affairs (about which something is said); and the hearer (whose response is to be triggered). Bühler argued that previous theories of language had presented one-sided accounts of language, with the work of the psychologist Wilhelm Wundt typical of *Kundgabetheorie*, Husserl of the representational theory, and the Brentanian philosopher Anton Marty of the 'triggering' theory. Marty's observations on 'triggering' also become important for the shape of the theory of dialogue that Voloshinov develops, but it is Bühler's account of the utterance which plays a central role in shaping the Bakhtinian account of discursive interaction.

Bühler also introduced into language theory an element that had previously been developed in cognitive psychology, in which he had been a prominent researcher. This was the observation that a single perceptual complex appears differently against various backgrounds. The background was called the 'field' and the complex the 'ground'. Bühler now extended this to language, arguing that the language user has to actively discern the meaning of a word in use against the fields in which it is set. He outlined two different fields. The first is the verbal context of the utterance (that is, its place within a larger body of discourse such as a sentence, a paragraph, a novel, a conversation, and so on), which he called the symbol field (*Symbolfeld*). The second is the spatio-temporal situation in which language users find themselves and within which the word is uttered, which he called the 'index' or 'deictic' field (*Zeigfeld*). Bühler insisted that a sharp distinction between these fields should be maintained, as only this could allow a coherent and non-reductive account of language in use to be developed.

Voloshinov restates (without acknowledgement) Bühler's 'organon model', with just the added glosses that the speaker may also be a writer, the represented object may also be a person (the utterance's hero), and the listener may also be a reader (SZSP 72; DLDP 17). Furthermore, he recasts the familiar dichotomy between art and life in terms of Bühler's 'two-field' theory: meaning in life is more heavily dependent on the deictic field than meaning in poetry where the symbol field predominates. The very title of Voloshinov's article draws upon this distinction. Voloshinov argues that in life, discursive interaction involves more than the linguistic aspect (for example, words, phonemes, sentences). It also involves a common non-verbal situation which has three moments: '(1) a common spatial purview (the unity of what is visible – the room, the window and so on); (2) a common knowledge and understanding of the situation and finally (3) a common evaluation of the situation'

(DLDP 11; SZSP 66). This is illustrated by an imagined situation in which two people are sitting in a room and one says the word '*Tak!*' ('well').

The meaning of the word is unclear to us, even if we know the intonation of the word, unless we know that (1) two people looked through the window and saw that it was snowing; (2) it was May and the winter had been protracted; and (3) both were anxious for spring and irritated by the snowfall. Voloshinov's conclusion from this recasts Bakhtin's earlier insistence on the co-participation of the I and the other in the 'event of being' in new terms: 'The utterance consequently depends on their real, material belonging to one and the same piece of being, which gives their material commonality ideological expression and further ideological development' (DLDP 11; SZSP 67). Again we have the idea of an act, in this case a discursive act, being a Janus-faced affair that looks in two directions: the utterance looks at the language as a sphere of objective validity (culture) and at the same time towards the implied extraverbal context (life). This opposition has, however, now been correlated with Bühler's two-field theory. Furthermore, the 'emotional-volitional tone' that surrounded the act now becomes the intonation of the utterance: 'Intonation always lies on the border of the verbal and non-verbal, the uttered and the unuttered. In intonation the word directly makes contact with life. And above all it is precisely in intonation that the speaker makes contact with the listeners: intonation is social par excellence' (DLDP 14; SZSP 69). Intonation is evaluative intentionality in language use, the directedness of a linguistic unit from the speaker towards both the topic of conversation (the 'hero') and the listener in an intentional act called the utterance.

We will return to Voloshinov's work on language in life a little later, and now turn to discourse in art. The relation of the utterance in life to that in art is parallel to Bakhtin's earlier theory of the relation between the act in each of these realms, but the new element of Bühler's symbol field is introduced. Whereas in life the extraverbal situation (Bühler's deictic field) is directly implied in every utterance, this is not possible in art. Where Bakhtin, following Simmel, had argued that aesthetic activity is a timeless moment of phenomenological intuition in which the essence of an 'event' is realised, Voloshinov argues that 'the poetic work is a mighty condenser of unexpressed social evaluations: every word of it is saturated with them. These social evaluations also organise artistic form as its immediate expression' (DLDP 19; SZSP 76). Language in poetry is the 'material' of the work that is subject to aesthetic activity. This involves the divination, from the words themselves, of the actual relationships between the author and the depicted world, and between the author, the world and the 'spectator'. The relations between people are realised in the material of words and it is this that constitutes the artistic 'event'.

Where in Bakhtin's early work it was argued that the types of intersubjective relations were given artistic form in the work of art, Voloshinov treats degrees and kinds of distance as bestowing a stylistic flesh on the skeleton of language. Here again, however, we find the question of social structure coming to the fore in Voloshinov's work: certain evaluative perspectives which find stylistic embodiment are correlated with certain social groups and the interaction between groups of different or the same social rank. Thus style and social perspective are fused in the mind of the speaker: 'style ... is the individual and his social group in the figure of its authoritative representative – the listener – the permanent participant in the inner and outer discourse of the person' (DLDP 27; SZSP 83–4).

Sociological poetics and Formalism: Medvedev's *Formal Method* (1928)

Voloshinov's text is at least in part a further engagement with contemporary Russian Formalists, who are criticised for abstracting form from content and looking for the meaning of the work in the material. In a passage curiously omitted from the English translation, Voloshinov argues that: 'the significance [*znachenie*], the sense [*smysl*], of form does not refer to the material but to the content' (SZSP 77). This is a position very close to that taken by Bakhtin in his early attack on Formalism for ignoring architectonic form, and it is restated in the Circle's most sustained critique of Formalism, Medvedev's *Formal Method*. Medvedev argues that the 'content' of literature is the 'reflection and refraction' of the 'reflections and refractions' of 'socio-economic being' that constitute the other spheres of ideology (FMLS 16–17; FML 22–3). These are all discursive. In elaborating this perspective Medvedev acknowledges that the conception derives from Hermann Cohen's aesthetics, in which art is seen as an original type of superstructure over other ideologies, over the actuality of cognition and the act. Actuality thus enters art cognised and ethically evaluated. However, this actuality of cognition and ethical evaluation is for Cohen, as for the most consistent idealist, the 'ultimate actuality'. Cohen does not know the real being that determines cognition and ethical evaluation. Deprived of its concreteness and materiality and synthesised into an abstract systematic unity, the ideological purview is Cohen's ultimate reality. (FMLS 24; FML 30)

Medvedev, whose own acquaintance with neo-Kantianism predated his meeting with Bakhtin by several years (Medvedev 1998), here seeks to recast this perspective according to a Marxist account of the ideological superstructure, and this account is again one that derives from Bukharin.

As well as dividing the superstructure into a relatively unsystematised 'social psychology' and a more structured realm of ideology proper, Bukharin tried to show how different elements of the superstructure exist in equilibrium. Each area of the ideological superstructure proper corresponded to a certain specialised division of labour, and it was fairly straightforward for the Circle to correlate these areas with the different sciences outlined by Cohen and the Marburg School. The result is that literature does not reflect and refract[9] material reality directly, but refracts the linguistically embodied images of 'being': ethics, politics, religion, and so on. Literature does not, however, take up already systematised ethics, politics, and so on, it takes them 'directly from the very living process of the becoming of cognition, ethics and other ideologies' (FMLS 16–17; FML 22–3), that is, it takes them from what Voloshinov called life-ideology and Bukharin called social psychology. It is for this reason that works of art often anticipate developments in other spheres of ideology.

The literary work removes life-ideology from its 'pragmatic' connections in social life and turns it into 'content', but this does not imply the simple removal of life-ideology from that life; it rejoins social life in a new form. It rejoins life as an element of an artistic work and does so through the artistic work as a whole. It has become, to use the terminology of the early Bakhtin, an aesthetic object, and it thus occupies a different region of being: aesthetic validity. As a specific work, an act of artistic objectification, art is active in social life, and this activity is as important as the social phenomena that it models. All of this is broadly consistent with the early Bakhtin's approach. Medvedev then goes on to argue that only Marxism is able to make the correct correlation of the 'specific actuality of literature with the ideological purview reflected in its content' that is necessary to avoid turning the work of art into a thing (FMLS 26; FML 33). Following Marx's discussion of 'commodity fetishism' in *Capital*, which Simmel had claimed he was generalising in his discussion of objective culture, Medvedev terms this reification of the work of art its 'fetishisation' (FMLS 151; FML 167).[10] This tendency was considered characteristic of much contemporary poetics, from the vulgar 'sociologism' of P.N. Salukin, in which literature is treated as a thing determined only by external social forces, to the Formalists' assertion of the non-social structure of artistic works. Each of these positions was a specific variety of positivism, that is, an attempt to treat art as an object to be studied in the way the natural sciences study physical entities. Thus, where Bakhtin had brought Marxism and neo-Kantianism together as provisional allies in a common struggle against 'theoretism', and Voloshinov had done so in a more wholehearted way in his battle against biological determinism and psychologism, Medvedev now brought the two trends together in a common struggle against positivism. According to Medvedev, what was needed was the development of a 'Marxist poetics', and this was seen as synonymous with a 'sociological poetics'.

Specification and differentiation of the different regions of the ideological superstructure and of their interrelations are seen as the task of a Marxist 'science of ideologies', and a 'sociological poetics' is one region of this. Literature must be studied as a specific part of the ideological environment, and is determined both from within and from without, since other ideologies are its content and its form is the form of that content. Formalism is seen as being in conflict with this approach:

> The specifying tendencies of our Formalists are diametrically opposed to Marxism. They consider specification as the isolation of a given region of ideology, as sealing it off from all other forces and energies of ideological and social life. They see specificity, individuality as inert and hostile to all other forces, i.e. they do not think about individuality dialectically and are therefore unable to combine it with living interaction in the concrete unity of socio-historical life. (FMLS 37; FML 45)

Here, once more, we have as the focus of criticism Formalism's theoretism, its tendency to divide life and culture into sealed realms. Marxism is once again cited as an effective counter to positivism and theoretism.

Medvedev begins his critique by arguing that Russian Formalism, as developed by Viktor Shklovskii, Boris Eikhenbaum, Iurii Tynianov and others in OPOIaZ (The Society for the Study of Poetic Language) was actually a branch of a Europe-wide movement that included the work of Wilhelm Worringer, Heinrich Wölfflin and Oskar Walzel. Here Medvedev had an area of expertise unrivalled in the Bakhtin Circle. This movement originally developed with reference to the visual arts, and is shown by Medvedev to have developed in opposition both to 'idealism' (or more exactly 'abstract ideologism', which saw art as simply continuous with the ideological environment) and to positivism, which emptied art of all social meaning:

> The struggle with positivism and naturalism, which rendered art meaningless, had an enormous significance for the European formal method. If the idea of the closed constructive unity of the work was mainly raised against idealism and all general abstract ideality in understanding art, then as a counterweight to positivism it steadfastly underlined that every element of artistic construction is profoundly saturated with meaning [smysl]. (FMLS 48; FML 55)

This is seen as a positive development since the splitting of the work into isolated aspects of form and content was eliminated: both form and content are seen as simultaneously ideological *and* constructive elements of the closed unity of the work. This, as we saw in our discussion of the early Bakhtin, is the significance of *architectonic form*, but it is now recast in new terms. The example given is Worringer's analysis of stylistic development as characterised by an alternation between naturalism (as a principle of empathy) and abstraction (withdrawal), which are expressive of a positive attitude towards and trust in the world and a hostility to the world respectively. Different styles are thus expressive of different modes of 'artistic volition', and as such have an ideological significance. Thus, rather than a lessening of the ideological significance of the work of art, 'there occurred only a transfer of the ideological centre from the object of representation and expression, taken as independent of the work, to the very artistic construction of it' (FMLS 51; FML 59).

Worringer's and Wölfflin's ideas about visual art had already been applied to literature by Walzel, whose work appeared many times in Russian translation in the 1920s and was championed as a superior alternative to the ideas of the Russian Formalists by the prominent literary scholar Viktor Zhirmunskii (1881–1971). Walzel analysed literary style as a result of the close connection between content in the sense of what is said (*Gehalt*) and its appearance (*Gestalt*). He explicitly connects this use of *Gestalt* to von Ehrenfels's theory of Gestalt qualities (Val´tsel´ 1923: 48), which was discussed in Chapter 1.[11] This was most clearly expressed in Chapter 4 of Walzel's 1920 book on German poetry since Goethe, which appeared in Russian translation in 1922. Here Walzel explored the decline of art that represents 'passive' sense impressions (impressionism) and the rise of interventionist art (expressionism) in Germany before and after the First World War, and he then linked this to the shift in philosophical ideas in the same period. Drawing on Wölfflin's ideas discussed above, he argued that changing literary forms are the external aspect of changing world-views (Val´tsel´ 1922).

Against this point of comparison the Russian Formalists fare badly because they assume that the 'constructive significance of an element of a work is acquired only at the price of losing its ideological sense' (FMLS 49; FML 56). In this, Medvedev argues, the Formalists were too closely associated with a particular tendency in poetry: that of the Russian Futurists, who concentrated on formal experimentation at the expense of concrete meaning. The clearest expression of this was so-called *zaum´*, or transrational poetry, associated with the poets Velimir Khlebnikov (1885–1922) and Aleksei Kruchenykh (1886–1969). The Formalists made the error of seeking the specificity of literature in 'poetic language' as understood by linguistics, which itself had a tendency to divorce form (phonetics, syntax, and so on) and meaning. A principled opposition between 'practical' and 'poetic' language was assumed but, objected Medvedev, there is no such thing as 'poetic language', and one can only speak of language carrying out different *functions*, among which is the poetic function.[12] It carries out this 'function' only when used in the context of a work of literature: it is this context that must serve as the basis for the specificity of literature, rather than a mythical 'poetic language'. This is, of course, a restatement of the principles behind Voloshinov's 1926 article. Now the analysis of poetic forms of discourse does not require linguistic analysis as such; rather the work is a particular type of *utterance* and requires a type of analysis that corresponds to this, some of the outlines of which we have already seen. It is 'social evaluation' that endows each utterance with meaning because it 'establishes an organic connection between the unique individuality of the utterance and the generality of its sense'. The specificity of the poetic utterance is that

> Here the utterance is detached both from the object as it is given apart from the utterance, and from action. Here social evaluation is complete within the utterance itself ... The actuality of the utterance serves no other actuality. Social evaluation pours out and is completed here in pure expression. Therefore all sides of the material, sense and the concrete act of realisation without exception become equally essential and necessary. (FMLS 126; FML 141)

From this arises the problem of the whole: genre, which from this time becomes a recurrent theme in the work of the Circle.

The Formalists had considered genre chiefly as a particular collection of artistic devices with a certain hierarchy that could be analysed after cataloguing the devices themselves. To this Medvedev objected that genre is not defined by the devices used, but the 'devices' by genre. Medvedev here explicitly links genre with the perception of form as understood in Gestalt theory (FML 56; FMLS 49). The work of art, as we saw with the work of Kagan and then with Bakhtin, is more thoroughly completed than other spheres of ideology, but now genre is 'a complex system of means and methods for the cognitive seizure and completion of actuality' (FMLS 133; FML 149). Genre is a 'two-fold orientation in actuality', being oriented towards the percipient and the specific conditions of performance and reception on the one hand, and 'in life' from within by the thematic content on the other. 'Every genre is in its own way oriented on life, on its events, problems etc.' (FMLS 131; FML 147). These orientations are interdependent and define the genre as such as a dynamic and creative form of the whole within life, but one that at the same time encapsulates an aspect of life and makes it an element of culture.

With Voloshinov's analysis of discourse in life and poetry in mind, we can see that Medvedev's notion of genre is similarly an application of Bühler's Gestalt model of the utterance, with the two-fold orientation corresponding to the utterance's object of representation and the receiver. We have seen that Bühler's model also incorporated elements of cognitive psychology, specifically the two-field theory, and this once again becomes part of the new perspective developed by the Circle. The notion that genre provides a means for the 'cognitive seizure' of actuality derives from the Gestalt notion that a percipient is oriented towards an object and acquires information about that object according to his or her 'set', 'attitude' or 'disposition' (*Einstellung*). In Medvedev's reworking the attention of the artist is directed according to certain tendencies that are both internal to the work of art as part of the history of art, and external to art, as the history of art exists as but a subdivision of general history. It was perhaps in response to Medvedev's criticism that the Formalist Iurii Tynianov was later to redefine the work of literature as a Gestalt, and 'literariness' as the *Gestaltqualität,* that is, the quality that derives from the perception of the whole (Erlich 1969: 199).

The history of literature is, for Medvedev, a history of two-fold orientations as described above: a dialectic of 'intrinsic' and 'extrinsic' factors in the process of becoming (*stanovlenie*). The Formalists had treated literary evolution as the self-enclosed development of a 'datum' external to consciousness, but Medvedev insisted that 'to understand the becoming of literature and the isolated work is possible only within the whole ideological purview', which is itself racked with conflicts and contradictions:

> The work of art is also drawn into these conflicts and contradictions. It is penetrated by and it absorbs some elements of the ideological medium and others external to it are repulsed by it. Therefore 'inner' and 'outer' dialectically change places in the process of history, of course not remaining self-identical as they do so. That which today lies outside literature, extraliterary actuality, may enter literature tomorrow, as an inner constructive factor of it. Similarly, that which is literary today may turn out to be an extraliterary actuality tomorrow. (FMLS 154; FML 169)

Medvedev argued that the Formalist dichotomy of poetic and everyday language excluded such an approach: literary evolution can in the Formalist understanding only be considered as the alternation of dominant and subordinate devices.

Medvedev's argument has here been presented in a much-abbreviated form, but the main features are clear. The formal and sociological methods are incompatible. However, it is a matter of some debate as to how accurately Medvedev presents the practice of the Formalists as opposed to their polemical programmes, or to what extent he accounted for the significant shift in their work in the late 1920s that occurred under pressure from their many Marxist critics. Medvedev's critique differs from that of the less sophisticated Marxist critics of the time in recognising the value of the Formalists 'work in focusing attention on key questions of literary analysis', and he concludes with a call for Marxist critics to value this 'good opponent more highly than a poor ally' (vulgar sociologism). However, the impression remains that Formalism is singled out as an example of positivism in literary scholarship and is analysed only to the extent that it conforms to this characterisation. This allows Medvedev to advocate a Marxist eclecticism (FMLS 28; FML 35) that finds common cause with neo-Kantianism, life-philosophy, Gestalt theory and what he calls 'European formalism'. Furthermore, the very contrast of formal and sociological 'methods' has more in common with neo-Kantian philosophy than with Marxism, as does the aim to create a 'science of ideologies'. It is significant that by 'ideology' Medvedev repeatedly refers to the 'ethical, cognitive and other contents of literature' (FMLS 16–17; FML 22–3), that is, to the 'good', the 'true', the 'beautiful' and so on that constituted 'universal validity' as defined by the neo-Kantians. Ideology becomes simply the content of culture, and literature draws from this in the process of its creation in 'life'. The only specifically Marxist feature is the addition of the adjective 'socio-economic' to the term 'being' wherever it occurs. At all points, however, the socio-economic is in effect bracketed out: there is no discussion, for example of the relationship between forms of literature and the rise and fall of certain classes in society, or of the development of the publishing industry which underlies literature as an institution. These are not considered to be relevant to the development of a 'science of ideologies'. A full discussion of the extent to which literary studies can ignore or 'bracket out' such factors is, of course, beyond the scope of the present study.

This said, however, Medvedev's book is certainly full of insight and represents a significant contribution to the work of the Circle. It is undoubtedly the most comprehensive and even-handed critique of the work of the Formalists in the whole Soviet period, and still rewards a careful reading today. It also shows how the aesthetics developed earlier by Bakhtin was recast according to discursive principles and a different type of sociological analysis that allowed correspondences to be drawn between neo-Kantianism, Gestalt theory and Marxism.

The Formal Method was intended as only the first in a series of works, and this is perhaps indicated in its subtitle, 'A Critical Introduction to Sociological Poetics'. Archival materials suggest this was to be followed by a work provisionally entitled *Sociological Poetics, Volume 1: Thematics* (Medvedev 1998: 31). This plan was not to be realised, and the very project of a new 'sociological poetics' was lost. In 1934 a heavily revised version of *The Formal Method* was published under the title *Formalism and the Formalists* (FF). Here, while a significant portion of the book remains unchanged, certain sections have been omitted, some key sections revised and a new chapter on 'The Collapse of Formalism' added. The result is a much more polemical and less interesting work, which is now a destructive attack on Formalism rather than a constructive critique of the Formalists as a springboard for the development of an outline of a 'sociological poetics'.[13] This change is a good illustration of the transformation of the ideological climate in the intervening years.

Voloshinov's *Marxism and the Philosophy of Language* (1929)

Voloshinov's 1929 book on language is perhaps the culmination of the development we have been examining in this chapter: the turn towards semiotics. It is also the text in which a phenomenological account of intersubjective interaction is fully transformed into an analysis of forms of dialogue, and in which the corresponding type of sociological analysis becomes apparent. After some general comments on the dearth of Marxist accounts of language and its significance for the development of Marxism, Voloshinov begins with a repetition of the attack on psychologism that we saw in the Freud book. The claim that ideology exists in the consciousness misses the fact that 'consciousness can only realise itself and become an actual fact in the material embodiment of signs' (MPL 11; MFIa 223). The sign is also described as wholly determined by social communication, indeed it is the 'materialisation of this intercourse'. Thanks to its neutrality, it can carry out 'ideological functions' of any type: 'scientific, aesthetic, ethical, religious'. This neutrality allows it also to embody 'life-communication' as well as already specified spheres of ideology: 'the material of life-ideology is primarily the word'. Moreover, it is also the 'semiotic material of inner life – consciousness (inner discourse)'. The word thus becomes an essential ingredient of any conscious act, even accompanying all other forms of ideological sign such as pictorial representation and musical composition (MPL 12–15; MFIa 225–8).

In a significant footnote Voloshinov records that neo-Kantianism has now moved away from an abstract conception of consciousness and placed symbolic representation at the centre of its attention. The work that is singled out for attention is the first volume of Ernst Cassirer's *Philosophy of Symbolic Forms* (1955a [1923]), which Voloshinov was translating at the time. We will later return to the question of to what extent Cassirer's work can still be regarded as simply 'neo-Kantian', but again we have here an attempt to present neo-Kantianism as compatible with Marxism because of their shared anti-psychologism. In Cassirer the sign becomes a means of presenting conscious 'images' of being, which Voloshinov recasts as the 'refraction' of 'socio-economic being'. In a recently published plan for the book, Voloshinov writes that in Cassirer's work

> 'the word' becomes a *partition* between transcendental validity and concrete actuality, a 'third realm', as it were, lying between the cognising psycho-physical subject and the empirical actuality surrounding him on the one hand, and the world of a priori, formal being on the other ... It is precisely on the ground of the philosophy of language that the Marburg School's scientism and logicism and the Freiburg School's abstract ethicism are presently being overcome. (LDV: 87)

While Voloshinov draws quite heavily on Cassirer's book for information about and philosophical criticism of current philosophy of language, and recommends the assimilation of the valuable material therein (LDV: 88), he also further develops his association with Gestalt theory and with the ideas of Bühler. The notion of *refraction* is a case in point. On the one hand this term echoes the 'reflection theory' of perception developed by Lenin in his 1908 book *Materialism and Empiriocriticism*, but it also has strong connections with Gestalt theory, especially as developed by the Graz School. This trend also influenced Bühler (Cattaruzza 1996). For the Graz School, the percipient *produces* a Gestalt from a given stimulus complex by means of a form of activity. While this at first sight appears compatible with Cassirer's neo-Kantian notion of production of an object of knowledge, it is actually fundamentally incompatible with it. What is produced is completely dependent on an autonomous formation being perceived (seen, heard, and so on) rather than being produced from and in consciousness, by thought. Unlike all forms of neo-Kantianism, the Graz School maintained a fundamental distinction between perception and cognition. These are two different classes of mental phenomena: presentation or direct awareness (seeing, hearing, and so on) and thinking or the reordering of perceived reality under concepts (Stucchi 1996: 149–50; Kanisza 1979).[14] The notion of refraction seems to reiterate this distinction. Bühler criticised Cassirer on precisely this basis. For Bühler, Cassirer was guilty of throwing the 'baby' of knowledge of the extradiscursive world out with the 'bathwater' of spurious claims that this world and language were directly connected. For Bühler there are 'mediated co-ordinations' between the two, with the representative capacity of language following the 'natural lines' of the stimulus complex even though the discursive subject is guided by a particular 'set' (*Einstellung*) on reality, i.e. is 'intentionally oriented toward experience' (Innis 1988: 90). Cassirer was accused of an idealistic 'epistemologism' (Bühler 1990: 215). It is significant that while seemingly not perceiving the incompatibility between the two positions, Voloshinov appears much closer to Bühler's version while, as we shall see, in his later works Bakhtin adopts a position closer to Cassirer's idealism. Thus, only Voloshinov and Medvedev use the term 'refraction' to describe the *perception* of a given, extradiscursive formation, while Bakhtin does not,[15] indicating an ambivalent realism on the part of the Marxist members of the group which the idealist Bakhtin does not share. This distinction has generally been lost in critical literature on the Circle.

Voloshinov also retains and even deepens his association with Bukharin's work (Tihanov 1998a), as can be seen from such comments as 'Ideological actuality is the immediate superstructure over the economic base. The individual consciousness is not the architect of the ideological superstructure, but only its tenant lodging in the social building of ideological signs' (MPL 13; MFIa 226). Language, as for Bukharin (and, as we shall see, for Marr), is consigned to the superstructure, but it is no longer simply regarded as a part of it. It is the very stuff of which the superstructure is made. Verbal interaction becomes the material embodiment of 'social psychology' as delineated by Bukharin, because the word is 'omnipresent' in all social interaction. Social psychology is the 'transitional link between socio-political structure and ideology in the narrow sense (science, art etc)'. Where Bukharin argues that 'class psychology is based on the aggregate of the conditions of life in the classes concerned, and these conditions are determined by the position of the classes in the economic and social-political environment' (Bukharin 1926: 212), Voloshinov notes that 'productive relations and the socio-political structure immediately conditioned by them determine all possible verbal interactions between people, all forms and means of their verbal intercourse'. It is for this reason that verbal interaction registers social changes, even if at an elementary stage: words are the 'most sensitive indicator of social changes' even when they have not stabilised into ideological systems. The social organisation of participants in dialogue and the immediate conditions of their interaction affect the type of utterance, the 'discursive genres' of verbal intercourse in which social psychology exists. As we have seen, this is a development of what Bakhtin termed the architectonic form of the work: the utterance is treated as a form of the verbal whole within which the aesthetic object is realised. So now Voloshinov argues that the study of social psychology must analyse both the 'content' and the 'forms of utterance' that exist in verbal 'material'. This necessitates a typology of discursive forms within which social world-views are manifested and which relate to the hierarchical organisation of society (MPL 18–21; MFIa 231–4). The study of social psychology is therefore transformed into a study of 'discourse in life'.

Between the 1926 essay and the 1929 book there has occurred a significant development in Voloshinov's view of language. In the later work language is no longer treated as simply having an evaluative moment, but now actually *embodies* a social world-view. This perspective had originated with Johann Herder (1744–1803), and had been systematically developed by Wilhelm von Humboldt (1767–1835), who argued that a language embodied the 'spirit' of an individual and a nation. Opposing the growing tendency towards positivist linguistics, Humboldt argued that language should not be studied merely as '*ergon*' (a finished work), but also as '*energeia*', an activity. This position was adopted by the romantic philosophers of language Benedetto Croce (1866–1952) and Karl Vossler (1872–1949), who argued that if we accept the idea that language is 'spiritual expression', then 'the history of linguistic development can be nothing other than the history of spiritual forms of expression, that is to say, a history of art in the broadest sense of the term' (Cassirer 1955a: 175). Voloshinov, it seems, follows the line of interpretation presented in the first volume of Cassirer's *Philosophy of*

Symbolic Forms, which argued (disputably) that von Humboldt's original formulation had been based on the work of Kant, but that the later developments had been based on the new psychologism that grew out of the work of Wilhelm Wundt (1832–1920): 'Language, it was held, is built up in the individual's mind by the interaction of the various mechanisms of sound production on the one hand and of the psychological mechanism of associations on the other; it becomes a whole, but a whole which we can understand only by dissecting it into physical and psychological elements' (Cassirer 1955a: 172). Croce and Vossler had translated this into terms of artistic creation. While viewing language as having an aesthetic dimension, Voloshinov remained close to Bühler's two-field theory, being unwilling to erase the division between discourse in life and discourse in art. Similarly, while accepting the close link between language use and the extraverbal context in which the unique utterance is created, Voloshinov was unwilling to accept the sort of psychologistic interpretation of the phenomenon that derived from Wundt. In this, Voloshinov found close allies in both Bühler and Cassirer. Once again we have the constellation of Marxism, Gestalt theory, neo-Kantianism and anti-psychologism.

This constellation required an analysis of the philosophy of language and 'objective psychology', which comprises the third chapter of *Marxism and the Philosophy of Language*. According to Voloshinov the 'most important philosophical and methodological event of the first two decades of our century' was the work of the Marburg and Baden Schools of neo-Kantianism and the birth of phenomenology, while the counterpart at the present time (1929) was life-philosophy, particularly as represented by Dilthey and Simmel. These, the author argues, were waves of anti-psychologism and psychologism respectively which needed to be synthesised by means of 'the philosophy of the word as the ideological sign *par excellence*' (MPL 32–3; MFIa 246–7). Both Dilthey and Simmel were thinkers who had traced an incomplete evolution from a notion of 'understanding' that concerns the psychological reconstruction of mental processes toward an interpretation of artefacts which are originally generated by mental processes, but which become detached and acquire an autonomous existence. We have already seen how Simmel developed an account of the development of an objective culture that resulted in an eternal conflict with forms of life. Presenting the work of these philosophers as contemporary forms of 'psychologism', Voloshinov now offers a rather more subtle evaluation of psychologism and anti-psychologism than in the Freud book:

> *Anti-psychologism is correct in refusing to derive ideology from the psyche.* Moreover, the psyche must be derived from ideology. Psychology must be based on the science of ideologies. The word must have been born and matured in the process of the social intercourse of organisms in order then to enter an organism and become an inner word.
>
> *However, psychologism is also correct. There is no outer sign without an inner sign.* An outer sign that is incapable of entering the context of inner signs, i.e. is incapable of being understood and experienced, ceases to be a sign and is transformed into a physical thing. (MPL 38–9; MFIa 254)

The account of the interplay of inner and outer sign is viewed by Voloshinov as the forte of Simmel's work, although the interpretation of this interplay as a tragedy of the individual personality creating culture is considered unacceptable.

As we have seen, Simmel argued that in developing objective culture the subject constructs a self-sustaining entity that ultimately undermines the individual consciousness itself. Following Goldstein and Cassirer (1996: 16–17), however, Voloshinov argues that this view is based on a misunderstanding of the relations between psyche and ideology in which the sign is common to both. The psyche is 'inner discourse' and social intercourse is 'outer discourse'. All ideological content is understandable because it can be reproduced in the material of inner signs, while, conversely, ideological creation originates with inner signs and is engaged in new contexts. Inner and outer signs are not qualitatively different but only quantitatively so; the difference is the orientation of the sign inward or outward:

> If the content of the individual psyche is just as social as ideology, then on the other hand ideological phenomena are also as individual (in the ideological sense of the word) as phenomena of the psyche. Every ideological product bears the stamp of the individuality of its creator or creators, but this stamp is also as social as all other particularities and features of ideological phenomena. (MPL 34; MFIa 248–9)

In Simmelian terms, both life (as *energeia*) and culture (as *ergon*) consist of the same material (the sign); the distinction is one between that which is within the psyche and close to the life of the organism and that which is closer to structured ideology proper. The material is, however, identical.

Voloshinov is now armed with an effective weapon with which to engage with what he regarded as the most recent form of linguistic positivism, what he calls 'abstract objectivism'. Saussurean linguistics embodies this trend and is summarised as follows:

(1) Language is a stable, immobile system of normatively identical linguistic forms that the individual consciousness finds indisputable for itself.

(2) The laws of language are specifically linguistic laws of connections between linguistic signs within a given, closed language system ...

(3) Specific linguistic connections have nothing in common with ideological values (artistic, cognitive or other) ...

(4) Individual acts of speech are, from the point of view of language, only accidental refractions and variations or simply distortions of normatively identical forms ... Between the system of language and its history there is no connection or common motifs. They are alien to each other. (MPL 57; MFIa 270–1)

Here Voloshinov identifies the features of 'theoretism' and positivism that are constant targets of the Circle, but also a consistent anti-psychologism. In fact what we are presented with resembles all the worst features of objective culture as identified by Simmel. The model of such a philosophy of language is the study by philologists of dead languages. Although this approach claims to be above ideological concerns, it is deeply ideological itself. The word coalesces with ideas of authority, power, holiness and truth (MPL 75; MFIa 290). The history of language is elided in favour of a synchronic study in which the individual utterance (*parole*) is presented as a catastrophic corruption of the pure system (*langue*).

Voloshinov's critique of 'abstract objectivism' can be summarised as follows: language is not a stable system of self-identical forms, but a system of signs adaptable to ever-new contexts. Utterances are not individual acts complete in themselves, but links in a chain of discursive communication that is in the process of becoming.

Language is a historically developing phenomenon rather than an arrested static system. The Saussurean approach ignores the compositional forms of the whole utterance in favour of an abstract understanding of the elements of language. The meaning of a word derives entirely from its (verbal and extraverbal) context and it maintains an evaluative accent in use, something that is ignored by Saussure. Language is not a ready-made product that is handed down but an enduring part of the stream of verbal communication. The system of language and its historical evolution are incapable of being reconciled by a Saussurean approach.

In addition, Voloshinov holds that Saussure's approach, which values a synchronic national-linguistic unity (*langue*), easily coalesces with oppressive political power. It derives from the tradition of Indo-European linguistics that prized a scholastic study of 'dead languages' over a more egalitarian study of vital and interactive living discourse. This evaluation of Indo-European linguistics derives from the work of Marr, and has important implications for Bakhtin's work of the 1930s. We will return to this in Chapter 5.

Voloshinov claims to have overcome the bifurcation of psychology and the philosophy of language into objectivist and subjectivist currents through a dialectical synthesis: verbal interaction (MPL 82: MFIa 298). He further argues that this is possible only on the basis of Marxism. Here we have the same strategy of argumentation as Medvedev developed in his book on the Formal Method, although there Marxism was to be the basis for a synthesis of vulgar sociologism and abstract Formalism, transcending the limitations of each. Bakhtin was to present his 'Discourse in the Novel' article of 1934 in a similar way, though with no insistence on the indispensability of Marxism. It is worth noting that this strategy of argument was a common one in the late 1920s when the 'Marxist reform' of academia was being pursued.

Dialogue, literature and 'inner form'

'Verbal interaction' is the germ of the Bakhtinian notion of dialogue that will be developed in the coming years. Dialogue as the discursive embodiment of intersubjectivity means the individual utterance is a social fact and, conversely, the linguistic form as a social fact is individualised. In dialogue, social interaction in 'life' is objectified in culture, and culture is part of life. Voloshinov tells us that dialogue, both inner and outer, is tightly bound up with the 'whole pragmatic run of life' and develops in close connection with the 'historical conditions of the social situation' (MPL 38; MFIa 236). It was, again, Bühler who had treated verbal interaction as the focal point for psychology, though without the Marxist gloss. In his 1927 book *The Crisis of Psychology* (although, as we have seen, the themes were anticipated in his earlier work) Bühler argued that the central issue for psychology is the 'mutual steering [*Steuerung*] of meaningful behaviour of the members of a community' (Bühler 1927: 21) and that this is closely bound up with the 'triggering' function of language.

Voloshinov was, however, in some ways still wedded to the idea that social interaction had a juridical basis, and he argues that the 'contractual' form of dialogue can be abstracted from the specific situation in which discursive exchange takes place. These are the 'laws of *axiological* (emotional) *correspondence*, a *dialogic thread*' (MPL 38; MFIa 236). Verbal interaction inherits many of the ethico-juridical features of intersubjective interaction that Bakhtin derived from Simmel, Scheler and Cohen, and this is brought to prominence in Bakhtin's subsequent work on the novel (Brandist 2001). If the forms of discursive interaction have a juridical or even a 'contractual' significance, then dialogue is the foundation of the legal person or discursive subject. Behind every utterance there is a unity of will and this unity in social interaction accounts for what von Humboldt called the 'inner form' of language.

The notion of the 'inner form' was a much debated issue among scholars in the humanities in the 1920s. It was foregrounded in the work of scholars led by Gustav Shpet at the State Academy for Research in the Arts (GAKhN) in Moscow (Freiberger-Sheikholeslami 1982; Poleva 2000) and elsewhere (Shor 2001; Ushakov 2001).[16] This ultimately resulted in Shpet's rambling book *Vnutrenniaia forma slova* in 1927 (Shpet 1996). While it is clear Voloshinov and Bakhtin both read Shpet's book with interest, Voloshinov was dissatisfied with the direction of work in Russia on the question and referred directly to the German material (LDV 88–90). Vossler had presented a Romantic and psychologistic version of the notion of inner form, in which the 'outer form' of language comprises the grammatical form (*ergon*) and the 'inner form' is a manifestation of the 'stream of mental life' (*energeia*). Thus, the meaning of words becomes 'equivocal' when the immediate context of utterance has passed because the 'stream' has moved on:

Who is able to breathe life again into a sloughed skin and for a second time recreate that unique thing, which has forever flown out of it and out of itself? That life was the inner form, which in the meantime has itself changed and now flows through life in new skins and language forms. (Vossler 1932: 181–2)

Voloshinov, as we have seen, followed Cassirer in rejecting the psychologism of Vossler's interpretation, and instead moved closer to an anti-psychologistic version based on the Brentanian notion of intentionality.

As Voloshinov acknowledged elsewhere (LDV 88–9), the person chiefly associated with this reform was the disciple of Brentano, Anton Marty. For Marty (1908), inner form describes the way in which the 'immanent content' of a word in use deviates from its 'ideal content' (the etymological meaning). The inner form associates sound and meaning, allowing a speaker to 'group an immense variety of semantic contents with the help of a rather small number of signs' (Kiesow 1990: 56). When speaking, the chief thing that is intended is a 'certain influencing or controlling of the alien psychic life of the hearer' (quoted in Smith 1990: 42) and this inevitably leads to a certain dichotomy between linguistic meaning and meaning as intention. Inner form is thus trans-subjective, registering the pattern of distortion of a word's 'ideal' meaning when the word is used in intentional patterns of mutual 'triggering'. The 'inner form' of language is no longer an element of a 'stream of mental life' but of a chain of discursive interaction. As Bakhtin was to argue some years later, it is 'not an undifferentiated discursive stream but concrete utterances corresponding with each other' (AZPRZ 271). Discursive interaction is now an embodiment of ongoing intersubjective social interaction with the forms of the whole of the utterance (discursive genres) corresponding to particular 'forms of sociation'.

It is on this basis that Voloshinov develops an analysis of how the 'outer form', or impersonal linguistic significance (*znachenie*), is filled with the 'inner form', or sense (*smysl*), in social interaction. Voloshinov sometimes argues that during dialogue the 'theme' of the utterance, its unitary sense, is bestowed on a language structure that is essentially meaningless. Thus significance does not 'belong to the word as such', but 'is realised only in the process of responsive, active understanding ... significance is the effect of the interaction of speaker and listener on the material of a given sound complex' (MPL

102–3; MFIa 321). Thus 'the sense of a word is entirely determined by context', the variety of which is potentially infinite, while the 'significance' of a word is only potential meaning. Although all social groups may belong to a single sign community, different social groups bestow different 'senses' on words, and this Voloshinov calls the 'inner dialecticality of the sign'. The ruling class strives to assign a 'super-class, eternal character' to the sign, 'to extinguish or drive inward the struggle of social accents that takes place within it, to make it monoaccentual' (MPL 23; MFIa 236). Here we see the cultural force of the 'ruling class' being treated as a manifestation of Simmel's 'objective culture', stifling the healthy and unrestrained meaning-bestowing interaction of 'life' in which words become the site of contested meanings. Thus words such as freedom, democracy, and so on have different meanings for different social groups, while the ruling class strives to have its own particular perspective accepted as authoritative, claiming it is the only true perspective.

There are undoubtedly strengths in this argument. However, since each word has a limited range of meanings that is relatively stable, Voloshinov's point may not hold true in such stark terms. It is, for instance, doubtful that if in a discussion over the nature of freedom between members of two hostile but English-speaking classes one were to substitute the word 'carrot' for freedom, this would lose its established connection with the vegetable for either side. Fortunately, however, Voloshinov on occasion argues a more defensible case. Rather than seeing the language structure as meaningless and the meaning of words as thereby infinitely adaptable, he sometimes argues that linguistic meaning is but a *necessary component* of the theme of an utterance, a meaning potential in a concrete utterance. At the end of the second part of the book, for instance, he argues that 'significance [*znachenie*] is an abstract self-identical element that is subsumed by theme, torn apart by its inner contradictions, in order to return in the form of a new meaning [*znachenie*] with the same sort of temporary fixity and self-identity' (MPL 106; MFIa 325).[17]

Voloshinov's exaggeration of the dependence of linguistic on social changes probably reflects the influence of N.Ia. Marr, who is referred to positively more than once by Voloshinov and who will be discussed in a later chapter. Consider for example the following quotation, which is typical of Marr at this period:

Upheavals [in thought: conditioned by changes in production] are so mighty, are so vast in the changes which are created following the upheavals, that new generations seem to be newcomers from another world in comparison with the former generations from which they have descended. On the two banks of the gulf which forms between them, two antithetical objects and, it would seem, antithetical concepts are denoted by a single word. One and the same word on the one side (the *abandoned* side) means 'head' and 'beginning', on the other side (the new side, which has won, of course, by struggle in the process of the development of production and productive relationships) means 'tail', 'end'; on the one hand the word 'fire', on the other, 'water'; on the one hand 'day', 'white', on the other 'night', 'black'; on the one hand 'top', on the other, 'bottom'. (Quoted in Thomas 1957: 78)

Voloshinov does not, of course, go to these extremes, and the notion of social 'accent' is probably designed to avoid the maximalism of Marrist claims. But as we have seen, there is a distinct ambivalence in Voloshinov's work between, on the one hand, individual and/or collective subjects[18] bestowing a prelinguistic meaning on a meaningless language structure and, on the other hand, different social groups using an already meaningful structure in different ways (style).

Although Voloshinov repeatedly stresses the impossibility of consciousness outside the sign, like Husserl he appears to be suggesting that the subject fuses an internal act of meaning with words, embodying sense in them and the utterance as a whole. This happens in dialogue. The notions of accent, tone, and so on, are manifestations of this fusion, stressing a connection with the voice, but it soon becomes clear that these have a broader, metaphorical meaning and are also apparent in written forms. This becomes a central focus of Bakhtin's 1929 Dostoevsky study.

One of Voloshinov's most important claims, which survives in Bakhtin's later work, is that style is a constant indicator of a unified ideological perspective (a unity of will), even though the object and context of discourse might change over time. As he puts it in the 1926 essay, 'style is ... a person and his social group in the person of its authoritative representative – the listener – the permanent participant in a person's inner and outer speech' (SZSP 85; DLDP 27). Style is the discursive embodiment of the 'contractual' relations between persons in society and, as we have seen, this is held to be the source of those persons' unities of will. This mapping of subjective-social identity and ideological unity on to style was, however, developed from the idea of *Gestaltqualität*, which was itself a transformation of the Aristotelian notion of 'substantial form' into a principle of perception. Aristotle argued that 'figure and shape' is a 'sort of *quality* that belongs to a thing' even when the matter of that thing changes. Thus, a certain dog remains the same dog even though the individual cells of its body are replaced in the course of its life. The form (structure) of the dog is what defines its identity. Ehrenfels had moved this from the ontological to perceptual level so that a Gestalt, such as a melody, remains the same Gestalt throughout changes of key (Macnamara and Boudewijnse 1995: 412–13). Now, in the work of Voloshinov and Medvedev, style is the Gestalt quality, the principle of unity, the 'inner form' of an ideology.

Voloshinov also noted that this notion of 'inner form' had become a central aspect of art and literary history, and this was further developed by Medvedev. Here the linguistic theory of inner form was combined with another position which had been outlined by Johann Herder (1744–1803) and Johann Goethe (1749–1832), but which had been developed by Walzel in his 1918 essay 'Die künstlerische Form des jungen Goethe und der deutscher Romantik' (The artistic form of the young Goethe and the German Romantics) (Val´tsel´ 1928b). Linking the notion of inner form to the philosophy of Simmel, Walzel argues that the form of art is the outward aspect of the inner dynamic of life, and that the artist has an ethical responsibility to embody this inner form rather than capitulate to the conventional 'outer form' of his or her time. Form must be only the surface aspect of the inner dynamic of life and must be dependent on the latter's inner laws. The changing forms of literature are thus an index of changing forms of life, of what Simmel called 'forms of sociation'; this position is reworked by the Bakhtin Circle to mean changes in the forms of discursive interaction.

The notion of dialogue is forced to bear all these senses, and it is hardly surprising that it often fails to bear such a semantic load without distortions.

Conclusion

The fascinating works dealt with in this chapter have been the subject of heated debates over the status of the Marxism to be found in them. The truth of the matter now, however, appears more complex than a simple affirmation or rejection of Marxism. They include a rather specific type of Marxism, which was open to

complex hybridisations with phenomenology and forms of contemporary idealism. The formulations that result, and which
decisively influence Bakhtin's later work, are unthinkable without
the Marxist element, but they are by no means pure exercises in
Marxist theory. However, the significance of these works for the
development of the ideas of the Circle as a whole is greater than the
use of Marxism. Language from this point becomes a central focus
of the Circle's work and intersubjective relations are now analysed
as they are manifested in discursive forms of various types. We next
turn to an examination of how this is developed into an analysis of
narrative literature in the final part of Voloshinov's text and the
1929 Dostoevsky book.

It should be stressed, however, that the works of Voloshinov and
Medvedev are much more than transitional stages on the way to
Bakhtin's more mature work. They present distinctive arguments
and utilise specific theoretical resources. Voloshinov, in particular,
was a very promising young scholar, being only 25 years old when
he published *Marxism and the Philosophy of Language*, a book that
placed him at the forefront of incipient Soviet semiotics. His work
had much potential for development, but progress was curtailed by
political conditions at the end of the 1920s and his premature death.
Bakhtin's own fame, and the subsequent attempts to ascribe the
works to him, have also overshadowed their distinctive character. It
is to be hoped that a proper appreciation of the incipient realism
found in the works of Voloshinov and Medvedev will lead to a
reassessment of the theoretical legacy of the Bakhtin Circle.

4 From Verbal Interaction to Dialogue: Dostoevsky and the Novel

Bakhtin's first Dostoevsky study of 1929 is in many ways a recasting of the problems developed in *Author and Hero* in terms of the 'semiotic turn' that we have been examining. Since only the 1963 version of the book has been translated into English, it is important to set out the distinct features of the 1929 book.[1] *Problemy tvorchestva Dostoevskogo* (*Problems of Dostoevsky's Art*, 1929) is basically a static phenomenological analysis of Dostoevsky's work, but *Problemy poetiki Dostoevskogo* (*Problems of Dostoevsky's Poetics*, 1963) is a much more substantial analysis of Dostoevsky's place in literary history. The influential 80-page chapter on genre, which discusses the connection of the novel with the Socratic dialogue, the features of the Menippean satire and the concept of carnival, was introduced only in 1963, while the unambiguously phenomenological terminology of the first edition was adjusted to appear more ambivalent. These major differences aside, most of the central argument of the 1929 edition remains in the later version. Before turning to Bakhtin's 1929 book, however, we need to examine the account of reported discourse that constitutes the final part of Voloshinov's book on language, for it is here that the transformation from a phenomeno-logical to a dialogic approach to literature is most clearly visible.

Voloshinov: 'Sociological Method and Problems of Syntax' (1929)

The first, limited, application of the incipient dialogic philosophy of language to Dostoevsky was undertaken by Voloshinov in the 1926 essay on discourse, and Dostoevsky is again invoked for illus-trative purposes in the 1929 book on language. As we have seen, Voloshinov was familiar with the philosophy that formed the basis of Bakhtin's *Author and Hero*, but as a trained linguist who numbered the linguist L.P. Iakubinskii among his advisers, Voloshinov played a crucial role in Bakhtin's recasting of intersubjectivity as dialogue. Iakubinskii was an early ally of the Formalists who had dissociated himself from the movement and whose 1919 article 'On dialogic discourse' was held by Voloshinov to be the first work on dialogue in Russia by a linguist. It is in the final part of Voloshinov's book on language that there emerges an analysis of literature proper based on a syntactical analysis of the various forms of indirect discourse. Varieties of 'discourse within discourse, utterance within utterance and at the same time discourse about discourse, utterance about utterance' (MPL 115; MFIa 331) become the linguistic embodiments of the recontextualisation of the hero's intention by an external, authorial consciousness that concerned the early Bakhtin. Specific forms of reported discourse correspond to specific modes of inter-subjective interaction, with various linguistic forms prevailing in different languages at different times and among different social groups with different aims.

It is appropriate to discuss this aspect of Voloshinov's work separately from the main part of *Marxism and the Philosophy of Language* because archival evidence shows that this section of the book was originally conceived as a separate project to be called 'The Problem of the Transmission of Alien Discourse [*chuzhaia rech*]: An Experiment in Socio-linguistic Research'. In it Voloshinov draws heavily on a collection of articles published in German in honour of Karl Vossler in 1922 entitled *Idealistische Neuphilologie* (*Idealist Neophilology*). Bühler's article on syntax, which Voloshinov translated, first appeared here, and there are several other articles that proved crucial to the development of Voloshinov's and later Bakhtin's work. These included works by Oskar Walzel, Eugene and Gertraud Lerch and Leo Spitzer. This shows that the empirical work of the Vossler school was very important for the Circle, even if they had serious doubts about its philosophical underpinnings.

Volosinov adopts from Worringer a distinction between two types of pictorial representation and, like Walzel before him, applies this to verbal art. Unlike Walzel, however, Voloshinov's focus is specifically discursive, and he details two basic tendencies within reported discourse, within which there is a plurality of subtle variations. The first 'linear' direction is characterised by an attempt to establish robust boundaries for the reported discourse, protecting it from incursions by the authorial intention and maintaining its linguistic particularities. The second 'pictorial' direction is characterised by an erosion of the boundaries between discourses, leading to an infiltration of the reported discourse by the responses and commentary of the author's discourse. Here we have a linguistic manifestation of

Bakhtin's 'outsideness' and its potential 'crises'. The first direction varies according to the level of differentiation a given language community assigns to the reported discourse, and within this the extent to which the stylistic qualities, choice of words and so on are regarded as bearing significant social values. If the focus of attention is conceptual content (what is said), such considerations are moved into the background and the reported discourse is depersonalised. Related to this is also the 'degree of authoritarian perception of the discourse, the degree of its ideological surety and dogmatism'. The more dogmatic the discourse, the more sharply the contrast between truth and falsehood is accentuated and thus the more depersonalised it becomes. According to Voloshinov such forms are typical of, for example, Middle French, Old Russian, seventeenth-century French and eighteenth-century Russian. The second direction individualises the reported discourse much more fully even though the exact, external contours are compromised. Reception now focuses on the linguistic peculiarities of the discourse as much as on the conceptual meaning. The two main varieties within this type are:

(a) The authorial discourse gains prominence and penetrates the reported discourse, permeating it with its own humorous, ironic, scornful intonations and so on. The reported discourse's claims to authority are compromised and the social values borne by the discourse are relativised. This is seen as characteristic of the Renaissance.

(b) The reported discourse becomes dominant over the authorial discourse. The authorial discourse recognises itself as relative and 'subjective'. In narrative literature a fluid, questionable narrator replaces the author, who feels unable to bring a more authoritative perspective to bear. This is seen as characteristic of the work of Dostoevsky, the major novelist Andrei Belyi and recent Russian prose writers (see MPL 119–21; MFIa 335–8).

The first direction is represented in traditional direct and indirect discourse, while the second is manifested in what we now call free-indirect discourse (*nesobstvenno-priamaia rech´*, what the English translation of *Marxism and the Philosophy of Language* calls 'quasi-direct discourse'). The classic examples of this in Russian are to be found in the work of Dostoevsky, but the technique has now become generalised and signifies a 'general, profound subjectivisation of the ideological word-utterance'. This is a cause of concern for

Voloshinov, since the responsible word 'from one's own mouth' (Bakhtin's non-alibi in being) is now supplanted by the piecing together of the words of others, with the direct word only alive and well in the natural sciences. It is with this warning that Voloshinov's book closes.

Voloshinov acknowledges that his book is only a first stage in the development of the study of language in 'concrete utterances', and he is open about the fact that the sources for his analysis of dialogue are primarily the works of the 'individualistic subjectivists' criticised in the early parts of the book. The Vossler School, which looked at language in literature throughout history, was no doubt respected by Voloshinov even as he sought to overcome its psychologism. This shows that, faced with a choice between Saussurean and Vossleran philosophies of language, he remained closer to the latter, for all his criticisms of both trends. It could be said that Voloshinov reads the work of the Vossler School through a philosophy derived from the work of neo-Kantian and phenomenological philosophers (primarily Simmel, Cassirer, Marty, Bühler and Scheler) and connects it to a particular version of Marxist sociology as developed by Bukharin.

Bakhtin's *Problems of Dostoevsky's Art* (1929): Dostoevsky's polyphonic novel

Moving from Voloshinov to Bakhtin, one is immediately struck by the latter's completely different evaluation of the significance of Dostoevsky's work, even though the type of analysis involved is very similar. Whereas Voloshinov and, as we have seen, the early Bakhtin, regarded Dostoevsky's work as symptomatic of a profound crisis of authorship and of the utterance in general, Bakhtin now celebrates the great Russian novelist's work as indicating the way forward for a new and better type of novel. Furthermore, whatever Dostoevsky's own particular opinions on socio-political questions, the architectonic form (what is now called the author's 'form-shaping ideology'), is regarded as the epitome of progressive and democratic culture. Why the change?

Undoubtedly the deteriorating political situation for intellectuals in the Soviet Union at the time of the book's composition was an important factor. Literature and culture had, from the end of the Civil War until 1928, been an agitated field of experimental techniques and groups, giving rise to an impressive range of valuable works. This field began to narrow quite sharply in 1928 with the

inception of Stalin's 'revolution from above'; a destructive dictatorship was granted to the bellicose advocates of proletarian culture
grouped under the name of RAPP (*Rossiiskaia assotsiatsiia prole-
tarskikh pisalelei*; Russian Association of Proletarian Writers), who
harassed those non-conformist writers who spurned traditional
narrative techniques. The so-called fellow-travelling writers who
were subject to particularly harsh treatment were by and large the
heirs of the techniques developed by Dostoevsky and Belyi, to which
Voloshinov referred. Bakhtin presents his own study of Dostoevsky
as being built on the tradition of Dostoevsky criticism that was established by the Russian Symbolists such as Belyi, and most notably
Viacheslav Ivanov in his book *Dostoevsky and the Novel-Tragedy* of
1916. Although composed before the RAPP dictatorship was established, Bakhtin's book may to some extent have been a response to
the polarisation of the cultural field that preceded the monumental
changes of 1928. This needs to be kept in mind when we consider
the claim that Dostoevsky was the innovator responsible for the
polyphonic novel based on principles antithetical to the
'monologism' that underlies 'the principles of all ideological culture
of the new times' (PDP 80; PTD 61). However, one should not be too
eager to draw political conclusions since the point made extends to
'modern times', and the illustrative material is German idealism and
European utopian socialism. It is, of course, quite possible that a
parallel is being implied. In any case, the focus of concern has shifted
from what Voloshinov termed 'pictorial' relations to 'linear' relations
between discourses.

In a recent article Brian Poole (2001a) has shown that Bakhtin also
drew on new intellectual sources in the Dostoevsky book that led to
a significant revision of the 'finalising' theory of authorship found
in 'Author and Hero'. Central to this was the work of the German
novelist Friedrich Spielhagen (1829–1911).[2] In his critical works
(1883; 1898) Spielhagen advocated a minimisation of direct narra-
torial intervention in the novelistic text and the maximisation of
dramatic dialogue to allow the hero to reveal his or her own distinct
view on the world. The narrator should *show* rather than *narrate*
characterisation, and this leads to a new type of literary objectivity
– a quality that Bakhtin repeatedly attributes to the work of
Dostoevsky. The significance of this change was also cast in ethical
terms by Spielhagen, who argued that the hero's autonomy should
be respected by the author, who should not talk about the former
'behind his or her back', as it were. In adopting this perspective

Bakhtin also deviated from the work of his colleague Lev Pumpianskii, who had been the first in the Circle to publish on Dostoevsky. Pumpianskii argued that the novel is rightly an aesthetic court (*sud*) where it is the hero's character and not his or her deeds that are subjected to 'an uninterrupted passing of judgement' (KT 382). The quasi-juridical model of the novel remains in Bakhtin's formulation, but the right of the author to sit in judgement is undermined.

In the 1929 Dostoevsky book we are for the first time presented with a socio-historical account of literary form but, as we shall see, this account remains undeveloped. Bakhtin begins his book with a critical overview of recent Dostoevsky scholarship, which supports Otto Kaus's contention that Dostoevsky's presentation of a 'plurality of equally authoritative ideological positions' must be seen in relation to the development of capitalism in Russia:

> The polyphonic novel could really only come into existence in the capitalist era. Moreover, the most favourable soil for it was precisely in Russia, where capitalism arrived almost catastrophically, and where it encountered a variety of untouched social worlds and groups not weakened in their individual isolation by the gradual process of capitalist encroachment, as in the West. (PDP 19–20; PTD 29)

Although Kaus is criticised for not exploring the structural particularity of the novelist's work, the connection between sociological conditions and artistic form is validated. Dostoevsky's work thus grows out of the conditions of modernity as experienced in Russia, but it is structurally incompatible with the ideological principles of 'modern times' to which we referred above, and which were typified by German idealism or, rather, a simplified version of Hegelianism. Thus, interpretations such as those of the literary scholar Boris Engel´gart (1887–1942), which while correctly presenting the idea as an 'object of representation' in Dostoevsky interpret the novel as a dialectically unfolding and unitary spirit, are missing a central point of Dostoevsky's work: its irreducible pluralism. Dialectical progression and Dostoevsky's pluralism are deemed incompatible: 'The Hegelian concept of a single dialectical spirit in the process of becoming can give rise to nothing but a philosophical monologue.' In Dostoevsky's world 'planes were not stages but *camps*, the contradictory relations between them were not the rising or descending course of a personality, but the condition of society' (PDP 26–7; PTD 37–8). Simultaneous juxtaposition, not dialectical progression, is characteristic of Dostoevsky's method, and the absence of progression means that the acts of a character are free of determination.

Bakhtin's historical analysis can proceed no further because from this point onwards we are presented with a contrast between two compositional *methods* or, more exactly, two *logics* which underlie culture. In a rather typical move for a neo-Kantian of the Marburg type, these principles are abstracted as methodological principles that exist outside historical time: mono*logic* and dia*logic* principles. The former is a logic of causality and determination, the latter is a logic of unrepeatability and freedom:

> Therefore in Dostoevsky's novel there is no causality, no genesis, there is no explanation drawn from the past, from the influence of surroundings, upbringing and so on. Every act of a hero is completely in the present and in this regard is not predetermined, it is thought of and represented by the author as free. (PDP 29; PTD 40)

The same applies to Bakhtin's analysis. He follows the neo-Kantian trend of treating individuals not as concretely singular and embodied beings subjected to material, economic and social influences, but as juridical persons who are exclusively considered as bearers of rights and responsibilities.[3] As in the juridical process, all causal influences are to be bracketed out if persons are to be held personally responsible for their actions, discursive or otherwise. This inevitably imposes a particular character on work that adopts such a principle and this should be clearly recognised before Bakhtin's categories are employed in literary analysis today (Brandist 2001b).

Dostoevsky is, in 1929, presented as an innovator in terms of representational *method* ('form-shaping ideology'), which can be separated from the novelist's actual opinions on social questions. There is no discussion of the forebears of the 'polyphonic novel', and this is one of the main differences between the two versions of the study. Here, the phenomenological and historical approaches are mutually exclusive, and Bakhtin chooses to develop a static, 'juridical' and phenomenological study of the Russian novelist's work at the expense of the incipient historical study. This is important to recognise since, as Tihanov has shown, the 1929 Dostoevsky study is not the celebration of social dialogue that it has often been presented as (Tihanov 2000b: 190–202). It is, rather, an account of how Dostoevsky establishes a way for the authorial voice to find its own unique and unrepeatable place in relation to the characters of the work without imposing a causal and determinist logic on them, thus overcoming the crisis of the responsible word that Voloshinov spoke about at the end of his study. Dostoevsky's main characters are embodiments of an ability to find their own position among the discourses of others, while the narrator is unwilling, or unable, to present a more authoritative perspective. In this sense, the 1929 study maintains a continuity with Bakhtin's early work, but the new, semiotic rendering of the argument and the (compromised) incipient historicism of the study anticipate what is to come.

Despite the new semiotic terminology, the most visible philosophical presence behind the Dostoevsky study is still Scheler, and more specifically the final chapter of Scheler's book on sympathy called 'The Perception of Other Minds'. Bakhtin is still engaging in a phenomenological description of intersubjectivity, but now in discursive forms. He refers to Scheler as a pioneer in the critique of monologism in a footnote to the first Dostoevsky study (PTD 62), but this is omitted in the 1963 book. Nevertheless, in both editions Dostoevsky is shown to present his heroes exclusively as 'other minds' embodied in discourse: 'Dostoevsky's hero is not an image, but a fully-weighted discourse [*slovo*], pure voice; we do not see him – we hear him'. Dostoevsky's artistic dominant is the representation of 'self-consciousness', the hero's 'discourse [*slovo*] about himself and his world' (PDP 53; PTD 52). The discourse of the hero is something like a testimony delivered to the novelistic court.

Scheler argues that 'a man tends, in the first instance, to live more in others than in himself; more in the community than in his own individual self', and that this is also characteristic of the child in his or her family environment:

Rapt, as it were, and hypnotised by the ideas and feelings of this concrete environment of his, the only experiences which succeed in crossing the threshold of his inner awareness are those which fit into the sociologically conditioned patterns which form a kind of channel for the stream of his mental environment. Only very slowly does he raise his mental head, as it were, above the stream flooding over it, and find himself as a being who also, at times, has feelings, ideas and tendencies of his own. And this, moreover, only occurs to the extent that the child *objectifies* the experiences of his environment in which he lives and partakes, and thereby gains *detachment* from them. (Scheler 1954: 247)

Dostoevsky's heroes, such as Raskolnikov in *Crime and Punishment* or the 'Underground Man', are devoid of any stable 'sociologically conditioned patterns' that could channel the 'stream of their mental environment'. Furthermore, they are subject to an environment in which monologic 'linear' discourse is dominant, with the result that the hero is constantly being objectified, indeed, reified, and devalued by others. This is at the root of the pathologies typical of the Dostoevskian hero, who struggles against being turned into a 'thing' but is unable to find a firm and stable position from which to objectify his or her experiences. The idea of which the hero is an image is either repudiated or accepted by the monologists who surround the hero, but the author's relationship to the hero is different, it is dialogic. It is significant that Bakhtin characterises Dostoevsky's relationship to his heroes' consciousnesses in terms that directly echo Scheler's account of phenomenological distance in intersubjective interaction that we examined in the chapter on the early work: 'Dostoevsky knew precisely how to *represent an alien idea*, conserving its entire meaningfulness as an idea, but at the same time also maintaining a distance, not supporting and not merging it with his own expressed ideology' (PDP 85; PTD 66).

Dostoevsky is able to achieve this by removing all 'objectivisations' (images) of the hero from his own field of vision, and by doing so allowing the hero's words about himself, his self-consciousness, to take centre-stage. The object of authorial representation then becomes the hero's self-consciousness, not the hero as a physical object. Instead of seeking to go behind the discourse of the hero, to draw closer to his life with his own more adequate discourse from without, Dostoevsky seeks to abandon any such pretension in favour of an examination of the 'basic formative principle' behind the hero's discourse:

All the hero's stable, objective qualities, his social position, his sociological and characterological typicality, his habitus, his spiritual profile and even his very physical appearance – i.e. everything that usually serves the author for the creation of a hard and fast image of the hero – 'who he is' – becomes, in Dostoevsky, an object [*ob´´ekt*] of the hero's own reflection, the object [*predmet*] of his self-consciousness; the object of the author's vision and representation turns out to be the very function of this self-consciousness. (PDP 48; PTD 46)

The objects of the hero's life become, in Dostoevsky's work, subordinate to the 'function' of the hero's cognition and his discursive thinking. In describing this type of literary representation Bakhtin is here drawing on Spielhagen (Poole 2001a), but the terms in which Bakhtin's argument is posed directly incorporate more recent philosophical concepts. The concept of 'function' was one that had been used by phenomenologists to delineate the types of mental acts involved in cognition. Thus Bühler, as we have seen, states the three functions of language to be expression, representation and triggering. Here Bakhtin argues that the author 'brackets out' the external features of the hero, leaving only his or her mental relation towards those features. The external features are now only what Brentano called 'intentional objects' of the hero. Bakhtin's interpretation is, however, close to the neo-Kantian version presented by Cassirer, according to which the duality of the intentional object (the mental pointing towards something which may or may not exist) and the 'real' object that is mentally indicated renders the latter unknowable. This could possibly be the earliest trace of the influence of Cassirer's philosophy on Bakhtin's work. In his 1910 book on the 'exact' sciences, *Substanzbegriff und Funktionsbegriff* (The Concept of Substance and the Concept of Function), which appeared in Russian as early as 1912, Cassirer argues against the idea that we have knowledge of a world beyond discourse. As he puts it in a later book, the meaning of

> signs in the functional sense ... is not determined by looking out on the world of things but rather by considering the world of relations. The signs express the 'being', the 'duration', the objective value of certain relations, and hence they indicate 'forms' rather than material things. (Cassirer 1950: 65)

In the 1920s Cassirer developed this position into a philosophy of culture:

> If all culture is manifested in the creation of specific image worlds, of specific symbolic forms, the aim of philosophy is not to go

behind all these creations, but rather to understand and elucidate their basic formative principle. It is solely through awareness of this principle that the content of life acquires its true form. Then life is removed from the sphere of mere given natural existence: it ceases to be a part of this natural existence or a mere biological process, but is transformed and fulfilled as a form of the 'spirit'. (Cassirer 1955a: 113–14)

Bakhtin read Cassirer's philosophy of culture only in the 1930s, and the many ramifications of this 'reversal' are played out in Bakhtin's later work. However, here we can see Bakhtin arguing that Dostoevsky's innovation in novelistic form parallels Cassirer's account of the neo-Kantian innovation in epistemology, the theory of knowledge. The physical, social and other attributes of the hero are no longer treated as aspects of a sensible reality to be 'copied' in the artistic image, but are presented as things of which the hero is conscious, they become *functions* of the hero's own self-consciousness.

Unlike Tolstoy or Flaubert, who are used exclusively as a point of contrast in the study, Dostoevsky does not believe he can present a more authoritative perspective on the world than his heroes. Instead, he builds an aesthetic superstructure called the 'polyphonic novel' over the perspectives of his heroes similar to that we saw in Medvedev's *Formal Method*, and which was derived from Cohen's aesthetics. Dostoevsky consciously presents images of 'already cognised' being rather than seeking an image of what Kant called the 'thing in itself'. The extradiscursive world is, for Bakhtin's Dostoevsky, what it was for the Marburg School, an 'unknown X' which we endlessly define. It is nothing more than the totality of what Scheler called 'milieus', that is, sociologically distinct intentional (perceptual) horizons, but now organised systematically according to the 'objectively valid' principles of aesthetics. Dostoevsky thus becomes the first 'neo-Kantian' novelist who treats the world of nature as inaccessible to knowledge while culture, in all its many forms, is the only realm accessible to perception. The Romantic idea of the artist's 'vision' is translated into the terms of a phenomenological 'intuition of essences' in which the 'formative principle' behind each character's discourse is objectified. Everything in the novel is subordinate to this task. Thus, in a passage omitted from the 1963 edition, Bakhtin argues that even plot becomes a means to this end:

In Dostoevsky plot is completely devoid of any finalising function. His purpose is to place the hero in different positions, uncovering and provoking him, to bring people together and make them collide, in such a way, however, that they do not remain within the limits of the plot but go beyond them. Authentic connection begins where the plot ends, having fulfilled its service function. (PDP 277; PTD 78)

The authorial design is exclusively aimed at bringing together a variety of perspectives on a single issue and examining their 'formative principles'. The narrative event is now what Belinskii called the novel's 'most vivid and salient device for making the characters speak their thoughts' (Belinskii 1962b: 33).

In works of the monologic type, however, things are different. The author implicitly claims to have direct access to the extradiscursive world, and this is reflected in the structure of the work. The work does not attempt to present a plurality of fully valid perspectives with which the authorial perspective engages as an equal. In the monologic work the author's ideas are not represented, but either govern representation, illuminating a represented object, or are expressed directly without any phenomenological distance. In this sense the monological work of art is a testament to the dominance of a precritical type of consciousness.

The first part of the 1929 study is a philosophical excursus on Dostoevsky's method, a method which, though born in historical time, has for Bakhtin a validity that is quite independent of his own ideas on certain matters. By acknowledging the inability of discourse directly to capture extradiscursive 'reality', and by turning toward the types of intersubjective relations in their discursive embodiment, Dostoevsky shows that the authorial consciousness can adopt its own unique and unrepeatable place in being and thereby become ethically valid. The excursus ends with a typical neo-Kantian claim for Dostoevsky's work: 'His artistic method of representing the inner person, the "person in the person", remains exemplary in its objectivism for all epochs and under any ideology' (PDP 278; PTD 80).

Problems of Dostoevsky's Art: discourse in Dostoevsky

The second part of the 1929 study is subtitled 'an experiment in stylistics', perhaps reflecting Bakhtin's own recent adoption of extended discursive analysis. It is also experimental in that Bakhtin is now attempting to base stylistic analysis on a new philosophical ground derived from his earlier intersubjective phenomenology. It is important to note that the methodological remarks from the 1963 book, in which the concept of 'metalinguistic inquiry' is introduced (PDP 181–5; PPD 395–9), were added specifically for the later edition, and so the 1929 version begins directly with stylistic analysis of stylisation, parody, *skaz* and dialogue. These interest Bakhtin for their two-fold orientation towards an object (*predmet*) and towards another word, an alien discourse (*chuzhaia rech´*).[4] We thus have a return to the concerns of the final part of Voloshinov's book. However, Bakhtin undertakes a much more elaborate categorisation of the various forms of reported discourse in order to account for the various tones such discourses acquire (PDP 199; PTD 99). Unusually for Bakhtin, he quotes one of his sources on this question, although he leaves the quotation in the original German:

> When we reproduce in our own speech a portion of our partner's utterance, then by virtue of the very change in speakers a change in tone inevitably occurs: *the words of 'the other person' always sound on our lips like something alien to us, and often have an intonation of ridicule, exaggeration, or mockery.*

This passage comes from the 'individualistic-subjectivist' Leo Spitzer's 1922 book on Italian colloquial speech,[5] but Bakhtin interprets Spitzer in a phenomenological sense, arguing that 'on entering our discourse alien words inescapably acquire a new intention, our own, i.e. become double-voiced' (PDP 194; PTD 93).

In the 1929 book, the phenomenological terminology is overt, while in the 1963 version it is less explicit. In the above passage, for example, 'intention' is later replaced by 'interpretation', and it is this that is in the English translation. Another example is a passage on simple direct and indirect discourse:

> The directly intentional word is directed at its object and is the last meaningful [*smyslovoi*] instance within the limits of the given context. The object [*ob´´ektnoe*] word is also only directed at the object, but at the same time it is an object of an alien authorial intention. But this alien intention does not penetrate into the object word, it leaves it as a whole and, not changing its sense and tone, subordinates it to its task. (PTD 87)

The corresponding passage in the 1963 edition replaces the word 'intentional' (*intentsional'noe*) with 'fully-signifying' (*polnoznachnoe*) and 'intention' (*intentsiia*) with 'directedness' (*napravlennost'*), thus weakening the phenomenological coloration of the original version (PDP 189; PPD 402). It is thus hardly surprising that the philosophical principles of this work have been overlooked. However, this passage tells us something significant: there is no merging, or interanimation, of intentions reminiscent of Scheler's intersection of intentional horizons in either of these types of discourse. They remain single voiced.

Intersection of horizons is precisely what characterises the dialogic relations between discourses: double-voiced or 'hybridised' discourses are its manifestation and as such, an index of the type of intersubjective interaction. Thus, there may be a hidden polemic between discourses in which the authorial word is oriented towards an object but simultaneously strikes a blow at the discourse of another on the same theme. Although the words of the other are not reproduced, the whole structure and shape of the authorial discourse depends on this implied relationship. In stylisation and parody another's discourse is implied, but the authorial discourse poses as another's, or claims the other's discourse as his or her own. In each case, however, there is a fundamentally different type of intersubjective interaction: in the first case there is a marked antagonism, while in the latter cases there may be a variety of 'angles of intersection'. Other such varieties, which Bakhtin shows are very common in Dostoevsky's work, include the direct rejoinder, which, while still being directed toward an object, anticipates, answers and reacts to another's discourse.

A particularly important type for Dostoevsky is 'hidden dialogicality', in which while there is no second discourse represented, it is *as if* its presence was felt. The discourse reads like a transcribed dialogue in which one of the participants has been edited out. The first speaker thus appears to be responding to and engaging with another speaker, but that speaker is absent. Bakhtin illustrates this in a revealing analysis of part of Dostoevsky's first novel, the epistolary novel *Poor Folk* in which the hero Makar Devushkin writes anxiously to Varenka Dobroselova in such a way that it appears as if there were a third 'socially alien' participant. Devushkin's discourse, as well as his whole mental demeanour, is shaped as if in response to this 'third'. As Bakhtin puts it, using terms familiar from the *Author and Hero* essay:

The hero's attitude toward himself is inseparably connected with his attitude toward another and with the other's attitude toward him. His consciousness of self is always felt against the background of the other's consciousness of him, 'I for myself' against the background of 'I for another'. The hero's word about himself is structured under the continual influence of the alien word [*chuzhoe slovo*] about him. (PDP 207; PTD 109)

The effect on the discourse is as follows. Two rejoinders on the same topic are 'present', but

instead of following each other and being pronounced by different mouths, the discourse and counter-discourse are super-imposed one on the other and merge into a single utterance and a single mouth. These rejoinders move in different directions, collide with each other; therefore their superimposition and merging into one utterance leads to the most acute interruption. The collision of these rejoinders – singular and uniaccentual in themselves – is now transformed in the new utterance that results from their merging into the sharp interruptions of contradictory voices in every detail, in every atom of this utterance. The dialogic collision has gone within, into the most subtle structural elements of discourse [*rech´*] (and, correspondingly – elements of consciousness). (PDP 209; PTD 110)

To illustrate the point further Bakhtin intersperses the said passage with the invented rejoinders of the implied 'alien person'. The same phenomenon, though manifesting different modalities between discourses, is observed in the interaction between the discourses of Goliadkin and the narrator in *The Double* (PDP 210–27; PTD 112–30), and between the confessional first-person narrator of *Notes from Underground* and the implied addressee (PDP 227–37; PTD 130–41). In each case we have a hero's discourse with a 'sideways glance' at an implied or anticipated discourse of another and a discourse with a 'loophole' in which the hero evasively attempts to retain the pos-sibility of changing the final meaning of his or her own words. This evasiveness shows a hero unable to find a firm identity, his own individual and responsible discourse, among those of others that permeate his self-consciousness. Such heroes suffer from what Scheler called a 'heteropathic' inability to find a stable position outside the other.

Bakhtin's analysis of the various forms of internal dialogue in Dostoevsky's work is subtle and highly suggestive for the structural analysis of the modern novel. At the end of the study Bakhtin comments on the enormous variety of discursive forms in Dostoevsky's work, but then notes that everywhere the compositional principle of the 'polyphonic novel' is the same:

> Everywhere – *the intersection, consonance or interruption of external dialogue by the rejoinders of the inner dialogue of the heroes.* Everywhere – *a definite totality of ideas, thoughts and words pass through several unmerged voices, sounding different in each.* The object of authorial intentions ... is the passing of a theme through many and various voices, so to speak, its *multi-voicedness* and *vari-voicedness* that is in principle irrevocable. (PDP 265; PTD 177)

Passages like this one have led many observers to see in Bakhtin's first Dostoevsky study a celebration of the decentralising forces of dialogue in both society and the individual psyche. Such an interpretation would not, however, account for the overall tone of the book, which maintains important points of continuity with the earlier *Author and Hero* study. Dostoevsky now shows a way to overcome the 'crisis of outsideness' and of the responsible subject which motivated the early work. However much the psyches of the heroes of Dostoevsky's novels are disrupted by a variety of internalised discourses, within this 'a special place is occupied by the *penetrative word*'. It has a special 'function', being a 'firmly monologic, non-dissenting word, a word with no sideways glance, no loophole and no inner polemic'. It is that with which Voloshinov closed his book on language and which is possible only in 'real dialogue with the other'. To take up one's own unrepeatable position in the 'real' world is to adopt a responsible position outside the other. But while this position is only possible in relation to others in dialogue, 'it is necessary to subdue and smother the fictive voices that interrupt and mimic a person's genuine voice'. This is the emergence from the 'stream of otherness' that Scheler noted. Thus, in *A Meek One* we see the incipient emergence of a 'monologically firm and assured voice ... when the hero ... approaches the truth about himself, makes peace with the other and acquires his authentic voice, his style and tone begin to change'. Dostoevsky himself advocated a merging of the voice of the intelligentsia with that of 'the people', a joining of a religious chorus in which the word passes between voices with identical tones of 'praise, joy and gladness'. Bakhtin notes that despite this authorial ideology a battle of 'internally divided voices' more accurately describes the world actually presented by the novelist and is a testament to his realism and to the sociological significance of his work (PDP 248–50; PTD 155–7).

Dialogue is thus the denial of 'linear' monologism in which an external perspective is imposed on another's own unique position in being, but at the same time it can be the handmaiden of monologue in which one's own position is recognised and adopted. Dostoevsky's works examine the predominance of 'heteropathic' forms of consciousness in contemporary society, but they also present a possible way in which this pathology can be overcome and the individual become ethically responsible. Dostoevsky's authorial method is the epitome of this, for it shows the supremacy of 'function' over the object by reversing the urge to go behind discourse and draw closer to 'life'. For Dostoevsky it is only discourse itself, image worlds, that become objects of perception. The formative principle behind discourse is revealed in the process. The objectification of this 'stream of otherness', of the dialogic nature of consciousness, that constitutes 'life' enables the individual to raise his or her head above the stream, repressing alien voices within the self, and to adopt a unique, unrepeatable and responsible position in being.

The 1929 Dostoevsky study is simultaneously the culmination of Bakhtin's 'phenomenological' phase and the beginning of a move beyond it by means of the philosophy of language. However, a movement beyond this stage required a return to and nurturing of the seeds of historicism that are only just discernible beneath the static structure of the 1929 Dostoevsky book. This movement was to come when, in his first years of internal exile, Bakhtin turned his attention to the novel as a genre rather than to the work of a single writer. This move led to a series of difficulties for Bakhtin because, while not abandoning his elaborate phenomenology of authorship, he was compelled to deal with impersonal, or suprapersonal, bodies of discourse that interacted within generic structures with their own history. For all of Bakhtin's inventiveness in combining different ideas, he was faced with an impossible task: how to apply a synchronic method in consideration of a diachronic problem. The effort was to break apart the coherence of Bakhtin's theory, but in so doing it led to Bakhtin's most important work.

5 The Novel and Literary History (1934–41)

After publication of the 1929 Dostoevsky book Bakhtin was not able to publish anything of substance until the revised edition of the book in 1963. He was clearly intellectually active, however, and by 1934, when he began his now famous essays on the novel, he had modified his approach. The main development is that questions of cultural history have taken centre stage, while the phenomenology still dominant in the Dostoevsky study has taken a subordinate position. This is a change every bit as significant as the 'semiotic turn' we discussed earlier, for the whole structure of his thinking undergoes some fundamental revisions. In order to understand these developments we must first examine the way in which the last generation of Marburg neo-Kantians gravitated towards a revised version of Hegelian philosophy, and the type of historicism that resulted.

Cassirer and the Hegelian shift

We have seen how one of Bakhtin's main concerns in his early work was the need to bridge the gap between life and culture (Tihanov 2000a), existence and knowledge, which the neo-Kantians, like Kant, regarded as essentially separate. Such concerns inevitably demanded a significant encounter with the philosophy of Hegel, who regarded life and culture as aspects of a dialectical and teleological process: becoming. This stress on 'becoming' became a central aspect of life-philosophy, which, however, maintained the fundamental split between the two. On the one hand there was the realm of becoming, of life, and on the other was the realm of timeless validities and values that constituted culture. This rigorous dualism was already breaking down in the last works of Paul Natorp, but it was in the work of Cassirer that the shift towards a Hegelian resolution was definitively stated.

Cassirer combined a rationalistic neo-Kantian account of knowledge with a Hegelian evolutionist and holistic approach to argue for a unity of gradually unfolding forms of life that maintained the neo-Kantian distinctions between the object domains of the sciences. In *The Philosophy of Symbolic Forms*, these 'forms of life' were redescribed as 'symbolic forms' within which the dialectical process that Hegel had highlighted occurred. For Hegel, phenomenology studies the way *Geist*[1] (mind/spirit) 'appears', that is objectifies itself in things in order to appear 'for itself' as something opposite to itself. Cassirer similarly argued that symbolic forms such as art, myth, language and so on study and recall the various objectifications of life. This 'recollection' is not only historical, but, like Hegel's phenomenology, is the study of what is essential. The philosophy of *Geist* is characterised by Hegel as the representation of the route to true knowledge that consciousness takes as a matter of necessity. 'Essence' must ultimately 'appear' at the end of a course of development. Cassirer replaced Hegel's account of dialectical logic with an account of the 'law of symbolisation', and argued that all symbolic forms necessarily move through 'mimetic' and 'analogical' stages before reaching a 'purely symbolic' phase in which the essence of the form 'appears'. Cultural history (now separated from the history of 'civilisation') becomes a mind-driven liberation from immersion in the world of sensation. However, while Hegel argued that in the final stage all perspectives on being are transcended by a final transparent concept, Cassirer maintained that each form must maintain its integrity. Thus, while accepting Hegel's narrative, Cassirer complained that for Hegel philosophy deprives 'various cultural forms ... of their autonomous and independent value and subordinates them to its own systematic purpose. Here is the point of contrast with Kant' (Hendel 1955: 34). Bakhtin, as we shall see, follows this selective appropriation of Hegel.

Voloshinov, who was the first in the Circle to engage with Cassirer's *Philosophy of Symbolic Forms* in a sustained fashion, was well aware of the significance of the work. In his 1928 plan for *Marxism and the Philosophy of Language* he notes that Cassirer's book shows that

It is precisely on the ground of the philosophy of language that at the present time the scientism and logicism of the Marburg School and the abstract ethicism of the Freiburg School are being overcome. By means of *the inner form of language (as a semi-transcendental form)* movement and historical becoming is being introduced into the petrified realm of transcendental-logical forms. It is also on this basis that an attempt to re-establish the idealist dialectic is being made. (LDV 87–8)

This is central to Bakhtin's reorientation for, as we have seen, dialogue becomes the 'inner form' of language. In Cassirer's volume on language, the first, 'mimetic' stage of the dialectical progression is reached when, by means of uttered sounds, primitive man tries to reproduce a sensory impression as faithfully as possible. Cassirer argues that this stage breaks down as different cultures and languages come into contact with each other, and as a result of the growth of an analysis of language. At the next 'analogical' stage, the sign *refers* to reality and communicates the speaker's relationship with reality. Ultimately any mediated or immediate relationship between reality (thing) and symbol is seen to be untenable and understanding is liberated from close adherence to the concrete world of sense impressions. Attention turns towards the activity of the subject and towards the full realisation and application of the symbolic character of interpretation, so that the symbolising process becomes self-conscious and self-referential. In a key passage from the volume on language, Cassirer argues that the value and specific character of both linguistic and artistic formation lies in the 'progressive removal' from 'the immediately given', for 'the distance from immediate reality and immediate experience is the condition of their being perceived, of our spiritual awareness of them' (Cassirer 1955a: 188).

For Cassirer, all symbolic forms must 'be emancipated from the common matrix of myth ... Theoretical, practical and aesthetic consciousness, the world of language and morality, the basic forms of community and the state – they are all originally tied up with mythico-religious conceptions' (Cassirer 1946: 44). In the second volume of the *Philosophy of Symbolic Forms*, which we know Bakhtin read in detail, Cassirer shows that myth, like art, science and language, is a configuration *towards* being, and that the specificity of myth lies not in its content but in 'the intensity with which it is experienced, with which it is believed – as only something endowed with objective reality can be believed' (Cassirer 1955b: 5–6). Mythic thought allows no detachment, it stands in awe of what confronts it, having 'no will to understand the object by encompassing it logically and articulating it with a complex of cause and effects; it is simply overpowered by the object' (Cassirer 1955b: 74). The mythical world is one of conflicting powers: every natural phenomenon is filled with those powers and is therefore perceived as if permeated by emotional qualities. Everything in the mythical world is friendly or hostile, alluring or repellent, fascinating or threatening because the primitive mentality views nature as *sympathetic*, that is, as a fundamental '*solidarity of life*' in which the viewer has no unique and privileged place.

Scientific thought aims systematically to liberate the observer from observed phenomena and obliterate all trace of mythical perception, but such activity only restricts myth to certain spheres, it does not, and indeed cannot, destroy myth itself. Myth remains in the 'expressive function' of symbolism, where there is no difference admitted between 'image and thing, the sign and what it designates' (Cassirer 1955b: 72). Art, like myth, is dependent on the perception of expression, but there are significant differences between the two. Myth is overwhelmed by this perception, whereas art couples depth of feeling with 'the distance accompanying the universality of objectification'. Human life is 'bound and fettered' in mythical experience, whereas in art it becomes 'aesthetically liberated' (Krois 1987: 139). As well as an ideal history of the unfolding of autonomous symbolic forms from the common matrix of myth, Cassirer's work also presents a theory of conflicting social forces. The main conflict is that between mythical and non- (or anti-) mythical conceptions of the world. Cassirer presents a dialectic of mythical and critical symbolic forms. Although a distinct and irreducible symbolic form, myth can and does enter into combinations with other forms and has a particularly close kinship with both language and art. Critical thought must minimise this influence by showing the fundamental gap between sign and object signified.

Cassirer's influence on Bakhtin was profound. As a former pupil of Simmel and a critical enthusiast for Scheler, this last major Marburg neo-Kantian's endorsement of a neo-Hegelian historicism was bound to weigh heavily in Bakhtin's estimation. Furthermore, a major project to publish Hegel's complete works in Russia was under way at the end of the 1920s, and his status as a precursor of Marxism was being stressed. This position entered literary scholarship, where Georg Lukács was attempting to create a Hegelian Marxist theory of the novel (though with his own neo-Kantian twist), culminating in his 1935 article on the novel for the *Soviet Literary Encyclopedia* and a major debate on the novel at the Moscow Communist Academy in 1934–35. Hegel thus had scholarly and ideological respectability in Russia at a time when censorship was extremely tight (Tihanov 2000b: 269–70), and this provided Bakhtin with a perceived opportunity for publication at just the time when he was discovering Cassirer's original way of wedding neo-Kantianism to Hegelianism. Furthermore, the debate on the novel in the Soviet Academy opened the way for Bakhtin's philosophical ideas to be combined with observations drawn from work on literary history by Russian and Soviet scholars such as Aleksandr N. Veselovskii (1838–1906), Ol´ga M. Friedenberg (1890–1955) and the Formalists.

Marrism

There is one more important feature of the distinctly Soviet reception of Cassirer that should not be overlooked. Cassirer's idea of the distinct stages through which all symbolic forms must pass, which he supported with empirical data taken from the work of the French anthropologist Lucien Lévy-Bruhl, was selectively incorporated into what by the mid 1930s had become the dominant theory of linguistic and cultural evolution, the so-called 'New Theory of Language' developed by Nikolai Marr and his followers (Skorik 1952: 137; Moss 1984: 82–109).[2] 'Marrism' was impossible to ignore or escape in the humanities in the Soviet Union at this time. As Slezkine notes:

> By the end of 1934 most ethnological disciplines (but not most ethnologists) had been proclaimed to be Marrist; Marrism had been proclaimed to be a subset of Marxism; and Marr himself had been decorated with the Order of Lenin, buried beside Lomonosov, and beatified through a series of 'memory immortalisation' decrees. (Slezkine 1996: 851–2)

By the time Bakhtin wrote his now famous articles on the novel the dominant position of Marrism, which had been officially pronounced 'Marxism in linguistics', could not be challenged directly, although its prestige throughout the humanities generally declined from this highpoint until after the Second World War. Throughout this period, however, Marr remained in the 'Marxist pantheon', but this does not mean that the Circle merely paid lip-service to Marrism. There is clear evidence of a genuine interest in Marr's work among members of the Circle from as early as 1922, when adherence to Marrism was quite optional (L 621; GTP 448, 450; NT 208–9; LT 42–3). In 1958–59, long after Stalin's denunciation of Marr in *Pravda*, Bakhtin was still speaking about Marr as a 'remarkable scholar' and the creator of 'linguistic paleontology', even though he had been criticised for his 'philosophical views' (Tihanov 2000b: 160; LIZL 89). As this evaluation suggests, despite its notoriously exaggerated claims and administrative excesses, the influence of Marrism was not unambiguously negative in all areas of study.

According to Marr and his followers, all languages pass through distinct stages in a 'single glottogonic process' beginning with a prehistorical stage of 'primordial thinking', which corresponds to Cassirer's 'mythical thought', and which can be excavated according to a 'paleontological analysis' (Thomas 1957: 61–84; Moss 1994). Marr gave this a Marxist gloss, arguing that 'primordial thinking' belonged to the time of 'primitive communism', and that from that time onward all language has a class character, embodying class perspectives and developing according to the development of productive forces.[3] While Marr's own 'linguistic paleontology' led to the fanciful claim that all languages derive from four archaic elements: *sal*, *ber*, *yon* and *rosh* (Alpatov 1991: 32–78), many thinkers found productive elements in Marrism (Slezkine 1996: 852–3; Alpatov 1991: 55). As the scrupulously fair Viktor Zhirmunskii noted in retrospect, Marr's 'theoretical ideas and separate pronouncements', though 'in most cases not fully worked out and chaotic', contained

> ... productive and fruitful thoughts that most of us (especially Leningrad linguists) were bound to find chiming with our own work. I mainly have in mind such things as Marr's struggle against the narrowly Eurocentric theory of traditional linguistics; the stadial-typological approach to the development of languages, and comparison of them regardless of their common line of descent; research into the realm of the interrelations of language and thought; and what might be called the semantic approach to grammatical phenomena. (Bazylev and Neroznak 2001: 18)

Furthermore, the 'paleontological' approach was particularly fruitful in literary and folklore studies where Ol´ga Freidenberg and the biblical scholar Israil´ Frank-Kamenetskii (1880–1937) were Marr's main disciples. Both Voloshinov and Medvedev, it seems, knew Freidenberg personally, with Medvedev actually planning a joint project with Freidenberg and Frank-Kamenetskii (Medvedev 1998: 31).[4] The Marrists developed certain ideas central to the historical poetics and folklore studies of nineteenth-century Russian scholars like Veselovskii and Aleksandr Potebnia (1835–91), according to which artistic forms and typical forms of expression can be traced back to forms of primitive collective consciousness (Perlina 1991: 373; Toporkov 1997). For the Marrists, behind 'literary plots, tropes and motifs' could be revealed 'prehistoric meanings – and hence prehistoric social realities'. Such features survived as 'semantically transfigured but physically recognisable relics of earlier cognitive-linguistic stages' (Slezkine 1996: 847). In a book of 1932, which Bakhtin cited (LIZL 89, 140), Freidenberg outlines the method as follows:

> ... Paleontological analysis (genetic and sociological analysis) proceeds from 'finalized' phenomena and moves to their background, discovering, step by step, the multistage development of such phenomena ... It demonstrates that artistic forms that are supposedly 'fixed once and for all' are in fact historically fluid and their qualitative changeability is prompted by the worldview of society as conditioned by the base. (Freidenburg, 1991: 57)

Literature is a product of class society, and its earlier stage was folklore, which in turn developed from myth, the symbolic form of 'protoclass society'. Certain stages are transitional in this progression, thus:

> In the feudal period, the literary plot is implemented in a form that is literary in character but nevertheless borders on folklore. It is precisely in the plot that we can see with particular clarity the entire path of development from the origins of the worldview of primitive society to the myth, and from the myth to the simplest literary cell. (1991: 57)

As we shall see, this approach is very significant for Bakhtin's work on Rabelais and carnival, but it is also important for understanding the idea of the chronotope, and of recurrent generic forms in the history of literature in general and the novel in particular. However, the influence of Marrism on the Bakhtin Circle was already well established. It is especially apparent in Voloshinov's work, where Marr's work is referred to positively more than once,[5] and Marr's 'new doctrine on language' conditioned the terms of Bakhtin's account of language in society in the 1930s and 1940s, when Marrism was the only acceptable theory of language.

Heteroglossia

Bakhtin's first (failed) attempt to enter print at this time was with the long essay 'Discourse in the Novel', written in 1934–35, at the height of the dominance of Marrism.[6] In accordance with the Marrist agenda, Bakhtin argues that traditional scholarship not only accepts the givenness of such categories as the unitary national language, and the standards of traditional poetics, but participates in their propagation. Indo-European linguistics, ethnography and literary scholarship have thus become instruments of 'ideological manipulation by a dominant social force'. As Boris Gasparov, perhaps the first person to recognise the systematic nature of the influence of Marr on Bakhtin,[7] argues:

> Such a force [for Bakhtin and for Marr – CB] – be it prestigious 'high culture' or a Eurocentric notion of the community of 'Indo-European' nations – always strived to maintain its dominance by imposing its own values on the world of culture as a whole and by suppressing the multitude of voices that actually coexist and amalgamate in any speaking community, at any stage of its development. (Gasparov 1996: 143)

For Marr, the dictatorship of artificial linguistic and literary standards opposes the 'natural life of languages', especially those of oppressed socio-economic groups, and progressive scholarship should consider all languages equally, irrespective of the development of their written forms or integration into modern culture (Slezkine 1991: 478–9; 1996: 832–3).

Bakhtin argues that as a result of this relationship between language, traditional scholarship and power, culture becomes an arena of struggle between official (national) unity and popular heterogeneity. Every concrete utterance is a microcosm of this struggle between 'centripetal' and 'centrifugal' forces that simultaneously unify and stratify language at all stages of its historical existence. As academic disciplines, linguistics, stylistics and the philosophy of language were all shaped by the centralising currents of culture; they have ignored the 'dialogised heteroglossia' (*raznorechie*) that constitutes the authentic linguistic environment. As we have seen, Voloshinov had already attacked Saussure's mythical '*langue*' as an expression of such authoritarian forces in 1929, and in doing so he approvingly citied Marr in support. For Marr, '... the approach to this or that language as a so-called national culture, as the mass native discourse (*rech´*) of a whole population, is unscientific and unrealistic, the national language as an all-class (*vsesoslovnyi*), non-class (*neklassovyi*) language is still a fiction'. Marr also argues that national languages are the result of the crossing (*skreshchenie*) of 'simpler elements', and 'intertribal communication brought about by economic needs' (MPL 76; MFIa 291–2).

Bakhtin now echoed this line of thinking in a new way, quietly dropping Marr's correlation of language and class and replacing it with a more general type of social stratification derived from classical sociology. This results in the now famous notion of heteroglossia (*raznorechie*):

> At any given moment of its becoming, language is stratified not only into linguistic dialects in the strict sense of the word (according to formal linguistic markers, especially phonetic), but, and this is fundamental for us, into socio-ideological languages: languages of social groups, 'professional' languages, 'generic' languages, languages of generations and so on. (DN 271–2; SR 85)

In this recasting of the Marrist 'class-character' (*klassovost´*) of language, Bakhtin was drawing quite strongly on neo-Kantian and phenomenological ideas. Heteroglossia, the socially stratified national language, is 'anonymous and social as language' (like the neo-Kantian realm of objective validity) but it is simultaneously 'concrete, filled with specific content and accentuated' in each individual utterance (it is *actualised* in life, that is in social dialogue). Words do not relate to their 'object' singularly but, as we saw with Dostoevsky, they encounter other words directed toward the same object:

> Directed toward its object, a word [*slovo*] enters a dialogically agitated and tense medium of alien discourses [*slovo*], evaluations and accents, becoming intertwined in complex interrelations, merging with some, recoiling from others, intersecting with a third group; and all this may form a discourse essentially, leaving a trace in all its layers of meaning [*smysl*], complicating its expression and influencing its whole stylistic profile. (DN 276; SR 90)

Here once again we have a phenomenological position in which an 'intentionally impelled' discourse encounters others in a complex fabric of intersubjective relations. However, the social medium has a much more structured nature than previously and suggests relatively stable patterns of social relations or *institutions*. As previously, however, these remain 'bracketed out' of Bakhtin's account of discursive stratification. What are actually institutional questions relating to economic and political structures now acquire an *ethical* significance that renders the relations between forms of social organisation and modes of discursive interaction unclear. Decentralising forces are always ethical and centralising forces unethical.

This position is actually difficult to maintain in historical analysis, and it is a good example of Bakhtin collapsing politics into ethics. A more reasoned political analysis is provided by Antonio Gramsci, who opposed the educational reforms of Giovannni Gentile, Mussolini's minister of education, partly on the grounds that it made no provision for the teaching of normative Italian in state schools. Class divisions thereby became 'juridically fixed', while the lack of a national language 'creates friction' among the masses. This situation could only benefit Fascist domination and obstruct the construction of a popular-democratic mass movement (Gramsci 1985: 182–7; Crowley 2001).

The direct or indirect source of Bakhtin's idea of the opposition between centrifugal and centripetal forces is most probably the 1892 *Ethics* of Wilhelm Wundt (see especially Wundt 1907–08: I, 262–3; III, 269–72). Here, as in his famous *Völkerpsychologie* (*Folk Psychology*),[8] Wundt celebrates the triumph of the centralisation of language, literature, world-view and social life within a nation over the 'centrifugal' forces of different classes and associations. This was all part of Wundt's ethical philosophy that recommends the transcendence of individual organisms by the collective organism of the state, with the moral goal of the creation of intellectual goods. In this project society is necessarily divided into an active upper class and a passive lower class. Wundt's work played an important role in the development of intellectual foundations for German nationalism, and the glorification of the state undoubtedly had unpleasant connotations for an egalitarian intellectual like Bakhtin living in Stalin's Russia. Wundt's attitude towards language and literature was, moreover, quite the opposite of the programme delineated by Marr.[9] Wundt had also long been regarded as a *bête noire* by ethical socialists, neo-Kantians and the Würzburg School, and it is therefore unsurprising that Bakhtin should treat this type of ethics in a negative fashion. Nevertheless, Bakhtin adopted an important element of Wundt's theory, even if the evaluation of this feature was diametrically opposed to that of its original author. Thus, Bakhtin was to regard questions of linguistic and wider cultural centralisation as ethical rather than political questions by treating the institutional structure of society as the expression of ethical principles.

Heteroglossia and the novel

According to Bakhtin, literary language is but a specific stratum of language and, furthermore, even literary language is stratified according to genre, period and so on. The novel is special, however, because it is based on heteroglossia itself. Heteroglossia is an a priori precondition of the novel as a genre.

> The internal stratification of a single national language into social dialects, group manners, professional jargons, generic languages, languages of generations and age groups, languages of trends, languages of authorities, languages of circles and passing fashions, languages of socio-political days, even hours (every day has its slogan, its vocabulary, its accent) – this inner stratification of every language at any given moment of its historical existence is a necessary precondition of the novelistic genre. (DN 262–3; SR 76)

The first section of 'Discourse in the Novel', subtitled 'contemporary stylistics and the novel', shows how it was only in the 1920s that the 'novelistic prose word' began to find a place in stylistic analysis. However, Bakhtin argues that the pioneering studies of the 1920s used categories designed for an analysis of poetic discourse, and that these are unsuitable for studying the novel, which is a very specific artistic genre. Stylistically speaking, unlike poetry the novel is made up of a variety of social discourses or 'heteroglossia' (*raznorechie*), and sometimes it includes a variety of languages [*raznoiazychie*] and of individual voices [*raznogolositsa*]; all of these are organised artistically.

Using a musical metaphor not unlike that of polyphony in the Dostoevsky book, Bakhtin argues that themes are 'orchestrated' in the novel by means of this stratification of the national language, making it particularly inappropriate to use a Saussurean-type analysis, based on a homogeneous language system (*langue*) and individual discursive acts (*parole*). The Saussurean approach may be productive in the analysis of most poetic genres in which a single language system and an individual poet's discourse are assumed, but it is not suitable for the 'heteroglot' novel. Some, such as the Russian phenomenologist Gustav Shpet (1879–1937) and the linguist Viktor Vinogradov (1895–1969), tried to explain the difficulties that arose from analysing the novel with such categories by arguing that the novel is a rhetorical rather than a poetic genre. Bakhtin, however, disagreed, arguing that the fact that the novel does not fit into the official canon of poetic genres as defined by Aristotle does not mean that it is not an artistic genre.

Poetry and the novel

According to Bakhtin, the artistic image presented in the novel is based on heteroglossia and the interanimation of intentionally impelled words, while the poetic image naively presumes only the interaction of word and object. Where in poetry 'the word forgets the history of the contradictory verbal recognitions of its object, as well as the heteroglossia of its present recognition', in the novel 'the dialectics of the object are interlaced with the social dialogue around it' (DN 277–8; SR 91–2). This is a crucial passage that opposes the common assumption that Bakhtin posited dialogue simply as an alternative to dialectics. The truth is more complex. Here we see that the novelist, whom Bakhtin champions, is a critical thinker who sees the object of cognition in the process of becoming (in neo-Kantian terms, its general, endless production in cognition) and who also perceives the plurality of discursive perspectives that constitute the object as a social fact. The poet, on the other hand, is a mythical thinker who believes that he or she can have direct access to the object in a language that is indisputable. Thus, even if poetry recognises the shifting, dialectical nature of the object, it does not recognise the equally valid status of other discourses that surround that object. If noticed, such languages are treated as objects of what Voloshinov called 'linear' reception. The boundaries of other discourses remain intact and the relation of outsideness is total and dogmatic, so that the poet's discourse is granted an authoritative status (DN 287; SR 100). Thus 'the poet is defined by the idea of a single and unitary language and a single, monologically sealed utterance. These ideas are immanent in those poetic genres in which he works and determine the means by which the poet orients himself in the actuality of heteroglossia' (DN 296–7; SR 109). The poet thus adopts a stance towards other discourses that is conservative and authoritarian, making poetic genres highly conducive to employment by officialdom in a heteroglot society. The counter-tendency is relegated to those 'low' comic and satirical genres that have been marginalised by 'official' poetics and constitute one of the main sources of the novel. Poetry is literature approaching the limits of 'objective culture', while the novel is literature in its closest proximity to 'life'.

In poetry proper, other voices are simply cut out. The presence of another speaker would be strictly locked within quotation marks or set apart in some other way, to show the fundamental separation of the second voice from the poet's own voice. This is not the case in the novel. Here many characters interact and the voice of the narrator becomes simply one among others, even if in certain cases the narrator's voice is given a higher status. In any case, the narrator has to take account of the perspectives of others in a serious manner because any novel that was simply an occasion for the voicing of the narrative perspective would not be a novel so much as a philo-sophical treatise, a sermon or some other genre. Bakhtin's point is that high poetic genres have been held up as some sort of ideal, while the narrative prose genres such as fairytales, anecdotes and other popular stories such as the bawdy *fabliaux* and *Schwänke* are relegated to a second division and treated as unworthy of forming part of a great tradition.

Here, for the first time, we have a conjunction that becomes central for Bakhtin's work from this point onwards: mythical con-sciousness is aligned with poetic genres, monologue, unitary language, objective culture and officialdom, while critical con-sciousness is aligned with the novel, dialogue, discursive plurality, 'life' and 'the people'. The conjunction is a particularly populist one based on Cassirer's dialectic of symbolic forms and the dichotomy of life and forms that derives from life-philosophy. As a genre spurned by traditional literary studies, the novel also fits into the camp of marginalised subjects as delineated by Marr. We will return to this below. It is, however, important to note that the phenomenological aspects of Bakhtin's work are still present. Discourse, we are told, is intentionally directed towards an object, but the language is always 'populated' with the intentions of others, making the relation between language and its object problematic. All writers must work amid the sociologically stratified discourses that result from this variety of intersecting intentions, but the ways in which the poet and the novelist respond to this challenge are quite different. The poet qua poet must assume complete mastery over his or her language, and thus ignore the other intentions that populate the words in order to make it serve his or her purpose; but such an attitude is a mark of mythical consciousness. The novelist, however, utilises the 'already populated' words and compels them to serve his or her own, secondary intention, leading to a variety of reflections and refractions of that intention in the heteroglot system:

> On entering the novel heteroglossia is subject to an artistic reworking. The social and historical voices that populate language, all its words and forms, which provide language with definite concrete senses, are organised in the novel into a structured stylistic system, expressing the *differentiated* socio-ideological position of the author in the heteroglossia of the epoch. (DN 300; SR 113)

The novel as such now becomes the means by which interacting discourses are transformed into artistic images, rendering their intentional essences intuitable. To use more contemporary language, the ideological structure, the genuine half-concealed motivations are made visible. The 'authoritative' attempts to establish a hierarchy between discourses are rendered palpable by the author's manipulation of contexts to bring discourses into contact. However, the novel also shows how one's own discourse can emerge from the plurality of 'internally persuasive' discourses that compete within the individual psyche. As consciousness begins to work critically, it becomes sceptical of claims to encapsulate truth in an 'authoritative' discourse. That discourse is objectified, allowing the emergence of one's own perspective (DN 342–6; SR 154–8). Here we have the same process, derived from Scheler, that was discussed in the 1929 Dostoevsky study, but transposed to a much more general level and given a socio-political edge. These features of the polyphonic novel are now generalised into features of the novel as such, even if a special place for the Russian novelist is maintained within the history of this particular 'symbolic form'. One such example will suffice. At one point (DN 304; SR 117) Bakhtin quotes from Dickens's novel *Little Dorrit*:

> It was a dinner to provoke the appetite, though he had not had one. The rarest dishes, sumptuously cooked and sumptuously served; the choicest fruits, the most exquisite wines; marvels of workmanship in gold and silver, china and glass; innumerable

things delicious to the senses of taste, smell, and sight, were insinuated into its composition. *O what a wonderful man this Merdle, what a great man, what a master man, how blessedly and enviably endowed* – in one word, what a rich man!

This passage begins in a high poetic style associated with the epic, glorifying the hero. The basis of glorification is undermined, however, because the narrator unmasks the real ideological structure behind the employment of such terms as 'wonderful', 'great', 'master' and 'endowed' with reference to Merdle – the respect generated by his wealth. All these terms, the words of a second interlocutor – probably Merdle's own unspoken self-image – can be replaced by the single word 'rich', revealing the value structure of the second person. The comic and satirical aspects of the novel are expressions of the linguistic scepticism that Bakhtin had already detected in the work of Dostoevsky, and Bakhtin examines further passages from Dickens and Turgenev, among others, to show that to a greater or lesser extent these strategies are characteristic of the novel as such. As the dialogic form *par excellence*, the novel is now engaged in the systematic debunking of the pretensions of 'authoritative discourse'.

The 'becoming' of the novel

All the features of the novel and of the social stratification of language that is its precondition are presented as timeless and unchanging. Heteroglossia is a semi-transcendental condition for the novel's existence, and the novel has a timeless set of forms. This is in keeping with the principles of the earlier work, but we now have an account of how the novel 'unfolds' in history and of how its 'essence' as a genre 'appears'. Although Bakhtin invokes interacting, differentiated social groups and nations as preconditions of the 'decentralisation of the verbal-ideological world' (DN 367–8; SR 179–80), his adherence to a neo-Kantian isolation of culture from civilisation leaves such suggestions hanging in the air. The relation between forms of social interaction and forms of discursive culture can be traced from Russian prerevolutionary criticism (Veselovskii) and through the Formalists to contemporary Soviet theory (Freidenberg),[10] but Bakhtin is linking these features of the theory of the novel to Cassirer's idealist dialectic. This is especially clear when he argues that the novel is the expression of a 'Galilean perception of language', echoing Cassirer's insistence on Kant's 'Copernican revolution' in philosophy. The idea is that where Copernicus and Galileo showed that the Earth is not the centre of the Universe, neo-Kantian philosophy shows that the centre of attention is no longer the object (thing) as in classical accounts of realism, but the cultural forms through which the object is 'produced'. Bakhtin goes on to advocate the same convergence of linguistic philosophy and idealist dialectic as Voloshinov (above) had in 1928:

> In order that an artistically profound play of social languages might be possible, a radical change in the feel for the word on a literary and general linguistic level was necessary. It was necessary to come to terms with the word as an objectual, characteristic, but at the same time [as an] intentional phenomenon. It was necessary to begin to sense the 'inner form' (in the Humboldtian sense) in an alien language and the 'inner form' of one's own language as alien; it was necessary to begin to sense the objectness, the typicality, the characteristicness not only of actions, gestures and separate words and expressions, but also of points of view, world-views and senses of the world that are organically united with the expressions of their language. (DN 367; SR 179)

The precondition for this new attitude is the 'fundamental intersection of languages in a single, given consciousness' which relativises established languages of authority. This leads to a discussion of the 'absolute rule of myth over language' in prehistoric times, the continued influence of mythical thinking in ancient societies, and its vestiges in modern poetic discourse. The germs of the novel appear in those ages when the religious and political authority associated with a ruling discourse is in decay and society becomes ideologically decentralised. Again we have Bakhtin applying German idealist philosophy to literature by reworking the observations of contemporary literary scholarship in accordance with his adopted philosophical position.

In 'Discourse in the Novel', the account of the history of the novel is quite sparse, but we are presented with two paths of novelistic development: one path approaches heteroglossia 'from above', from an ennobled position of 'literariness'; the other approaches from below, from the 'heteroglot depths', and overwhelms the literary language. Characteristic of the first path is sentimentalism and pathos, and of the second is parody and comedy, often incorporating figures from the 'low' comic genres such as the rogue (*picaro*), the clown and the fool. In this second line we have the greatest examples of the genre, such as the novels of Cervantes and Rabelais, in which a new attitude to language emerges. From such 'prenovel-istic', minor parodic genres (*fabliaux*, *Schwänke*, and so on) 'street songs' and so on, the second type of novel adopted an implicit 'philosophy of discourse', in essence, a 'profound distrust of discourse as such'. What concerns such genres is not the direct meaning or emotional content of the word but

> the actual, always self-interested *use* of that meaning [*smysl*] and the way it is expressed by the speaker, a use determined by the speaker's position (profession, estate etc.) and by the concrete situation. *Who* speaks and under what conditions he speaks: this is what determines the word's actual meaning [*smysl*]. All direct meanings [*znachenie*] and direct expressions are false, and this is especially true of emotional ones. (DN 401; SR 212)

Thus, in the novel of the second type we have a genre displaying complete scepticism toward the representational adequacy of language. It is, however, an attitude with a positive side, as Cassirer noted in his volume on language. In seeking to expose the 'nullity' of knowledge and language, scepticism ultimately demonstrates something rather different: 'the nullity of the *standard* by which it measures them':

> In scepticism the 'copy theory' is methodically and consistently demolished by the self-destruction of its basic premises. The farther the negation is carried in this point, the more clearly a positive insight follows from it. The last semblance of any mediate or immediate *identity* between reality and symbol must be effaced, the *tension* between the two must be enhanced to the extreme, for it is precisely in this tension that the specific achievement of symbolic expression and the content of the particular symbolic forms is made evident. For this content cannot be revealed as long as we hold fast to the belief that we possess 'reality' as a given, self-sufficient being, prior to all spiritual formation. (Cassirer 1955a: 188)

The second type of novel thus develops a 'purely symbolic' attitude toward language.

This is, however, an extremely Hegelian way of approaching literature. In ceasing to believe that thought can capture sensuous reality, Hegel argues that consciousness begins to recognise that spirit (*Geist*) is its own object. Similarly in Bakhtin, the novelist ceases to try to present direct images of 'reality' in an authoritative discourse and turns to providing images of languages, each of which presents an image of a tiny portion of being. This formulation still bears the influence of Cohen's aesthetics that we saw in Medvedev's book, for the novelist builds a 'superstructure' over these linguistically embodied world-views to present a simultaneity of dialogically implicated perceptions. However, the Hegelian line is foremost. At one point we see that the novel plays a role in cultural becoming like that of philosophy in Hegel and Cassirer: the coming-to-self-consciousness of spirit:

> In the novel literary language possesses an organ for the cognition of its own heteroglot nature. Heteroglossia in itself becomes, in the novel and thanks to the novel, heteroglossia for itself: languages are dialogically correlated and begin to exist for each other (like rejoinders in a dialogue). It is precisely thanks to the novel that languages mutually illuminate each other, literary language becomes a dialogue of languages that know about and understand each other. (DN 400; SR 211)

In the second line of the novel, the genre becomes 'what it actually is', its essence appears. However, in a typically neo-Kantian gesture the novel has a never-ending task: to present 'all the socio-ideological voices of an epoch, that is, all the languages of the epoch that are in some way essential; the novel must be a microcosm of heteroglossia' (DN 411; SR 222). Even at this most Hegelian moment, the ethical tone of Bakhtin's work asserts itself once more: the 'is' and the 'ought' never coincide, for they are fundamentally distinct aspects of being.

The novel and history

The new conception of the novel that is developed in 'Discourse in the Novel' draws only a very tentative correlation between the ideal narrative of the novel's coming-to-be and history. This correlation is more fully elaborated in the series of essays that follow, which were posthumously published as 'Forms of Time and of the Chronotope in the Novel' (1937–38) 'From the Prehistory of Novelistic Discourse' (1940), 'Satire' (1940) and 'Epic and Novel' (1941). The first of these, which was subtitled 'a sketch of historical poetics', introduces the concept of the 'chronotope' or spatio-temporal relations in culture, and this acts for Bakhtin as the main link between aesthetic form and history. The application of the categories of space and time to the empirical world was a central theme of Kant's theory of knowledge, but for Kant these categories did not fundamentally change, being a priori, transcendental forms. For Bakhtin, however, these categories are part of the world of objective validity and so have only a semi-transcendental nature. Each epoch is characterised by certain senses of space and time. The term 'chronotope' derives from a 1925 lecture given by the physiologist Aleksei Ukhtomskii (1875–1942) that Bakhtin attended (FTCN 84; FVKhR 235) in which Ukhtomskii argued that only the 'fusion of space and time is not relative' (Ukhtomskii 2000: 79). Yet the specific usage of the concept was to a large extent based on Cassirer's analysis of space and time intuitions as represented in language and myth (FTCN 251; FVKhR 399; Cassirer 1955a: 198–226; Cassirer 1955b: 83ff.). The concept of the chronotope allows Bakhtin to present a historical typology of the architectonic forms of literature: specific works are expressions of certain historically specific senses of space and time.

While Bakhtin's inventive use of this line of analysis is striking, the history of European cultural development that he outlines is not a particularly new one. It derives from the grand narratives that one finds in nineteenth-century German idealism. Following an argument that is consistent from Hegel to Wagner, Bakhtin argues that the collapse of Athenian democracy and the interaction of cultures in the conflicts of the Hellenistic period led to a splintering of the harmonious cultural scene dominated by tragedy and the epic and to the rise of comic genres which parodied the official culture. Thus begins a historical period that culminates in the Renaissance liberation of the human spirit from church dogma and the fixed hierarchies of the ancient and feudal worlds. The history of the novel is a microcosm of this coming-to-modernity, for the minor, serio-comic prose genres that resulted from the collapse of antiquity come together to form the modern novel in the work of such Renaissance novelists as Rabelais and Cervantes. The 'appearance' of the novel's 'essence' is thus presented as a dimension of the 'growth of individual freedom of thought and expression, the full development of self-conscious personality and the evolution of moral autonomy' that German idealism saw as culminating in the Renaissance (Ferguson 1948: 182).

The German idealist historians, such as Jakob Burckhardt, on whom Cassirer and Bakhtin drew inherited the Hegelian narrative of cultural development even though they disavowed any Hegelian influences. The point of contention was the evaluation of each development along the way. Thus, while Wagner and many others saw the collapse of Athenian democracy as a negative development, the philosopher and historian of autobiography Georg Misch, who Bakhtin also read, saw it as the time of the 'discovery' of individuality. He celebrated Hellenistic imperial expansion for facilitating this through 'the extension of the field of view to previously unknown peoples, with different ways of living'. Drawing on the works of Vossler and Spitzer, Bakhtin developed this cultural history into an account of how Homeric Greek encountered other languages, leading to a 'polyglot' awareness of linguistic 'otherness' that allowed the language to evolve in relation to others rather than remain in isolated stasis. Similarly, Misch saw the collapse of the Athenian *polis* and the growth of the bureaucratic state as ushering in a period in which the 'private existence of the individual' was realised for the first time. Freed from 'conventionally imposed participation in the life of the city state' which 'had given his life the character of an integral part of the whole', the individual now had to establish unity of personality from within. Bakhtin similarly argued that on the Greek public square, which constituted the state and all official organs, there was as yet 'nothing "for oneself alone", nothing which was not subject to public-state control and account. Here everything was entirely public' (FTCN 131–2; FVKhR 283). With the formation of an official stratum, Misch argued that 'a vast number of spheres and objects appeared in the private life of the private individual that were not, in general, open to the public ... the human image became multilayered and complex' (Misch 1950: 69, 180–1). Thus, new genres began to replace those expressive of wholeness – the epic and tragedy; these were the precursors of the novel. Non-canonical literature, and ultimately the novel, now became the organ for the disclosure of the multilayered and multi-faceted individual, which Bakhtin, following Misch, saw first emerging in ancient autobiography. A comparison of Bakhtin's and Misch's discussions of autobiography indicates just how heavily the former borrows from the latter. Moreover, Misch is undoubtedly an important source for Bakhtin's celebrated discussion of the history of the representation of personality in the novel.

The chronotope essay also presents a typology of forms of the novelistic whole from the various forms of ancient autobiography discussed above through the static, 'vertically organised' world of Dante's *Divine Comedy* and Dostoevsky's novels to the ritual inversions which abound in Rabelais's novels. These are correlated with the ages in which they emerged, so that the static architecture of the artistic worlds of Dante and Dostoevsky expresses their respective location in 'threshold' ages, on the border between medieval and Renaissance worlds and Tsarist hierarchy and capitalist dynamism respectively.[11] Representative simultaneity expresses the compression of that which was and that which will be into a single moment in which ethical decisions for action are to be made. Rabelais, however, showed a world between medieval stasis and the new absolutist monarchies of European states, in which the old hierarchical order of social values was relativised and the new official stratum yet to crystallise. Rabelais, we are told, attempted to re-establish the 'fully exteriorised' image of personality in the Renaissance without the stylisation typical of the literature of antiquity. This grows out of a discussion of the roles in the novel of the *picaro* (or rogue), clown and fool who wear the masks of the public square and thus re-establish the public image of the person. Their ability to provoke parodic laughter facilitates this view from outside. Although such characters as the fool play important roles in some Renaissance plays, such as Shakespeare's *King Lear*, *Henry IV*, and so on, Bakhtin argues that it is through the 'low' genres of the *fabliaux* and *Schwänke*, and then in the novel, that their role takes on its most structured form. These characters live, as it were, in the theatrical 'chronotope' of the interlude, which allows them to unmask the conventions of the moment by not understanding, and finding nothing in common with, the world around them. In the 1940 essay 'Satire', written for a planned but unpublished volume of the *Soviet Literary Encyclopaedia*, Bakhtin leans heavily on Freidenberg to trace these figures back to the comic festivals of ancient Greece and Rome, the *Lupercalia* and *Saturnalia*, in which everyday life, its hierarchies and conventions were suspended and in some cases inverted (S 17–19). The entry of these features into literature facilitated a new mode of representation, opening up hitherto forbidden and secret, 'private' spheres of life to artistic depiction.

We will examine the specific importance of Rabelais for Bakhtin in the next chapter. Here we are concerned with the role of the novel in cultural history. The modern novel is a product of a cultural-historical tendency that begins with the collapse of antiquity and reaches its decisive stage in the Renaissance. It is a tendency that is also correlated with changes in the nature of discursive interaction. The collapse of the *monoglot* Athenian city-state in Hellenistic times gave rise to the *polyglot* interaction of national languages, and the decentralising trend finally resulted in the interaction of different social classes and groups as the fixed hierarchy of the medieval period was undermined in the Renaissance. The history of literary genres that corresponds with this movement is the collapse of the epic and of tragedy leading to a plurality of serio-comic and satirical genres and the subsequent development of a new major narrative form which incorporates these developments: the novel. Both these processes also involve the collapse of the absolute rule of a single official discourse and poetics and a liberation of the various vernacular languages and popular genres, leading to the establish-ment of a plurality of social dialects that are recognised and 'imaged' in the novel. In the Renaissance, sandwiched between the rigid hier-archies and ecclesiastical dogmas of the Middle Ages on the one side and the rise of absolutist monarchies and new official languages on the other, the modern world-view arose with the intermingling of different nations and social strata, the latter facilitated by a flowering of popular festive culture: carnival. Carnival will also be discussed in the next chapter. However, here we have a parallel dialectical development of language and literary genres akin to Cassirer's 'law of symbolisation' as the 'inner form' that runs through all 'symbolic forms'. The broad periodisation that we have outlined is, however, as specific as Bakhtin ever is with regard to questions of history. The neo-Kantian separation of fact and value, civilisation and culture allows him to speak in terms of general correlations rather than dealing with the fundamental connections between institutional structure and cultural production.

Laughter and critique

One of the most striking aspects of Bakhtin's work on the novel is the important role he assigns to laughter. In 'From the Prehistory of Novelistic Discourse' we are told that along with 'polyglossia' laughter was the crucial factor in the development of critical literature, and that it even becomes the organising force for the representation of alien discourse (FPND 50–1; IPRS 418). In the pre-novelistic genres that arose from the collapse of the monoglot ancient world the small, parodic genres laid the foundations for the novel by establishing a 'linguistic Saturnalia' (FPND 77; IPRS 440) in which the authority of an official language was etched away by the corrosive effects of laughter.

There are two main sources for Bakhtin's conception of laughter: the work of the French life-philosopher Henri Bergson, and that of Cassirer.[12] Bergson insisted on the fundamentally collective and social nature of laughter. It is a 'social gesture' that constitutes the 'corrective' of 'a certain rigidity of body, mind and character' in the interests of maximising the 'elasticity and sociability' of society's members (Bergson 1956: 73–4). This concentration on laughter as corrective of autonomatism and inelasticity is developed by Bergson in a variety of areas of comedy, from verbal wit to physical mimicry, but everywhere the motif of 'something mechanical encrusted on the living' is revealed (Bergson 1956: 84). The argument is that excessive rigidity in the form of dogmatism or an inability to be flexible in one's conduct is a threat to the social organism and that laughter acts as a benign force within society by 'correcting' this deviation. Bergson's own explanation of this phenomenon often recalls his other writings on the '*élan vital*' or life-force, but Bakhtin was less interested in this aspect than in the potential the analysis offered when combined with Simmel's dichotomy of life and 'objective culture'. Laughter now became a collective corrective to all culture that has hardened into a damaging incrustation on life, but again a populist twist was added: it is a popular-democratic corrective of the dogmatic pretensions of the official culture. In Bakhtin's reworking laughter retains its vital, fear-banishing, inverting, self-conscious, moral and corrective nature from Bergson (Tihanov 2000b: 274–5), but this is integrated into a perspective derived from Cassirer in which laughter becomes the weapon of critical thinking against myth, undermining the truth-claims and authoritative pretensions of a discourse and thus showing that the process of symbolisation is itself the object of knowledge. The connection of laughter with sceptical deflation and critique, along with the privileging of the Renaissance as a golden age of the comic spirit, was outlined in the last chapter of Cassirer's 1932 book *The Platonic Renaissance in England*.[13] Here Cassirer, like Bakhtin after him, celebrated the comic writing of Rabelais, Hans Sachs, Cervantes,

Boccaccio and the like for presenting laughter as the 'objective criterion of truth and falsehood':

> To the pedant, as to the zealot, freedom of thought is an abomination; for the former takes shelter behind the dignity of knowledge, the latter behind the sanctified authority of religion. When both retrench themselves behind a false gravity, nothing remains but to subject them to the test of ridicule and expose them. Then only will knowledge and piety appear in their true character, which is not inconsistent with the enjoyment of life, which, on the contrary, is the finest expression of the enjoyment of life and of an affirmative attitude towards the world. (Cassirer 1953: 184)

Although Cassirer does not explicitly make the connection between scepticism in the philosophy of language, which he discussed in his volume of language, and this critical aspect of laughter, it was a very small step for Bakhtin to do so. Similarly, the link between Bergson's writing on laughter as the corrective to the rigidification of life and Simmel's hostility to objective culture as an incrustation on life was fairly straightforward. However, the fusion of all these elements into a coherent perspective and their application to the study of narrative literature was a considerable achievement.

Bakhtin's most sustained work on laughter is the Rabelais study, to which we will turn later. However, we must note here that the serio-comic nature of the novel is a crucial aspect of its nature as a critical genre. This is particularly well developed in the discussion of the relationship between the two most important narrative genres of the ancient and modern worlds respectively, the epic and the novel.

Epic and novel

The 1941 essay on the epic and the novel was originally called 'The Novel as a Literary Genre' and in line with this title it comprises a catalogue of characteristics of the genre. As Galin Tihanov has shown, the essay is organised around a contrast between the two major narrative genres and to a considerable extent is a response to a major work on the same topic by Lukács. In his 1935 essay on the novel for the *Soviet Literary Encyclopaedia* (Lukács 1935), Lukács argued that the novel was the 'bourgeois epic', which strove for epic totality but which could present only a debased version because of the divisions of community and the alienation of the individual in the bourgeois world. In the new socialist society the epic would once again take its place at the vanguard of literary life, presenting a total perspective on reality in its historical becoming. In a series of articles written in the 1930s, Lukács attacked the bourgeois decadence of writers who refused to strive for epic totality and instead developed modernist techniques of non-linear narrative. Lukács's conception was rooted in a particular reading of Hegel's comments on the epic in his *Aesthetics*, and this reflected Lukács's own earlier romantic anticapitalism in which he yearned for the organic totality of the precapitalist world. This had been evident in his pre-Marxist work *The Theory of the Novel* (1916), in which he also presented a comparison of the epic and the novel. There, too, he stressed the organic totality of the epic world lost in the contemporary age:

> The novel is the epic of an age in which the extensive totality of life is no longer directly given, in which the immanence of meaning in life has become a problem, yet which still thinks in terms of totality. (Lukács 1978: 56)

In the later interpretation, the coming of socialism would re-establish an 'extensive totality of life', but at a higher level.

Bakhtin offers a quite different contrast between the epic and the novel. In addition to the features of the novel that he had discussed in the preceding essays, he now adds a final point of contrast between the epic and novel: the former is enclosed within a concluded and ennobled 'absolute past', presenting an image of the world at a remote distance from the present, while the latter is 'in contact with the spontaneity of the incomplete present' (EN 27; ER 470). Here we see Bakhtin apparently evoking the celebration of capitalist dynamism over feudal stasis found in Marx and Engels, suggesting the role of the novel as the genre of modernity. The epic, it seems, is the narrative genre of a static and monologic age that has long passed, the epoch of classical antiquity, while the novel is the genre of the modern age, produced by and participating in its dynamism. However, Bakhtin still argues the Marrist case that the roots of the novel lie in folklore (EN 38; ER 481), and he refers to the dynamism of 'the people' as against the static nature of the official strata.[14] Here again we have evidence of Bakhtin's populist recasting of life-philosophy.

The epic is 'walled off' from life, it presents an image of the world
that is at the extreme of 'objective culture', with the conditions of its
own birth in historical time obscured by the 'absolute' nature of the
epic past, which renders all points equally distant from the present
(EN 19; ER 463). The epic presents a series of 'firsts and bests', of
heroes who are gods and demigods and events the integrity of which
is unquestioned. As a time of unparalleled grandeur and unapproachable triumph, the epic past can only be an object of awe for
those in the present; it is immune from questioning or doubt and
must be simply accepted in its enclosed totality. Heroes like Homer's
Achilles or Virgil's Aeneas are presented as the greatest of heroes,
whose stature is above anything in the contemporary world, while
the themes are the defining moments of great civilisations. In this
way, the epic is an expression of the rule of myth over language. Any
critical engagement with the world of the epic is denied. The novel,
on the other hand, is close to life, it maintains a maximal proximity
to the present, to all that is incomplete, that is, to the process of
becoming. This makes it incompatible with the epic. The world
depicted in the novel is recognisably *our* world; even if it is set in the
past, this is a recognisable past, it does not resemble a mythical past
that is held up as an unapproachable ideal. Where Cassirer saw the
task of the critical forms of culture to be to counter the mythical
forms and to consign them to strictly limited symbolic 'functions',
Bakhtin argues that the novel seeks to destroy the epic distance that
is integral to the mythical approach to the world. The main weapon
in this campaign is laughter, which is both the handmaiden of
critique and, being rooted in folklore, the agent for the popular
destruction of authoritarian dogmas. Laughter brings the object
close, demolishing all fear and piety before it, facilitating familiar
contact and in so doing laying the basis for free investigation:

> By bringing the object up close and familiarising it, laughter as it
> were delivers it into the fearless hands of investigative experiment
> – both scientific and artistic ... The comic [*smekhovoi*] and popular-
> linguistic familiarisation of the world is an exceptionally
> important and necessary stage in the formation [*stanovlenie*] of the
> free scientific-cognitive and artistic-realistic creation of European
> humanity. (EN 23; ER 466)

The organising centre of the novel is not only fundamentally
different from that of the epic, but is the antithesis of everything the

mythico-epic world-view is based upon. The novel is thus not an expression of a bourgeois world-view that must pass away, but the expression of critical thinking within literature as such. It is an orientation towards and within life that, while coming to fruition in historical circumstances, has a more general, objective validity for all ages and social systems.

Bakhtin's theory of the novel in the 1930s is thus a particular combination of a variety of intellectual trends forged in specific social and historical conditions. All of these factors need to be considered in assessing its originality and significance. We have distinguished a number of threads which make up the theory: the neo-Kantian notion of objective validity and split between fact and value, civilisation and culture, is and ought, and so on; the Simmelian antagonism between life and objective culture; Bergson's notion of laughter as the corrective of rigidity; Hegel's ideal narrative of the dialectical unfolding of spirit; Cassirer's notions of the dialectic of mythical and critical social forms and of the critical conjunction of laughter and scepticism; the tradition of German idealist and Russian literary writing about the novel; Misch's history of autobiography; the Vossler School's work on language and cultural history; Lukács's writing on the epic and novel; and a Russian Populist veneration of 'the people' against officialdom that derives from the tradition established by N.K. Mikhailovskii (1848–1904) and P.L. Lavrov (1823–1900) (Brandist 2000). There are undoubtedly other bricks to be found in this complex edifice, but these are surely some of the most important. Recognising the traditions with which Bakhtin's work intersected and worked is a precondition for an adequate grasp of his most important work, but we should not ignore the considerable originality of the theory that results, its many strengths and some of its contradictions and tensions. Bakhtin suggested a new and exciting way of looking at literary history and the dynamics of intergeneric interaction, but his work bears the marks of an attempt to reconcile ultimately incompatible ideas. The neo-Kantian demand that areas of being should be regarded as essentially separate and universally valid conflicts with a Hegelian stress on the historical unfolding of forms of life as a totality. The Hegelian strand demands a consideration of the economic and socio-political structure of the societies within which literature arises, while neo-Kantianism demanded that these factors be kept separate. The result is a vocabulary of formal categories that Bakhtin struggles to keep within literary works themselves while simultaneously registering all internal and external influences. It is thus not surprising that Bakhtin fails to devote adequate attention to the interaction of different areas of social life in an institutional context. This suggests that Bakhtin's work is in need of significant supplementation and revision, even as it presents an extremely significant and fruitful way of understanding literature within the development of culture as a whole.

The strengths and weaknesses of Bakhtin's approach become especially apparent in his sustained work on Rabelais, Goethe and Dostoevsky, to which we now turn.

6   The Novelist as Philosopher (1940–63)

Apart from the two editions of the Dostoevsky book, Bakhtin wrote only two other sustained works on specific writers: *The Work of François Rabelais and the Popular Culture of the Middle Ages and Renaissance* and a chapter on Goethe in the surviving fragment known as *The Bildungsroman and its Significance in the History of Realism*. These writers are studied by Bakhtin less as literary innovators than as the crowning literary representatives of their respective ages: the French Renaissance and the German Enlightenment. In these projects, Ernst Cassirer continued to exert a strong influence on Bakhtin's work, having written two works on the philosophies of these respective epochs, but where Cassirer viewed each period through the philosophical systems developed at the time, Bakhtin viewed each epoch through its literary works. Bakhtin's reliance on Cassirer's perspective is shown in his essay on the *Bildungsroman*, where without any reference, he cites a passage from Cassirer's *The Philosophy of the Enlightenment*, arguing that the Enlightenment should no longer be considered an 'unhistorical' epoch. However, Bakhtin then argues that the 'process of preparing and uncovering historical time took place more quickly, fully and profoundly in literary work (*tvorchestvo*) than in the abstract philosophies and the historical-ideological views of enlightenment thinkers themselves' (B 26; RV 206; Poole 1995: 41; Cassirer 1951: 197). The same principle applies to the Renaissance. Thus, Bakhtin argues that:

> In such novels as [Rabelais's] *Gargantua and Pantagruel*, [Grimmelhausen's] *Simplissimus* and [Goethe's] *Wilhelm Meister*, the becoming of the person ... is no longer a private affair. He becomes together with the world, reflecting in himself the historical becoming of the world itself. He is no longer within an epoch but on the threshold between epochs, the point of transition from one to the other. This transition is carried out in and through him. He is compelled to become a new, unprecedented type of person. (B 23; RV 203)

These works represent the dawning and growth of a new historical consciousness, the emergence of modern man. This is a liberation from the static and 'otherworldly' consciousness of the Middle Ages, which we touched upon in the previous chapter.

Bakhtin's works on these writers are thus certainly not simply exercises in literary criticism, although they involve literary-critical observations. Rather, each writer has a broader historical and philosophical significance. Indeed, one might argue that they are primarily treated as philosophers of history. Symptomatic of this is the extensive and unacknowledged borrowing from Cassirer's book on Renaissance philosophy in Bakhtin's book on Rabelais that has been clearly demonstrated in a recent article (Poole 1998). Indeed, in Bakhtin's book Rabelais becomes a sort of literary equivalent of the Renaissance philosopher Nicholaus Cusanus in that Rabelais is presented as writer in and through whose work the dawning of the modern age is both achieved and disclosed. There are, however, other important influences on the development of Bakhtin's classic account of Rabelais, which we have already identified, Bergson's and Simmel's life-philosophies being two of the most significant. In addition to this there are several Russian sources, including Ol´ga Freidenberg's 1936 book *The Poetics of Plot and Genre* (Freidenberg 1997), published shortly before Bakhtin worked on Rabelais, and the tradition of interpreting Nietzsche's *Birth of Tragedy* in Russia inaugurated by Viacheslav Ivanov. One particularly strong influence in the Rabelais book is, however, the populist tradition, which proved particularly open to incorporation into Bakhtin's analysis of the transition from the Middle Ages to the Renaissance. Here we have the definitive populist rendering of Simmel's dichotomy between objective culture and life, but with Bergson's and Cassirer's approaches to laughter added to the mixture along with important features from Freidenberg's research into folklore. All these factors underlie the central concept of carnival.

The origins of carnival

Along with dialogue and polyphony, the category of carnival has been enthusiastically adopted and variously applied, with little attention given to the philosophical roots of the idea. Bakhtin's vividly evoked image of the unrestrained festive vitality of 'the people' has been taken to heart by many modern writers seeking to break out of the narrow confines of the official canon of literature and establish popular culture as a legitimate object of study. It is by no means clear, however, that Bakhtin himself had any such agenda, as is suggested by the fact that he completely ignores perhaps the most important popular medium of his own age, cinema. Rather, Bakhtin is more concerned with the presence of the *forms* of past popular-festive culture in literature, and how they exercise a defining influence on the development of genre. Bakhtin outlines these *forms* and treats them as transitional stages between life and objective culture, stages which become reactivated at certain historical moments in order to address the rigidification of that culture. Galin Tihanov argues convincingly that this is at least partly due to the influence of Nikolai Marr's 'semantic paleontology' in which all humanity shares a common, indeed primordial, heritage of myth, features of which are preserved in later culture (Tihanov 2000b: 136–8, 159–60). Bakhtin traces the forms of carnival culture back to the comic festivals of antiquity, especially to Roman Saturnalia, which was considered a 'real and full (though temporary) return of Saturn's golden age to the Earth' (RW 7–8, TFR 12). He also suggests that festive forms go back even further, back into pre-history. In his discussion of the 'folkloric bases of the Rabelaisian chronotope', Bakhtin suggests that this temporary restoration of 'productive, generative time', which continues in carnival celebrations proper, can be traced back to the 'agricultural pre-class stage in the development of human society' (FTCN 206; FVKhR 355). This passage strongly echoes Freidenberg's more openly Marrist work on the 'primordial world-view' of 'primitive communism', with which she connects the 'cosmic' metaphors of food, death and rebirth, dismemberment, master and slave, laughter, praise and abuse, procession, and so on, that become central to Bakhtin's analysis (Freidenberg 1997: 50ff.). Bakhtin praises Freidenberg's book as an extremely rich source of 'folkloric material', which directly pertains to 'popular laughter-culture', but complains that 'this material is interpreted in the spirit of the theory of pre-logical thinking, and the problem of popular laughter-culture is still not posed' (RW 54; TFR 63). This single reference certainly does not do justice to the wealth of material Bakhtin evidently found in the book, as the following passage, which Bakhtin highlighted in his own copy of Friedenberg's book (Osovskii 2000: 133) shows:

> Ancient comedy has complete structural identity with tragedy; but the most remarkable thing is that in contradistinction to European

comedy, it presents itself not as an independent genre, but as a parody of tragedy. Meanwhile, parody in itself has a sacral origin and this lives on in folklore right up to modern times: its very cultic-folkloric forms bring to us both tragic elements, in the form of public worship and passion [strast´], and comic [elements] in the form of farces and obscenity. Beginning with antiquity, the festival of the new year, there is passion and Births – all days of the new suns and the new births – have a parodic beginning in the form of the feast of simpletons [glupets], the festival of asses, the feast of fools [durak] etc. After all we have said [in the course of the book – CB], there are for us no novelties; we are not surprised that the king [tsar] is chosen from the jesters, that the clergy swap clothes with the crowd, that public worship is parodied, that churches serve as an arena for obscenity and shame. Neither does it surprise us that we meet parody alongside all the acts of life – marriage, burial, birth, the administration of justice, commerce, government etc. And the main image is alongside the act of eating. Characteristic in this regard is the medieval 'liturgy of gluttons', which permeated the church during public worship: the clergy greedily ate sausage right in front of the altar, played cards right under the nose of the priests conducting a service, threw excrement into the censor and made a stink with it. (Freidenberg 1997: 275)

Freidenberg identified central 'semantic clusters' which recur in variously modified ways throughout literary history, and these same 'clusters' appear throughout Bakhtin's work on carnival.[1] Here one can sense the significance of Bakhtin's debt to Freidenberg's research, but there is no doubt that Bakhtin interpreted Freidenberg's material along different, indeed opposite lines. As Kevin Moss notes,

For Bakhtin parody is opposed to its original; for Freidenberg it is a shadow, but it affirms the same values. For Bakhtin parody is revolutionary, liberating, the epitome of free speech; for Freidenberg it reaffirms the status quo. Bakhtin sees in parody evidence of religious decline, a form ruthlessly driven from the official sphere by the church; Freidenberg sees in parody the apogee of religious consciousness that can use even laughter to affirm its forms. For Bakhtin, the model of parody is medieval carnival, with its rebellious freedom; for Freidenberg parody is the hubristic 'other aspect' of all that is real, authentic, official. (Moss 1997: 22)[2]

One can see that Bakhtin adapted Freidenberg's observations according to his own neo-Kantian philosophical predilections and populist political preferences. The former was not difficult, since Cassirer's work on myth had been an important influence on Marr's 'japhetic theory' and Freidenberg's work (Freidenberg 1997: 31–7; Moss 1984: 94–105), so Bakhtin only needed to restore the feature of Cassirer's work that the Marrists rejected: the neo-Kantian theory of knowledge. Parodic forms are, for Bakhtin, evidence of the growth of critical consciousness evident in the unfolding of symbolic forms, and the 'semantic clusters' that endure have the character of a priori elements necessary for thinking as such. Bakhtin's populist dialectic of official and popular forces could also find a correspondence in the Marrist idea of a primordial unity of all peoples.

Carnival as a 'proto-genre'

In an undated text which was probably written in the mid-1940s Bakhtin argued that he did not accept the notion of an identifiable mode of 'primordial thought'. He claims that 'there is nothing upon which to base talk about *prime*-ordial thinking, only about various types of ancient thought' (F 136). Here Bakhtin signals a shift away from the Marrist idea of 'primordial thought' as a stage through which all cultures pass and towards a more open conception of the categories identified by Lévy-Bruhl, Cassirer and Freidenberg as a typology.[3] However, Bakhtin continued to see traces of the common myth deriving from pre-class society reactivated in popular festive culture and novelistic literature. The status of such forms of consciousness as images and 'chronotopes' allows them to be incorporated into literary forms. Although Freidenberg had already discussed this feature, Bakhtin focused on the popular-festive rituals through which the images were mediated. One aspect needs to be noted about this, however: *Bakhtin does not base his discussion of popular festive culture on sustained historical research*. Instead, carnival is for Bakhtin a sort of 'proto-genre' described in terms of anthropology. This 'genre' reappears in different guises throughout the history of literature; indeed, specific and identifiable generic forms are considered to have existed in various manifestations at all points of history. This is especially clear in the new chapter on genre added to the second Dostoevsky book where, like Freidenberg, Bakhtin claims that genre 'preserves … undying elements of the *archaic*', but interprets this in a neo-Kantian fashion. Genre maintains 'the most stable, "eternal" tendencies in literary development', that is those aspects with 'objective validity'. A genre is therefore always both old and new, for the same features appear in new ways, renewed and 'contemporised' (PDP 106; PPD 314). Thus, the 'serio-comical' genres of antiquity, the Socratic dialogue and the Menippean satire among them, were all connected with 'carnivalistic folklore', with a 'carnival sense of the world', and the features of these genres are discernible in later literature, such as the novels of Rabelais and Dostoevsky. We shall return to these features of literary genres later, and now turn our attention to the features of popular festive culture proper. Bakhtin argues that the novels of Rabelais were connected with a resurrection of these practices in the early Renaissance, facilitating the renewal and 'contemporisation' of serio-comical literary genres. It is as if the upsurge of such festivities once again breathed life into forms that had become moribund and detached from that life: the chasm between life and objective culture was bridged by these pre-literary practices.

Carnival is therefore not a historically identifiable practice but a generic category: 'the totality of all varied festivities, rituals and forms of the carnival type', a *syncretic pageant* form of a ritual sort' which takes on particular characteristics according to the 'epoch, people and individual festivity' in which it appears (PDP 122; PPD 331). This notion of syncretism derived from Veselovskii's book on historical poetics (Veselovskii 1940), where it is argued that poetry emerged from a ritualistic 'union of rhymed dancing movements and song-music and the elements of words'. The content of literary forms becomes 'more variegated in correspondence with the differentiation of living-condition relationships' (quoted in Thomas 1957: 114–15). This conception made its way wholesale into the works of Marr and Freidenberg, and from here it becomes a basis for Bakhtin's idea of carnival. Carnival is the revisiting of the 'primordial' syncretic unity, with the effect that literary genres are renewed by the spirit of pre-class consciousness.

Standing midway between life and culture, carnival is a concretely sensuous experience of the world that, while being inadequately conveyed in abstract concepts, is quite open to being translated into artistic images and thus into literature. Literature thereby becomes 'carnivalised'. The aspects of carnival are most succinctly outlined in the 1963 edition of the Dostoevsky book:

(a) the suspension of hierarchical structure and forms of fear, reverence and etiquette connected with it;

(b) collapsing of distance between people, leading to their free and familiar contact;

(c) the flowering of eccentricity as a departure from the 'rut of life';

(d) a free and familiar attitude towards values, thoughts, phenomena and things leading to contacts and combinations of sacred and profane, high and low, and so on;

(e) profanation and blasphemy, obscenities and bringing down to earth by highlighting the reproductive powers of the earth and body;

(f) ritual mock crowning and uncrowning of a carnival king, based on the trope of perpetual death and renewal;

(g) celebration of the relativity of symbolic order.

The images of fire, birth, death, feasting, and so on, that Freidenberg had identified are combined in this generic complex. They thus gain a fundamentally ambivalent character in which the 'two poles of becoming' are always present: birth and death, praise and abuse, blessing and curse, face and backside, stupidity and wisdom, heaven and hell, sacred and profane, master and slave, and so on. Life is understood in a cyclical fashion, as the turning of a wheel, so that opposites are not separated but exist in a constantly shifting and self-renewing relationship. Death implies rebirth, hell heaven, blessing curse, and so on.

In carnival laughter becomes more than the corrective of rigidity; it is also linked to the death-rebirth cycle, bringing the target of the laughter down to earth and forcing it to renew itself. Thus, forms of parody destroy life's hierarchical incrustations while facilitating the rebirth of the object in a (re)new(ed) and creative form. Here one can see the influence of Cassirer once again. In a passage immediately preceding the quotation given in the last chapter in which Cassirer argued that laughter has precisely this effect, he argued that in the Renaissance laughter was understood as a 'liberating, life-giving and life-forming power of the soul' (Cassirer 1953: 183). This is associated in both the Rabelais study and Cassirer's study of 'mythical thought' with a primordial unity of the social and physical bodies (macrocosm and microcosm), with laughter performing a medicinal role in both spheres (Poole 1998: 548–9). The rigidification of the symbolic world and of the social hierarchy are presented as 'illnesses' of social life, which laughter treats, pricking the pretensions of the hierarchical discourse by bringing it into contact with the 'unseemly' creative organs of the social body. The old, worn-out parts of the 'body' are thus 'excreted', expelled from the bowels of society, but in the process this waste becomes fertiliser and so what is of value is reborn, for the image of defecation is associated with that of birth. This process is, of course, strongly associated with the agricultural cycle which dominated the lives of the peasantry, for it is only in this respect that excretion and birth of the new can be so closely related. The social body is open to the natural world, it is indeed continuous with that world, growing, dying and being renewed in connection with the seasonal cycle, the pivotal points of which are marked by festivals. These festivals evoke and celebrate the collective nature of social life, the unity of the social body through a collective, sensuous experience. In carnival the fixity of social roles is effaced, serious, hierarchical figures have their parodic doubles, the king is replaced by the fool, the priest by the rogue or the charlatan; indeed, the whole structure of society is for a time inverted, turned inside out and subjected to ridicule. In the collective experience of carnival, the fragmented nature of society is temporarily overcome, and the primordial mass of primitive, pre-class society is re-established:

> Even the very crush, *the physical contact of bodies*, acquires a certain meaning. The individual feels that he is an inseparable part of the collective, a member of the people's mass body. In this whole the individual body to a certain extent ceases to be itself; it is possible, as it were, to exchange bodies, to be renewed (changes of costume and mask). (RW 255; TFR: 281)

The grotesque

Bakhtin's extraordinary writings about the grotesque image of the body, with which Rabelais's novels are closely associated, must be understood in connection with the concept of carnival laughter. Indeed, it is a failure to connect the two phenomena that Bakhtin criticises in previous writers on the grotesque (RW 30–58; TFR 38–67). Bakhtin here draws on Cohen's *Aesthetics*, in which humour allows ugliness to become 'a stage of the beautiful' in art, for art embraces the ugly with love (Poma 1997a: 146). However, like that of Cassirer, Bakhtin's development is more anthropological. For Bakhtin the grotesque image of the body is part and parcel of carnivalised folklore. The symbolic dismemberment and re-combination of the parts of the body characteristic of grotesque imagery is linked to the collective and sensuous experience of carnival celebrations in which the social hierarchy is dismantled and reformed in parodic and eccentric ways. The physical body is a microcosm of the 'body' of the people. The corporeal focus of Bakhtin's exposition has misled many critics into missing the idealist philosophy that lies behind the notion of the grotesque. It is this that allows its apparently unproblematic transferral into the sphere of literature. Bakhtin's materialist rhetoric, which one finds throughout the Rabelais study, may well have been a deliberate attempt to make his doctoral dissertation, on which the published text was based, acceptable to the Soviet Academy while presenting the reader with a sugared dose of idealist philosophy.

As with much of Bakhtin's later work, one of the crucial elements of his ideas about the grotesque is a revised Hegelianism. There is only one passing mention of Hegel's conception of the grotesque in Bakhtin's Rabelais study. This refers to the three traits by which Hegel defines the term: 'the fusion of different natural spheres, immeasurable and exaggerated dimensions, and the multiplication of different members and organs of the human body'. Bakhtin criticises Hegel for ignoring 'the role of the comic in the structure of the grotesque' and then diverts his attention elsewhere (RW 44; TFR 53). Like many of Bakhtin's comments on Hegel, this is seriously misleading if taken at face value and again Cassirer stands as an important point of mediation between Bakhtin and Hegel. In an article of 1930 on Scheler's philosophy, Cassirer commended Hegel's preface to *The Phenomenology of Spirit* for issuing the demand that 'life open up, that it spread itself out and reveal itself', that essence should appear in a process of becoming (Cassirer 1949: 875). In this very passage, Hegel himself stressed the festive nature of this notion of truth as a 'Bacchanalian revel in which no member is not drunk' (Hegel 1977: 27). Although he comments only upon Indian art in connection with the grotesque in his *Aesthetics*, Hegel argues that the grotesque is the product of a particular contradiction between essence and appearance which leads to a split in that which was previously united. The result is a 'battle between meaning and shape' and attempts to 'heal the breach again by building the separated parts together in a fanciful way' (Hegel 1975: 1, 334). Bakhtin once again combines this Hegelian position with a populist dialectic of official and popular. Where Hegel sees in the grotesque image a 'frenzied oscillation' and 'fermentation' between the two elements, Bakhtin sees popular-festive rituals, ridiculing and parading the inadequacy of the rigid official identification of 'meaning and shape' and positing a new 'fanciful' combination of universal meaning and sensuous forms. It is now the *popular* imagination that 'drives particular shapes beyond their firmly limited character, stretches them, alters them into indefiniteness, and intensifies them beyond all bounds' (Hegel 1975: 1, 334). In Bakhtin, 'fanciful' resolution becomes the popular utopia that is implicit in festive forms but which can only be explicitly realised through the mediation of 'great literature' in general and the novel in particular.

As in Bakhtin, the grotesque metamorphosis of the body in Hegel's *Aesthetics* becomes an image of 'the universal dialectic of life – birth, growth, passing away, and rebirth out of death' (Hegel 1975: 1, 350). The inner meaning is now presented to our imagination through the outward shape, and the significance of the outer shape through the inner meaning. Art now expands the present to enshrine universal meanings, however limited and approximate. The natural phenomena or human forms which art brings before us hint at something beyond themselves, with which they still have an inner connection. The most perfect form for such a symbol is the human body, 'a form which appears elaborated in a higher and more appropriate way because the spirit at this stage already begins in general to give shape to itself, disengaging itself from the purely natural and rising to its own more independent existence' (Hegel 1975: 1, 353).

Hegel's argument is here couched in very different terms to that of Bakhtin, who celebrates the corporeality of the body, its protuberances, its excess, its waste matter, and so on. However, in stressing these features, Bakhtin seeks to underline the fact that the grotesque 'ignores the blank surface that encloses and limits the body as a separate, completed phenomenon' (RW 317–18; TFR 353). As the individual body is transcended, the 'body of historical, progressing mankind' moves to the centre of the system of images. The individual body dies, but the body of the people lives and grows; biological life ends but historical life continues. In the Renaissance, when Bakhtin saw the essence of the grotesque appear, 'a new, concrete, and realistic historic feeling was born and took form', and the novel of Rabelais is a high point of that awareness (RW 367; TFR 406). Rabelais is thus ultimately a philosopher of history as well as a novelist. The body now signifies not itself, but the 'universal dialectic of life', the inner movement of the spirit itself. The image-borne negation of the static, hierarchical, completed, epic and 'medieval' conception of the cosmos leads to a new, deeper and qualitatively different insight into the nature of the world, the creative process that is the structural basis of the cosmos becomes its own object. This, for Bakhtin, is both utopian and liberating:

> The grotesque actually frees us from all those forms of non-human necessity that permeate the ruling notion of the world. The grotesque uncrowns this necessity and makes it relative and limited. In any given epoch the necessity in the ruling picture of the world always appears as something monolithically serious, unconditional and indisputable. But historically the notion of necessity is relative and mutable. The laughter-principle and carnival sense of the world lying at the basis of the grotesque destroys limited seriousness and all pretensions to extra-temporal validity, the unconditionality of notions of necessity, and liberates human consciousness, thought and imagination for new poten-tialities. This is why large revolutions, even in the sphere of science, are preceded by and prepared for by a certain carnival consciousness. (RW 49; TFR 58)

Carnival in literature

Bakhtin argues that in the Middle Ages carnival culture existed only as small islands, isolated from the mainstream of cultural life, and was thereby ineffectual on the scale of what he calls 'great time'. As he puts it in the Dostoevsky study:

> One could say (with certain reservations, of course) that a person of the Middle Ages lived, as it were, *two lives*: one was *official*, monolithically serious and gloomy, subjugated to a strict hier-archical order, full of fear, dogmatism, reverence and piety; the other – *carnival-square* life, free and unrestricted, full of ambivalent laughter, blasphemy, the profanation of everything sacred, debasing and obscenities, familiar contact with everyone and everything. Both these lives were legitimate, but separated by strict temporal boundaries. (PPD 339; PDP 129–30)

This, however, changes in the Renaissance, when the self-enclosed nature of these 'lives' is terminated. This happens both in and through the development of the modern novel, in which the work of Rabelais has a crucial place. Thus, at the end of *Rabelais* Bakhtin argues that the modern novel grew on the border between these two world-views, world-views embodied in language, and it was precisely in the Renaissance that this 'dual language' broke down:

> An intense inter-orientation, inter-illumination of languages occurred. Languages directly and intensely peered into each other's faces: each cognising itself, its potentials and limitations *in the light of the other language*. This *boundary between languages* was sensed in relation to every thing, every concept, each point of view. *Two languages are two world-views*. (RW 465; TFR 515)

Here we have a recapitulation of the arguments developed in 'Discourse in the Novel'. However, Bakhtin undertakes a detailed analysis of parts of Rabelais's novels to show that carnivalised folklore exerts a structuring influence there, leading to a critical intersection of the official and popular world-views. Thus, in Rabelais's celebration of corporeality, his dwelling on images of collective feasting, of urination, defecation and the like, Bakhtin sees a presentation of the person as at one with the world, with ingestion and defecation showing the openness of the body which is incomplete and in the process of becoming along with the world. This is contrasted with the complete, perfectly proportioned body of classical aesthetics. Similarly in Rabelais's lively evocation of the language of the market place, in which praise is marked with irony and abuse is tinged with affection, Bakhtin sees the ambivalence of carnival; the celebration of obscenity and unseemly aspects of language is contrasted with the ennobled language of the social hierarchy, particularly as represented by Latin, which Rabelais often invokes. The two languages meet and illuminate each other's ideo-logical structure. Rabelais's lower-class characters, sometimes of titanic proportions (such as Gargantua), ruthlessly mock and parody the pretensions of their 'betters', yet their laughter is devoid of cynicism, being invested with the life-giving force of popular festivity. The one-sided, serious and official culture meets the ambivalent images and anti-conventions of the carnival world within the space of the novel. In and through the Rabelaisian novel these dimensions of spirit recognise each other and themselves from the point of view of the other.

Composed at the height of Stalinism, Bakhtin's text no doubt has a political subtext that applies to the present more than to the time of Rabelais. Indeed, there have been several critiques of Bakhtin's book from the point of view of historical scholarship that challenge the accuracy of some of the central claims of the book (for example, Berrong 1986). The celebration of the cyclical nature of agricultural labour and popular rural festivities which manifest a sort of primordial democratic spirit was written in the aftermath of Stalin's brutal drive towards the collectivisation of agriculture, breakneck industrialisation and the forcing of all ideological life into a monolithic mould. Bakhtin stresses the exceptional nature of the Renaissance as a pause between the stasis and hierarchical dogma of the feudal system and the new official culture that crystallised under the French absolutist monarchy, and it is not difficult to discern an implied parallel between the first years after the Russian Revolution and the Stalin regime. However, as in Bakhtin's other work of the period, the central arguments do not rest solely, or even mainly, on historical premises. The aim to present a neo-Hegelian 'history of laughter' is tempered by the neo-Kantian urge to discern objectively valid cultural principles and an attempt to present an eternal conflict between life and objective culture characteristic of life-philosophy. This allows Bakhtin to present the forms of carnival culture as elements of a wide variety of literary forms in different cultures and at different historical moments. In a series of notes designed as potential 'Additions and Changes to *Rabelais*' (DIR) Bakhtin broadens his analysis to encompass some Shakespeare plays (especially *King Lear*) and the Ukrainian stories of Nikolai Gogol´ written at the beginning of the nineteenth century. In the draft of a recently published article on the Russian poet Vladimir Mayakovsky (M) the same features are evoked once again, while the encyclopaedia article on satire (S) traces the recurrence of carnivalesque features throughout European literary history, though with a special emphasis on the Renaissance, when the 'essence' of carnival 'appeared'.

Socratic dialogue and Menippean satire

The most detailed examination of the carnivalisation of genre is in the second version of the Dostoevsky book, where the Russian novelist is presented not so much as a great innovator but as the heir to a tradition with its roots in popular festive culture. Indeed, it may be no exaggeration to say that whereas in the first version of the Dostoevsky book the polyphonic novel is seen as the result of Dostoevsky's individual genius, the author is here recast as the bearer of an impersonal or super-personal generic tradition. This places the second Dostoevsky study alongside the Rabelais study in Bakhtin's oeuvre and sets it apart from many of his other works. Here Bakhtin finds among the various carnivalesque ancestors of the modern novel the Socratic dialogue and, especially, the Menippean satire, which are united by the life-giving and transforming power of a 'carnival sense of the world' and an atmosphere of 'joyful relativity'. These 'serio-comical' genres share an orientation towards the 'living present', they 'consciously rely on experience' and 'free innovation', they are multi-styled and many-voiced, mixing elevated and lowly themes and language. They also incorporate other genres such as letters, parodies of 'high' genres, combine poetry with prose, incorporating dialects and jargons as the author wears styles as masks. As a result the discourse that represents is itself represented (PDP 106–8; PPD 314–16). While the serio-comical genres have this in common they do have specific features:

(1) The Socratic dialogue views the truth as lying *between* people, *between* their respective discourses rather than within any discourse as such. Bakhtin argues that although this *form* is based on the folkloric origins of the genre, it does not find expression in the *content* of any individual dialogue. It employs syncresis and anacrisis, the former being juxtaposition of points of view on an object, and the latter being the compulsion of one's interlocutor to speak, illuminating his or her opinions in all their falseness and incompleteness. Truth is thus *dialogised*. As such interlocutors are always ideologists whose opinions are tested in dialogue. Plot combines with anacrisis to provoke the word, placing the heroes in extraordinary situations such as the eve before their executions. This Bakhtin calls a 'threshold dialogue' that compels the speaker to reveal the deepest levels of his or her ideological being. Finally, the hero is an *image* of his or her ideological makeup, the two being inseparable (PDP 110–12; PPD 318–20).

(2) The carnival nature of the Menippean satire is much more pronounced. The higher profile of the comic and a distance from the conventions of the memoir are two of its most fundamental

features. The result is a much freer plot organisation and philosophical structure, allowing for the use of the fantastic in embodying and testing a discourse. Similarly, the Menippea is free to combine mystical and religious elements with the crudest 'slum naturalism' from scenes in brothels and taverns to portrayals of prisons and erotic orgies. Philosophical ideas are thus brought out of the rarified atmosphere of intellectual debate to encounter the most depraved and vulgar aspects of life, but this in no way compromises the satire's 'philosophical universalism', for the most important, even 'ultimate' questions are discussed in an extremely polarised syncresis. The common incorporation of topical, 'journalistic' elements does not replace but sharpens the discussion of these fundamental philosophical questions. Connected with this is a liking for extraordinary states of mind such as dreams, insanity, schizophrenia, and so on, which present the subject as open rather than whole and complete. Scenes of scandal, unseemliness and eccentricity as violations of accepted decorum are common, as are abrupt transitions within the social hierarchy, often combined with a social-utopian element. As with the Socratic dialogue, inserted genres and a multi-stylistic nature dominate the form of the Menippea (PDP 114–19; PPD 322–8).

Following Misch, Bakhtin argues that the Menippea was formed in an age when the 'national myth' of high antiquity was disintegrating: the Hellenistic era. At this time there was a hiatus between the stable hierarchies of antiquity and feudalism, while the novels of Rabelais are formed during the pause between feudalism and absolutism. Dostoevsky's novels, as we have seen, were formed between the decay of the Tsarist regime and the revolutions of 1917. All of these periods in literary history are particularly rich in carnivalesque elements and are distilled into literary forms that come to the fore at appropriate historical moments. The generic traditions of the Menippea and the Socratic dialogues that reaches certain periodic peaks, one of which is the work of Dostoevsky; these peaks show the 'essence' of the genre (*zhanrovaia sushchnost´*) appearing (PDP 177; PPD 348). One can here see how the Marrist idea of 'indestructible' semantic clusters reappearing at all points of social history is still maintained by Bakhtin into the 1960s. Each time the generic essence 'appears', however, it is at a new level, and between Rabelais and Dostoevsky Bakhtin discerns important points of mediation in the work of Balzac, George Sand, Victor Hugo and Gogol´.

Carnival in Dostoevsky

The new material found in the 1963 Dostoevsky book relates the Russian author to the carnival tradition by way of the Menippea and the Socratic dialogue. By the time of Dostoevsky the constitutive features of the Socratic dialogue and the Menippean satire have been raised to a higher unity through their incorporation into the modern novel:

> In Dostoevsky's work the carnival tradition … is reborn in a new way: it is interpreted, combined with other artistic moments serving its own particular artistic goals … Carnivalisation is organically combined with all the other particularities of the polyphonic novel. (PDP 159; PPD 373)

While the comic element is overt in his early works, the later works of Dostoevsky present carnival laughter in a 'reduced' form, as in the Socratic dialogue. Laughter remains in the image of the hero, in the dialogic relativisation of all dogma. Laughter is dissolved into the stream of becoming and bursts out loud only on certain occasions.

Carnivalisation is transformed into a unique form of phenomenological intuition, it is 'an extraordinarily flexible form of artistic vision, an original type of heuristic principle facilitating the discovery of the new and hitherto unseen' (PDP 166; PPD 381). Thus, St Petersburg, the scene of the novels, is transformed into a borderline realm between reality and phantasmagoria, becoming an extreme threshold that compels the hero to speak. Bakhtin finds a particularly clear illustration when discussing Raskolnikov's delirious dream in *Crime and Punishment* about the old woman he has murdered. This is an abnormal mental state of the sort beloved of the Menippea. Here we are presented with the image of the murdered old woman laughing, her laughter echoed by others in her flat. A crowd appears on the stairway and on the street below while Raskolnikov is at the top of the stairs. This is seen as an image of the carnival king-pretender being decrowned before the ridicule of the crowd. Thus we have a chronotope in which space assumes great significance with up, down, the stairway, the threshold and the landing representing points of crisis and transformation, transcendence leading to death or rebirth (PDP 167–70; PPD 381–5). Such 'threshold' scenes are found to be common in Dostoevsky's fictional world and serve as equivalents of the extreme threshold situations in the Socratic dialogue.

Dostoevsky's relationship to carnival culture constitutes a particular intersection with a formal tradition. This is mediated by the appearance of carnival forms in literary history beginning with antiquity passing through the serio-comical genres of Hellenism, the Renaissance and finally renewed in the European novels of the eighteenth and nineteenth centuries. As at each stage, however, Dostoevsky represents a renewal of the tradition rather than a simple reiteration of conventions. Carnival is what the young Bakhtin called an architectonic form, a form of intentional engagement with the cognised aspects of reality with the aim of transforming them into aesthetic objects, rather than simply a compositional form. We are dealing with the form of content (ethics, politics, and so on) rather than with the form of material (chapter, page, and so on). Dostoevsky, like Rabelais and others before him, inherited an intentional orientation towards the world that can be traced back to the era of primitive communism, but that world is in a perpetual process of formation, and thus the works that result are always different. The becoming of literature is therefore linked to the becoming of the world, that is, the world as it appears in the collective consciousness of an epoch rather than the world as it might exist independently of consciousness. This neo-Kantian principle remains constant in Bakhtin's work and can be most clearly seen in his work on the history of realism, and particularly on the place of Goethe in that history.

Goethe and realism

Goethe, it seems, was an important figure for members of the Bakhtin Circle from the 1920s onwards and he was a major preoccupation of some of their most important theoretical influences, notably Cassirer, Simmel, Walzel and Lukács. It is therefore not surprising that Bakhtin planned a whole book on the subject. *The Bildungsroman and Its Significance in the History of Realism* occupied him in the period 1936–38, between the composition of 'Discourse in the Novel' and the other essays on the novel. It also precedes *Rabelais*, and is concerned with many of the same problems. Indeed, realism is an important concern in both the *Rabelais* and *Bildungsroman* books and is the unspoken concern of the chronotope essay. This concern coincides with the formulation of the official doctrine of 'socialist realism' and its particular application to the novel as a genre in the 1934–35 discussion on the novel led by Lukács. Commentators (Todorov 1984; Tihanov 2000a) have been surprised how in the *Bildungsroman* essay we have a surprising reversion to viewing the novel as an epic form:

> The large epic form (the large epic), including the novel, should provide an integral picture of the world and of life, it should reflect the *entire* world and *all* of life. In the novel the whole world and all of life are given in a cross-section of the *integrity of the epoch*. The events depicted in the novel should substitute themselves for the whole life of the epoch in some way. (B 43; RV 224)

We already know from 'Discourse in the Novel', however, that the type of microcosm that Bakhtin has in mind for the novel is a microcosm of the 'heteroglossia of the epoch' (DN 411; SR 222). Bakhtin translates the Hegelian demand that 'life open up, that it spread itself out and reveal itself' into literary terms, resulting in a demand that the novel become an integrated totality of the world of verbal images that constitutes historical 'life'. Realistic depiction thus means nothing more than an accurate representation of the social consciousness of the epoch with all other factors 'bracketed out'. When Bakhtin argues the following we should take him quite literally:

> Three centuries ago the 'whole world' was a unique symbol that could not be adequately represented by any model, by any map or globe. In this symbol the 'whole world', visible and cognised, embodied-real, was a small and detached patch of earthly space and an equally small and detached chunk of real time. Everything else unsteadily disappeared into the fog, became mixed up and interlaced with other worlds, estranged-ideal, fantastic, utopian. The point is not that the other-worldly and fantastic filled in this impoverished reality, combined and rounded reality out into a mythological whole. The otherworldly disorganised and bled this present reality. (B 43; RV 224)

The world literally *was* that symbol, bled and disorganised by mythical thinking. The symbol did not represent the world badly, but it *was* the world itself.[4] That symbol could not be represented, it could not appear *for itself* but existed only *in itself*. Culture had no self-consciousness because the power of mythical thought was sufficient to prevent any such objectification.

It was in the Renaissance that 'the "whole world" began to condense into a real and compact whole', and by Goethe's time (1749–1832) the process had 'reached its culmination'. Goethe was perhaps the last 'Renaissance man', in that he excelled in an almost implausible variety of areas: as critic, journalist, novelist, poet, painter, theatre manager, statesman, educationalist and natural philosopher. Bakhtin is interested in the worldview that is common to all areas of Goethe's remarkable and voluminous writings, and in how this world-view represents a highpoint of the new stage of social consciousness. Now, the 'new, *real* unity and integrity of the world ... became a fact of concrete (ordinary) consciousness and practical orientation'. Visual equivalents could be found for invisible phenomena, so that the natural and social worlds became almost visible and perceptible (B 43–4; RV 224–5). Aesthetic vision (*vídenie*) now truly became an intuition of essences in which the objectively valid essences of culture become palpable to a wide number of people for the first time. Where Rabelais and Cervantes had been representatives of the first 'condensation' of the 'real' world ('grotesque realism'), Goethe now becomes the 'culmination' of this process. For Goethe 'everything that is essential can and should be visible; everything that is not visible is inessential' – crucial concepts and ideas can be given visual representation (B 27; RV 206).

As Tihanov (1998b) has shown, Bakhtin follows in his analysis a well-established tradition of interpreting Goethe's work that included Dilthey, Simmel, Gundolf and Cassirer, but as usual he adds his own particular twist. Unlike Dostoevsky in Bakhtin's 1963 study, Goethe is celebrated much more for his own individual artistic genius, particularly for his exceptional ability to 'see time in space' – both natural time and human time. He could discern the 'visible signs of time in human life' (B 30–1; RV 210), and his work represents one of the high points of the 'vision of historical time in world literature' (B 26; RV 205). This involves detecting the

> Visible traces of man's creativity, traces of his hands and his mind: cities, streets, houses, works of art, technology, social organisa-tions etc. The artist reads in them the complex intentions of people, generations, epochs, nations, social-class groups. The work of the seeing eye is here combined with the most complex

thought process ... Finally there are socio-economic contradictions – these motive forces of development – from elementary,
immediately visible contrasts (the social variety of one's
homeland on the large road) to their more profound and refined
manifestations in human relations and ideas. These contradictions necessarily push visible time into the future. The more
profoundly they are revealed the more essential and wide-ranging
is the visible fullness of time in the images of the artist-novelist.
(B 25–6; RV 205)

For Goethe, as for the neo-Kantians somewhat later, seeing and
thinking, perception and cognition, become a single process.
Goethe's artistic vision discerned 'multi-temporality', the process of
becoming, behind the simultaneous presence of many forms, 'multi-
formity', and this extended to his writings on natural history and
travel, and to his biographical novels. Traces of historical time are
detected in seemingly static phenomena. This is an interesting
recasting of Bakhtin's early writing on artistic intuition as the
detection and consolidation of 'a trace of meaning [*smysl*] in being',
of culture in life, of validity in existence (AH 115–16; AG 180–1).
Goethe's artistic vision detects the past definitions of the world by
human form-making activity, and in doing so it establishes culture
as the object of perception: in Goethe's writings culture becomes its
own object.

We have seen that, although the neo-Kantian insistence that the
object of perception is *produced* in human culture is present
throughout Bakhtin's work, the recognition of this fact comes to be
seen as a *historical* achievement only in the work of the 1930s and
afterwards. Goethe is particularly valued for this historical vision,
which allowed the production of cultural forms in spatio-temporal
context to be disclosed, thus overcoming the split between culture
and life that plagued Bakhtin from his earliest work. In Goethe's
work historical time is seen in its locality:

> The creative past must be revealed as necessary and productive in
> the conditions of a given locality, as a creative humanisation of
> this locality, transforming a piece of earthly space into a place of
> the historical life of people, a little corner of the historical world.

Even a small patch of cultivated greenery signifies '*a trace of the
planned activity of a single human will*' and as such it is '*an essential*

and *living* trace of the past in the present'. Goethe's vision alights on the 'necessary connections of the past and the living present', that is the 'necessary place of this past in the unbroken line of historical development'. This allows the past to be creative, to be 'active in the present'. 'Such a creative-active past defines the future; together with this present it also gives a certain direction to the future, to a certain extent predetermines the future. A *fullness of time*, indeed, a palpable, visible fullness, is thus achieved' (B 32–4; RV 212–14). Bakhtin's Goethe thus shows the future creation of the world to be a continuation of and an addition to all past creation; individuals are now presented as engaged in the never-ending task of co-creating their world and themselves as part of that world.

Bakhtin's perspective on human self-education and the formation of the self and the world that constitute the two aspects of the German *Bildung* (education and formation) is deliberately presented in terms that suggest connections with the Marxist idea of praxis. This was inevitable in the closed ideological environment in which he hoped to publish his work. However, close examination reveals that Bakhtin is concerned with what Cassirer called '*formative* energy, or the energy of pure formation [*Bildung*]' rather than '*efficient* energy'. Cassirer defined the distinction as follows:

Efficient energy aims immediately at man's environment, whether it be in order to apprehend it as it actually is and take possession of it, or in order to alter its course in some definite direction. Formative energy, on the other hand, is not aimed directly at this outer environment, but rather remains self-contained: it moves within the dimension of the pure 'image', and not in that of 'actuality'. Here the spirit does not directly turn against objects, but rather weaves itself into a world of its own, a world of signs, symbols and meanings. (Cassirer 1949: 868–9)

This is the real significance of Goethe's artistic vision [*vídenie*]. Goethe shows the formative principles behind the rise of the modern world-view, the rise of a new type of person in a new world liberated from the shackles of mythical thinking. Realism thus signifies an elaboration not of knowledge about an empirical world that lies beyond human consciousness, but of the process of creating the image world that is culture. The rise of the modern subject and the formation of the modern world here become a unity precisely because of Goethe's rejection of the duality of subject and object. As Bakhtin argued in a letter to Kanaev of 1962:

> The opposition of subject and object that is most the cardinal one for epistemology is profoundly alien to Goethe. The percipient is not, for Goethe, opposed to the perceived as a pure subject to an object, but is located in what is a mutually innate [*soprirodnyi*] part of what is perceived. Subject and object are made from one and the same chunk. The percipient, as a microcosm, contains within him- or herself everything that he cognises in nature (the sun, the planets, metals etc.; see 'Wanderjahre'). (EST 396)

While Bakhtin specifically refers to Heidegger here, to stress the contemporary relevance of Goethe's implicit philosophy, the idea that subject and object have their mutual origin in thinking is a central proposition of Marburg neo-Kantianism. Here, the logic of thinking is indistinguishable from the reality of being, so that 'being is the being of thinking: and thinking is the thinking of being (as being as object by being as subject: *genitivus objectivus* and *genitivus subjectivus*)' (Rose 1981: 9–10). Like Dostoevsky, therefore, Goethe is presented as a sort of spontaneous neo-Kantian thinker, 'not in clearly formulated theoretical propositions, but in the form of a tendency of thought, permeating his utterances and defining his methods of research' (EST 396).

Bakhtin was not the only member of the Bakhtin Circle to write a significant amount about Goethe. In 1957 Ivan Kanaev, who had met with Bakhtin again in 1951, also turned to Goethe as a major topic of study immediately after taking up a position in the Institute of the History of the Natural Sciences and Technology in Leningrad, and continued to work in this area as late as 1971. This resulted in several biographical articles and two books dealing specifically with Goethe's contribution to the development of scientific method (GN; GIEN; GL; VDG; SNRG; IVG; GKE), all of which Bakhtin is known to have read and prized very highly (EST 396–7). Interestingly Kanaev, like Bakhtin, specifically focuses on Goethe's 'realism' (GN 155ff.), pulls together his scientific and artistic works (IVG) and draws upon Cassirer in his exegesis. A serious study of the mutual influence of these thinkers, specialists in the natural and cultural sciences respectively, is an interesting prospect for the future.

Conclusion

The writers discussed in these remarkable works are thus simultaneously philosophers of culture and philosophers of history, but they are also important expressions of the rise of a scientific world-view. In their own unique ways their works both reveal and constitute a 'Copernican revolution' in culture that paralleled the cosmological revolution that bears the same name. The object of knowledge is distinguished from the 'thing in itself' (the world beyond consciousness), which is recognised as unknowable. Culture becomes the object of knowledge, producing itself consciously from within life, cultivating that life and in doing so making it into a historical life. Once again we see the complex of neo-Kantian, life-philosophy, phenomenological and Hegelian motifs that characterise Bakhtin's work.

These works together undoubtedly represent a major contribution to literary history and the philosophy of culture, and as such they have spawned a variety of productive works by critics working in a variety of areas. However, they bear the marks of the same irreconcilable tension between the static model of eternal principles derived from neo-Kantianism and its heirs and the developmental and totalising model derived from Hegelian philosophy that we noted at the end of the last chapter. Thus each genre has an eternal essence which remains identical, but which unfolds in historical time, never reaching a conclusion. Life and culture remain constant opposites, but they develop historically. Laughter has a history, but it remains constant. These contradictions are not easily negotiated. Similarly, Bakhtin is insistent on drawing an unproblematic correlation between forms of popular consciousness and forms of literature, with no consideration of such questions as the politics of literacy or the economics of publication. Applications of Bakhtin's work should not ignore these problems by reproducing his own formalisation. Such questions require a different type of analysis. In other words, the fundamentally idealist nature of Bakhtin's critique must be recognised if his work is to be developed and applied productively.

7   Final Methodological Works

Bakhtin's intellectual activity continued during his retirement years. Following the second edition of the Dostoevsky book his remaining works were largely dedicated to reflections on methodological questions in the light of the emergence of a school of Soviet structuralism in the 1960s and 1970s. The fact that it was in the field of linguistics that the new perspective began to appear was not accidental. In June 1950 Stalin published an article in which he denounced the teachings of Marr, which had dominated Soviet linguistics since the end of the 1920s, and opened the way for a plurality of perspectives at a time when narrow dogma reigned in all other branches of the humanities. As the Russian linguist Vladimir Alpatov argues, in 'Marxism and Questions of Linguistics', Stalin 'did not so much define the task of constructing a Marxist linguistics as remove it from the agenda, having established language as an object for study by the natural sciences'. We will see later how Bakhtin does precisely this with linguistics as narrowly defined. Although the 'Marxism' of Marr, his allies and opponents was largely a superficial grafting on to previously constituted theories of language (Alpatov 2000), Stalin's move was significant in removing the methodological straightjacket that had hampered thought about language for a generation, and this emboldened Bakhtin to return to the main issue developed by Voloshinov at the end of the 1920s: language in verbal intercourse.

However, we have seen that Bakhtin accepted certain aspects of Marrism, and the dethroning of Marr effectively made echoes of his work unacceptable. The leading position of Soviet linguistics that had formerly been occupied by Marr's student I.I. Meshchaninov, was now taken by Viktor Vinogradov, whose 1951 article on the 'Tasks of Soviet Literary Studies' seems to be an unspoken target of Bakhtin's important work on discursive genres (AZPRZ: 218–21). Here, as elsewhere, especially in the 1959 book *O iazyke khudozhestvennoi literatury* (On the language of artistic literature), Vinogradov strove to extend the realm of linguistics to incorporate literary stylistics (1959: 294), presenting the relation between discourse and language as one between the unitary linguistic consciousness and an impersonal language structure. Bakhtin quickly moved to oppose this trend, seeking to distinguish between language and discourse in a different way.

It was in the course of this engagement with incipient structuralism that some of the methodological principles of Bakhtin's final work were formulated. This is true principally of the reworking of the 1929 Dostoevsky book in the early 1960s, and the series of articles and sketches on the methodology of the 'human sciences' that were to conclude Bakhtin's long career. It is for this reason that Bakhtin's unfinished article 'The Problem of Discursive Genres' will be discussed here.

'The Problem of Discursive Genres' (1953–54)

Although previously translated as 'speech genres', the Russian *rechevoi zhanr* suggests genres of discourse, of language in use, more than of specifically spoken language, and it is clear from Bakhtin's article that he uses the term to refer to features common to both spoken and written genres. This is important to recognise since the central pivot of the article is the distinction between units of language and units of discourse, specifically between the sentence and the utterance. Utterances are held to have generic forms. Such a study is poised on the border between traditional disciplines, and thus Bakhtin can pose the question: 'Who should study the forms of utterance, i.e. discursive genres? The linguist? The literary critic?' (AZPRZ 226). The answer depends on how one understands the objects of linguistic and literary studies, and Bakhtin's understanding is diametrically opposed to that of Vinogradov. For Bakhtin, linguistics is incapable of dealing with the specifics of the forms of utterance: its competence effectively ends at the point where a syntactic unit becomes a unit of discourse. Yet traditional literary scholarship is also unprepared to deal with such a wide variety of generic forms, and therefore requires rethinking. Bakhtin, like Voloshinov before him, follows Croce's contention that 'the limits of the expression-intuitions that are called art, as opposed to those that are vulgarly called non-art, are empirical and impossible to define … The teacher of philosophy in Molière's comedy was right: "whenever we speak, we create prose"' (Croce 1978: 13–14).[1]

Those relatively stable types of utterance that prevail in everyday (mostly but not exclusively oral) interaction Bakhtin terms 'primary' (or 'simple') genres, those that arise in more complex and organised cultural communication (mostly written) Bakhtin terms 'secondary' (or 'complex') genres. The former range from the simplest interjection such as 'oh!' to rejoinders in a conversation about politics at the dinner table and personal letters, while the latter include artistic works, scientific tracts, philosophical lectures, monographs or articles. The latter are more systematically organised genres that may incorporate primary genres into their very structure. The novel, for Bakhtin, is the genre that has the greatest capacity to incorporate and reprocess both primary and secondary genres. A good example of this is the relationship between Dostoevsky's novel and the Menippean satire, which has itself already incorporated other genres. In this scheme we see a restatement of the familiar Bakhtinian theme of relations between life and culture, with culture comprising the realm of secondary genres that absorb and rework the primary life-genres. The concept of discursive genres is thus yet another attempt to relate the realms of life and culture, life and the spheres of objective validity, which Bakhtin inherited from the neo-Kantians and life-philosophers.

Like Voloshinov before him, Bakhtin's conception of the utterance takes the 'organon model' developed by Bühler, with its three functions (representation, intimation and triggering) and three relational foundations (object, subject and addressee) as its point of departure. However, Bakhtin does not maintain the idea that representation pertains to something given to consciousness, which we find in Voloshinov's notion of *refraction*. Instead, the object of discourse is, in typical neo-Kantian vein, seen as 'the content of an uttered thought' (PRZ 168; PSG 67). The still-pervasive neo-Kantianism of Bakhtin's account is not obvious from the surviving section of the essay itself, but it is clearly shown in recently published and extensive archival notes that Bakhtin made in the process of writing it. The neo-Kantian vocabulary is here quite plain to see:

> The speaker does not communicate anything for the sake of communicating, but has to do so from the objective validity [*ob´´ektivnaia znachimost´*] of what is communicated (its truthfulness [*istinnost´*], beauty, veracity [*pravdivost´*] necessity, expressiveness, sincerity). Intercourse requires objective validity [*znachimost´*] (in all its various forms depending on the sphere of intercourse), without it intercourse would degenerate and decay. All utterances in one form or another have dealings with objective

actuality regardless of the consciousness or will of people (speakers, those engaged in intercourse), and regardless of intercourse itself. (AZPRZ: 252–3)

Here we see that every utterance refers not to an independent formation beyond language, the extradiscursive world, but to the world as (re)constituted in intentional acts with reference to a priori object domains, the 'objectively validity' of which is simply assumed. Discourse in the primary life-genres is thus dependent on a pre-existing realm of cultural categories. However, the 'validity' of these categories remains merely theoretical if they are not realised in life: abstract thought needs to be intentionally validated in life, verbally embodied by being uttered. This all hinges on the use of the Russian word *znachimost'*, which means validity in the senses of logically consistent and actual (as in the sense of effective), but which is also semantically related to the word *znak*, meaning sign, and thus to *znachenie*, meaning meaning in the sense of significance. When put into words, abstract meaning (*smysl*) combines with linguistic meaning (*znachenie*) and becomes valid in life. Similarly, linguistic meaning (*znachenie*) remains a technical means for communication until it is infused with life-meaning (*smysl*), when it is related to 'objective validity' in a specific and unrepeatable instance:

What is important is the relatedness of these meanings [*znachenie*] *to real actuality*, their use in the goals of mastery (cognitive, artistic, active) by new moments of actuality. When speaking we do not combine prepared elements, but we *relate*, adapt them to actuality. (AZPRZ: 281)

Here we once again have the neo-Kantian recasting of von Humboldt's and Marty's distinctions between the inner and outer forms of language, which we saw in Voloshinov's work. Every time linguistic meaning is related to actuality (objective validity) a unit of language becomes a unit of discourse. This is the crucial distinction that Bakhtin draws between the sentence and the utterance and it is the defining feature of what in the second Dostoevsky book he calls his 'metalinguistics' (PDP 181–5; PPD 395–9).

Bakhtin closely associates style with utterance, and opposes style to units of grammar like the sentence, for style is language use considered in relation to the whole of an utterance (or discursive genre) while grammar is related to the linguistic system. Style changes along with changing discursive genres, both primary and secondary, and any new grammatical element is introduced after 'generic-stylistic testing and modification'. Thus, argues Bakhtin, adapting a metaphor previously used by Marr, discursive genres are 'drive belts [*privodnye remni*] from the history of society to the history of language' (PSG 65; PRZ 165).[2] These genres are relatively stable forms of utterance, which are 'metalinguistic' in nature. Their boundaries are set by a change of discursive subjects (speaker or writer). The sentence, as a linguistic category, is quite different. When a sentence is bounded by a change of discursive subjects it is transformed into a one-sentence utterance. Bakhtin argues that this change of subjects is crucial for understanding verbal communication, and has too often been obscured, leading to such conceptions as the undifferentiated 'verbal stream' which inform Romantic linguistics from Humboldt through to Vossler. Such a conception is monologic since it assumes a single, collective consciousness, rather than a plurality of consciousnesses engaged in active communication. Bakhtin prefers the image of utterances as links in a complex chain of discursive exchange. Each link in some way responds to the previous one and anticipates the next one, and this process exerts a decisive influence on the way each utterance is constructed.

According to Bakhtin, the utterance is a 'real unit' of discourse with clear-cut boundaries established by a change of discursive subjects. The floor is given over to an interlocutor with a 'silent sign' that the first subject has finished (*dixi*). Utterances thus presuppose another, active, participant, and this in turn presupposes 'dialogic relations' such as those between question and answer, assertion and objection, suggestion and acceptance and the like. However, such relations are not possible between linguistic units like sentences:

> As a unit of language the sentence lacks these properties: it is not bounded from both sides by a change of discursive subjects, it does not have direct contact with actuality (with the extralinguistic situation) or direct relations with alien utterances, it does not have semantic [*smyslovoi*] fullness and the capacity directly to define the responsive position of another speaker, that is, evoke a response … Sentences are not exchanged, just as words and combinations of words (in the strictly linguistic sense) are not exchanged – thoughts are exchanged, that is utterances, which are constructed with the help of units of language – words, combinations of words, sentences. (PSG 74–5; PRZ 176–7)[3]

One should note here that thoughts are exchanged 'with the help of' language, suggesting that there is a prelinguistic element to thought, something that many contemporary philosophers of language from both the poststructuralist and analytic traditions would reject. One other criticism could be that if response is enabled by a 'silent sign' that the speaker has finished (*dixi*) it is difficult to see what we are to make of an interrupted utterance or an objection to one sentence in a larger utterance. For example, on reading a student's essay I may feel that the proposition made in one particular sentence is mistaken or fails to follow logically from previous sentences, even though the general argument of the whole essay-utterance is correct. This is surely a response to a part of an utterance. Bakhtin could retort that in so doing we bring about a 'special syntactic aberration' in which the sentence acquires a degree of completion necessary for response to occur, it is 'thought into' (*domyslivat'*) a position where it is transformed into an utterance (PSG 82; PRZ 185–6). Treating the sentence in such a way is illegitimate, for Bakhtin, because it has not been transformed into an utterance by means of a complete meaning-bestowing, intentional act.

The problem with Bakhtin's treatment of this issue may be a result of the intellectual isolation Bakhtin endured in the Stalin years. Teaching at a provincial university meant that Bakhtin had access to few new works on the philosophy of language written abroad, and the Russian materials that were available were subject to the narrow dogmatism that characterised the time. Thus, Bakhtin was still drawing on philosophical sources from the first two decades of the century, but the field had moved on considerably in the meantime. However, Bakhtin's article is still full of fascinating insights. Bakhtin claims that the most important aspect of utterances is that the 'discursive will' of a speaker is manifested primarily in the choice of a specific 'discursive genre':

> This choice is determined by the specific given sphere of discursive intercourse, objectual-meaningful (thematic) considerations, the concrete situation of discursive intercourse, the personal make-up of its participants etc. And when the speaker's discursive intention with all its individuality and subjectivity is applied and adapted to a chosen genre, it is formed and developed in a definite generic form. (PSG 78; PRZ 180)

A discursive genre is therefore a bridge between life and the objectively valid object domains of culture, embodying a connection between the unrepeatable context of utterance and the impersonal, or supra-personal realm of objective culture. These relatively stable forms are the places where culture is vitalised (personalised) and life is cultivated, thus overcoming the widening chasm between life and culture that Simmel called the 'tragedy of culture'. All utterances, even those involved in everyday speech, are generic, but these genres are the most plastic and flexible types, while at the other extreme genres like the sonnet are the most inflexible and conventional. A sonnet, for example, must have 14 lines, usually in iambic pentameter, and one of three rhyme schemes, or it ceases to be a sonnet. Forms of conversational utterances are, however, free of any such rules. Everyday genres are informal and familiar while 'high', 'official' genres are formalised. The 'familiarisation' of high genres in the novel, often through the incorporation of parodies of formal genres, signifies an orientation towards the flexible everyday genres. Genres are thus cultural norms for the language user, since they are given as culture and yet adapted to each circumstance. Genres precede the individual utterance and must be mastered by the speaker if he or she is to engage in successful social interaction. An inability to communicate successfully in a given sphere of social interaction signifies an inability to use genres creatively and freely.

This conception resembles several other theories of language-in-use that also to some extent developed from the incorporation of Brentano's notion of intentionality into an analysis of discursive practice. Among these are the Munich phenomenologist Adolf Reinach's 1913 study of the 'a priori foundations of civil law', in which the structure of what he calls other-directed 'social acts' such as promises, commands and the like is analysed in a strikingly similar fashion (Reinach 1983).[4] It also resembles John Searle's famous account of 'speech acts' (1969),[5] and the notion of language games developed by Ludwig Wittgenstein in his *Philosophical Investigations* (1997). Here speech acts and language games are regarded as social institutions in the sense of being rule-bound self-referential collective practices (Bloor 1997: 27–42). It has subsequently been shown that the tenability of such a conception depends upon the acknowledgement of underlying economic and social structures which lend a relative stability to the perspectives and types of evidence that are regarded as authoritative and compelling in particular spheres of communication (Lovibond 1983; Bhaskar 1979: 79ff.).

Bakhtin is not, however, concerned with institutional factors. Instead, the notion of discursive *genres* allows him to remain firmly within the realms of aesthetics and ethics where social factors are limited to questions of intersubjectivity. The utterance as a whole becomes the means through which the individual endows language with an evaluative tone (PSG 90; PRZ 194). Here we have a restatement of the intonational coloration of the word that we saw as early as *Toward a Philosophy of the Act*, but now genre is the bridge between life and culture, whereas in that early work only the ethical deed was found. The selection of genre is now seen as the act of evaluation in discursive communication, while the philosophy of the act has become part of this philosophy of language. The immediate social situation within which an utterance is made is reduced to the knowledge each interlocutor has of that situation. Meanwhile, the sphere of 'objective validity' to which all utterances relate in one way or another is understood as the domain of academic disciplines. The consciousnesses that meet in communication and reciprocally shape their utterances according to the genres established in cultural traditions are not seen as subject to any influences beyond these factors. The extent to which this makes Bakhtin's work in need of amendment is an open question.

It is clear that although Bakhtin's theory of the utterance begins with Bühler's model, it is considerably more complex. Every utterance has components that include the speaker, alien (someone else's) discourse (*chuzhaia rech'*), the language system, the direct addressee, an assumed 'third' participant (to which we shall return), the conventions of discursive genres and the direct object (*predmet*) of discourse. This level of sophistication is a significant advance over Voloshinov's earlier contributions, though the idealist reorientation of the notion of representation is one that will disturb many, myself included.

In the final part of the essay Bakhtin discusses how utterances as links in discursive communication should be understood dialogically, as a chain of responses. Utterances 'mutually reflect' one another, and this determines their character. Their 'responsive reactions' can take many forms, incorporating elements of a preceding utterance and giving them a new accent: ironic, indignant, reverential or whatever. Accent expresses the speaker's attitude towards the utterances of another speaker. Traces of this process can be found in the finest nuances of the utterance, the 'dialogic overtones' that define the style of the utterance. Echoes of preceding and anticipated utterances are thus detectable in the very structure of every utterance as a link in a chain of communication. Central to all this is the 'addressivity' of an utterance, that is, its quality of being directed towards someone. The utterance will be different depending on whether it is addressed to an immediate partner in dialogue, a collective of specialists, 'the public', opponents, like-minded people, a subordinate or superior, and so on. This addressivity has an important effect on the shape of the utterance, affecting the selection of vocabulary, stylistic pattern, intonation etc. Such factors determine the formality or informality of the utterance, dependent on the type of relationship being enacted. Bakhtin notes that these considerations are important in explaining and assessing the new orientation towards familiar discursive genres in the secondary literary genres of the Renaissance in breaking down the medieval world-view.

The unfinished essay on discursive genres continues the themes of many of the earlier works, but attempts to establish generic study as a principle for the 'human sciences' in general. In this sense it is the first of a series of articles that Bakhtin was to work on at the end of his life. However, it also represents an attempt to update his early phenomenology in accordance with the concerns of the 1950s. Bakhtin's work resembles that of other philosophers of the period, but it retains a peculiarly Bakhtinian angle, to some extent thanks to the isolation of Soviet scholarship in the period. This illustrates the importance of understanding the intellectual roots that Bakhtin's work shares with much contemporary scholarship, for his original-ity and significance can only be correctly judged from within such an intellectual history.

The methodology of the human sciences

Bakhtin's last, fragmentary works in some ways represent a return to the principles of the Marburg School, in the sense not of a complete return to a 'pure' neo-Kantianism, but to an overriding concern with establishing a *methodology* for the definition of the object of the 'human sciences'. We now know that Bakhtin was making notes about the 'philosophical foundations of the human sciences' at least as early as 1946 (FOGN), but it seems that it was only in the 1960s that this issue became the main focus of his attention, perhaps as a result of his attempts to rework his book on Dostoevsky. Whatever the truth of this, we have at least 15 years of predominantly fragmentary work on these topics. In some notes from 1970–71 he delineates what he considers to be a crucial concern for any such methodology, the three types of relations with which science is concerned:

(1) Relations between objects: between things, between physical phenomena, chemical phenomena, causal relations, mathematical relations, logical relations, linguistic relations and others.

(2) Relations between subject and object.

(3) Relations between subjects – personal, personalistic relations: dialogic relations between utterances, ethical relations and others. Here are also all personified semantic [*smyslovoi*] connections. Relations between consciousnesses, truths [*pravda*], mutual influences, apprenticeship, love, hatred, falsity, friendship, respect, reverence trust, mistrust, and so on. (FN 138; IZ 342–3)

For Bakhtin (3) is exclusively the object domain of the human sciences while (1) is the domain of the 'exact' sciences; (2) is the methodology of the exact sciences, while (3) is the methodology of the human sciences. Bakhtin insists that these spheres should be kept separate: 'the more demarcation the better, but a benevolent demarcation. Without border disputes. Co-operation' (FN 136; IZ 341). In his final essay, Bakhtin expands on the question:

> The exact sciences are a monologic form of knowledge: an intellect cognises a *thing* and expounds upon it. There is only one subject here – the percipient (cogniser) and speaker (expounder). Only a *voiceless thing* stands over and against him. Any object of knowledge (man among them) may be cognised and perceived as a thing. But the subject as such cannot be cognised and studied as a thing, for as a subject he cannot become voiceless and remain a subject. Cognition of this can therefore only be *dialogic*. (MHS 161; MGN 363)

Here Bakhtin explicitly refers to Dilthey, whose distinction between explanation and understanding as the methods of the natural and human sciences was outlined in the opening chapter. This is important because it shows that for all his theoretical developments, his critique of neo-Kantian rationalism and the 'monologism' of Dilthey, Bakhtin to the end of his life remained within a paradigm fundamentally shaped by these traditions and thinkers. The insistence that there is no place for causality and explanation in the human sciences is based on the neo-Kantian oppositions that we have stressed throughout.

Bakhtin's late essays reveal not only that he was wedded to the methodological distinctness of the human sciences throughout his career but that his commitment to a juridical framework also persisted. In notes made in 1970–71 he argues that each subject is both witness (*svidetel´*) and judge (*sudiia*) in the creation of 'superbeing' (*nadbytie*). True, absolute, creative freedom lies in the ability of the subject to change the 'meaning of being' (*smysl bytiia*) through recognition, justification, and so on, rather than to change being as such. Similarly, intersubjective relations lead to the rise of the 'super-I' (*nad-ia*), the witness and judge of the whole human (*chelovek*), or the other (*drugoi*). This freedom is counterposed to the relative freedom which 'remains in being and changes the make-up of being but not its meaning. Such freedom changes material being and may become a force that is detached from meaning, becoming a crude and naked material force. Creativity is always connected with a change of meaning and cannot become a naked material force' (IZ 341–2; FN 137–8). The juridical person (super-I) is here counterposed to the material (biological) individual and, as for Kant, this is correlated with the opposition of the freedom of the morally legislative will (*der Wille*) versus that of the naturally determined will (*Willkür*). This all falls within the neo-Kantian opposition between value and fact, meaning and being, freedom and necessity.

The perceived need to transcend these Kantian dichotomies was what ultimately led to the rise of social theory: the split within social being was deemed to have historically specific preconditions. That Bakhtin never manages quite to break with the Kantian oppositions is symptomatic of the parlous state of social theory in post-Stalinist Russia. This contrasts with Voloshinov's and Medvedev's provisional though promising engagements with the relatively open and critical type of Marxism of the 1920s.

'The Problem of the Text'

In the late essays, Bakhtin's agenda is often set by the new structuralist philology, especially as represented by the Tartu School led by Iurii Lotman (1922–93), which he discusses briefly. Like Medvedev in the case of the Formalists, Bakhtin clearly respected the structuralists for their progress in 'specifying' textual aspects of literature. This can clearly be seen in his response to a question from the editorial board of the journal *Novyi Mir* in 1970 (RQNM 1–7; OVNM 328–35). However, he objected to the 'sequential formalisation and depersonalisation' at the core of the structuralist method, where there is only one subject and 'things are transformed into concepts' (the 'logical relations' of (1), above). Structuralism's methodology is characterised by (2), above, while only (3) can study the subject as a subject, and this is what interests Bakhtin: 'I hear *voices* in everything and dialogic relations between them' (MHS 169; MGN 372). This encounter with structuralism also lies behind the 1959–61 article 'The Problem of the Text', in which he quickly recasts 'text' as 'utterance', with generic forms understandable only according to dialogic principles. Bakhtin suggests that structuralism looks at *dialectical*, logical relations between elements in a text, whereas he is interested in *dialogic* relations between texts that permeate the text as a whole (PTLPHS 104–5; PT 308–9). This is again stressed in the final essay:

A text lives only on making contact with another text (with context). It is only at the point of contact between texts that a light flashes, illuminating both before and after, joining a given text to a dialogue. We emphasise that this contact is a dialogical contact between texts (utterances), and not a mechanical contact of 'oppositions', possible only within the limits of a single text (and not between a text and context), between abstract elements (signs inside a text) and necessary only at the first stage of understanding (understanding significance [*znachenie*] and not sense [*smysl*]). Behind this contact is a contact of personalities and not of things (at the extreme). If we convert dialogue into one continuous text, that is, erase the divisions between voices (the change of discursive subjects), which is possible at the extreme (Hegel's monologic dialectic), then the profundity (endless) of sense [*smysl*] disappears (we hit the bottom, reach a dead point). (MHS 162; MGN 364)

This passage is worth quoting at length because it shows that Bakhtin's most famous comments contrasting dialectics and dialogue refer specifically to structuralism rather than to dialectics per se. The stress on binary oppositions between signs within a single text is, of course, constitutive of structuralism as such. The reference to Hegel's 'monologic dialectic' may as easily suggest the possibility of a dialogic dialectic, perhaps of the sort Bakhtin develops in his own account of the interaction of generic forms. This is further suggested by his paradoxically Hegelian statement that 'dialectics was born from dialogue in order to return to dialogue at a higher level (a dialogue of personalities)' (MHS 162; MGN 364).[6] Bakhtin's argument, like that of Voloshinov before him, is that structuralism focuses exclusively on linguistic meaning (*znachenie*) to the exclusion of that dimension of meaning that is bestowed by communicating subjects in dialogue (*smysl*). The former is the object domain of the 'exact sciences', and the latter that of the 'human sciences'. Dialectics in the realm of the human sciences *is* dialogue: the interaction of text-utterances.

This idea lies behind one of Bakhtin's most famous and mistranslated assertions: that no sense is 'absolutely dead: every sense [*smysl*] will have its festival of rebirth' (MHS 170; MGN 373).[7] Every cultural artefact is an utterance that was created in 'life' as a unique orientation towards the realm of objective validity from a particular location in the infinite chain of utterances (dialogue within what Bakhtin calls 'great time'). The sense, or senses, of this utterance are a result of this unique correlation. The text is a microcosm, as it were, of that correlation whose facets are akin to an infinitely complex crystal in which images of the world are reflected. In some notes of 1961 Bakhtin says that 'in every word there are voices, sometimes infinitely distant, nameless, almost impersonal voices (of lexical nuances, of styles etc.), almost undetectable, and voices close by sounding together' (PTLPHS 124; ZAM 334). Every utterance is what Cassirer, following Nicholas Cusanus, called a *visio intellectualis*, a unity of an infinitely multiple number of relationships to being, the totality of which is inaccessible to any single perspective (Cassirer 1963: 36–8). Meaning is thus bottomless not in the sense of being a void (as in much poststructuralism), but in the sense of being endlessly incomplete and partial. We thus discover new aspects of the plays of Shakespeare unknown to previous generations, and indeed to Shakespeare himself, because our new perspective within 'great time' discloses yet another facet of their endless complexity. We discover new senses by establishing new correlations between ourselves and Shakespeare's works as orientations towards his own incomplete world in the process of becoming. This is the sense in which meanings are endlessly reborn. The significance (essence) of the novel, as we saw in the section on 'Discourse in the Novel', is that it *consciously* collects perspectives into a single unity and in so doing overcomes the mythical conception that a single perspective can grasp 'being' in its totality.

One of the most interesting formulations of the 1961 notes, and indeed of Bakhtin's late work in general, is the idea of the 'third' who is a structural precondition of all dialogue. This third is one who '*understands* a dialogue but does not participate in it' and acts as a sort of guarantor against the degeneration of plurality of perspectives into meaningless relativism. The importance of the third can be seen in the 1963 Dostoevsky book, where Bakhtin argues that 'relativism and dogmatism equally exclude all argument, all genuine dialogue, making it either unnecessary (relativism) or impossible (dogmatism)' (PDP 69; PPD 276). Bakhtin notes that the idea of the third is not a third person who is present, but is a structural prerequisite of dialogue. In a dialogue there is the first-person speaker, the second-person addressee and interlocutor:

> But apart from this addressee (the 'second') the author of the utterance more or less consciously supposes a higher '*super-addressee*' (the 'third'), whose absolutely just responsive understanding is supposed either at a metaphysical distance or in distant historical time (the loophole addressee). In different epochs and according to different understandings of the world this superaddressee and its absolutely correct responsive understanding acquired various concrete ideological expressions (God, absolute truth, the court of dispassionate human conscience, the people, the court of history etc.). The author can never yield all of himself and all his discursive work to the full and *finalised* will of present or nearby addressees (the nearest descendents may also be mistaken) and always supposes (more or less consciously) some higher instance of responsive understanding, which can move back in various directions. Every dialogue occurs as it were against the background of the responsive understanding of an invisibly present 'third', standing above all participants of a dialogue (partners). (See the understanding of the Fascist torture-chamber or 'Hell' in Thomas Mann as the absolute '*unheardness*', as the absolute absence of a '*third*'). (PT 126; ZAM 337–8)

The assumption of some absolute authority to which each discursive subject can appeal is thus constitutive of dialogue as such. The final, ultimate meaning of an utterance is never available to any empirical person, but the existence of an absolute meaning of the whole is nevertheless a necessary assumption for all utterances as such. This is a new version of the relation between the author and hero that we saw in the early work. There, the whole meaning of the hero's activity was perceptible only from the perspective of the author, who was able to view the hero's actions as determined against the background of the closed unity of the plot. The activity of the hero for himself was open, ethical action in the open 'event of being', and was thus only partially understood from within. The author was the ultimate 'other' who understood the meaning of the whole. In the 1961 text we have a situation in which the ultimate meaning of the speaker's utterance is guaranteed only by the presence of this assumed 'third', the absence of which deprives the utterance of its significance. The 'Hell' of 'absolute unheardness' is a complete collapse of any sense of oneself as a whole and the meaning of one's life in general.

The Marburg School principle that it is the *idea* of God that is important in human society, rather than God as a being with attributes, returns in the idea of the superaddressee. God becomes a symbol of the highest aspiration of human consciousness, the bond for the entire human race: the idea. The superaddressee is thus, for Bakhtin, a direction of consciousness determined by feeling rather than intellect: it is an object of will not of knowledge. This, then, is the 'never-ending task' that the Marburg School posited. As Natorp put it in his significantly entitled 1894 book *Religion innerhalb der Grenzen der Humanität* (Religion within the bounds of humanity) (Natorp 1908):

> ... the vista of an eternal, infinitely far, consequently non-empirical goal is thoroughly indispensable to the will. The empirically reachable can never be a final object, can never be the true goal of the will. In a finite goal it would come to rest – that means to die away, for its essence is movement. If the Eternal has a merely formal meaning for the will, so this formal meaning is the highest conceivable formal meaning, signifying here: 'setting the course'. Will, however, is altogether only the direction of consciousness. (Quoted in Saltzman 1981: 184)

The superaddressee is an 'infinitely remote' but 'validly posited' point of direction. Consciousness strives towards its infinite goal, co-creating the world as an object of cognition as it goes. However, the superaddressee also continues the juridical strand within Bakhtin's thought, which also derived from the Marburg School. It is the eternally deferred supreme judge who views the social world from without. The juridical world remains an interaction of juridical persons, with rights and responsibilities, but whose actions are not subject to causality.

Conclusion

Bakhtin's final works are widely regarded as valuable mainly for their methodological insights pertaining to the nature of language and of discourse, the problem of genre, and the distinctions between the human and natural sciences. In this last case it is clear that Bakhtin was still taking his point of departure from the philosophies of the early twentieth century which opposed the extension of positivistic methods from the natural sciences into the realm of the human sciences. Bakhtin clearly wants to delineate a clear and benevolent demarcation between these realms.

We need to be aware, however, that philosophy of science has moved on considerably since the debates out of which Bakhtin's writing emerged. Indeed, he seems to have been unfamiliar with the works of the most influential writers on the subject in the West: Karl Popper, Thomas Kuhn and Imre Lakatos. Similarly, Bakhtin's familiarity with developments in social science was severely limited, and this compelled him to fall back on the oppositions of German idealism. It would be shortsighted to adopt Bakhtin's models of the natural and human sciences today without reference to the thinkers who have transformed our understanding of science in the meantime. Furthermore, the traditional lines of demarcation between the natural and human sciences, which found their classical expression in the work of Dilthey, have, in recent years, been challenged from within both the natural sciences and the human sciences themselves. Newly developed theories such as emergent systems analysis, which has grown out of advances in information technology, quantum mechanics, which allots a role to the active observer within particle physics, and 'ecological psychology', which views physical structures as always already meaningful to an animal, require a fundamental rethinking of the validity of a clear division between natural and human sciences. These developments in cognitive science and elsewhere suggest that it may actually be possible adequately to account for 'mental phenomena' by adopting an explanatory form of questioning, and that mental cognitive properties may be ontologically transformable into natural ones (Roy et al. 2000: 43–9). Bakhtin's ideas on science are thus in need of significant, even systemic, revision. Yet it may well be that a good number of his observations will prove to be valuable elements of a future, more inclusive and flexible type of natural science that incorporates and acknowledges the specific and irreducible level of human relations and the structures thereof.

8 The Bakhtinian Research Programme Yesterday and Today

There is little doubt that the Bakhtinian research programme has proved progressive in literary and cultural studies. As Bakhtinian concepts have been applied to an increasing variety of problems with which they were not originally designed to grapple, they turned out to be impressively adaptive and seemed to explain a whole new range of phenomena. The application of Bakhtinian categories to modern drama, the visual arts, cinema, various aspects of social history, and so on, has led to the opening of new perspectives. Even where new material posed problems for the detail of Bakhtin's writings, it seemed that the main structure of the Circle's thought survived. Only what Lakatos (1970: 133–4) called the 'protective belt' of 'auxillary, observational hypotheses' was subject to refutation, rather than the 'hard core'. As a consequence of adjustments to the 'belt', qualifying and tightening up some of Bakhtin's looser contentions, progressive problem shifts have become clear to see. The concept of carnival, for example, has been refined and historically specified in a number of studies and applications, with the effect that the core of the idea has survived even if some of Bakhtin's specific contentions have been refuted. There seems little doubt, however, that enthusiasm for some of Bakhtin's ideas has often triumphed over methodological rigour. Much of the most valuable work that is critical of the ideas of the Circle has been confined to establishing the limitations of valid application. This type of work was encouraged by the publication of the early works, which cast new light on the better-known works on language and literary theory.

The achievement so far

In recent years the ideas of the Circle have been taken up by several thinkers working in the social sciences, where attention has especially fallen upon Bakhtin's early ethics and aesthetics. The return of ethics as a central problem of the sociology of culture has made Bakhtin's early work an important point of reference for some social theorists. Michael Gardiner (1996a; 1996b), for example, has argued that Bakhtin now stands beside such figures as Emmanuel Levinas and Martin Buber as pioneers of dialogical ethics. Subsequently, this trend has become an important part of the 'postmodern ethics' of, for example, Zygmunt Bauman (1993). This line of research does have its critics, myself included (Rose 1993; Brandist 1999b, 2001a), however, since questions of intersubjectivity tend to be isolated from the socio-economic structures of society which affect behaviour causally. This results in a distorted picture of human social life and tends to collapse politics into ethics. It remains to be seen whether Bakhtinian theory can be creatively shifted so as to push the research programme forward in this area or whether it cannot avoid entering a degenerative phase in which it fails to explain 'novel facts'.

The Marxist works of Voloshinov and Medvedev have been among the most influential of the Circle. Those decisively influenced have included Raymond Williams, Terry Eagleton, Stuart Hall, John Frow, Tony Bennett and many others. Through these figures the effect on cultural studies has been profound. The Medvedev book has in many ways set the agenda for interpreting the work of the Russian Formalists and is often cited as exemplary in its attempt to find a way to treat form and content as a single problem. Similarly, Voloshinov's critique of Saussure has often been regarded as the most satisfying Marxist engagement with structuralism, while the book as a whole is often seen as one of the most important Marxist statements on the philosophy of language. It has proved especially influential on analyses of the relationship between language and forms of power both in society at large and in popular culture.

Bakhtin's work on the novel has in many ways reshaped our understanding of literary history and of the relationship between the novel and other genres. David Lodge's 1990 book *After Bakhtin* was an attempt to sum up the potential of the analytical tools bequeathed by Bakhtin. Bakhtin's work on the novel has also transformed contemporary engagements with specific writers from different cultures, and has influenced such areas as post-colonial theory, which deals with the interaction of different national cultures. The two editions of the Dostoevsky book are regarded as landmarks in the study of the writer and of the threshold between the realism of the nineteenth-century novel and the modernism of much twentieth-century work.

Among the important developments in this area is Franco Moretti's work on 'the modern epic' (1996) and the *Bildungsroman* (1987), which, while taking issue with many of Bakhtin's formulations, takes them as a starting point for analysis. Furthermore, the dynamics of cultural history that Bakhtin describes in these works has proved productive in areas other than literary studies. These applications have supplemented the appeal of Bakhtin's work on the Middle Ages and Renaissance among historians.

The first of Bakhtin's works to have been translated in the West is also one of the most influential: the Rabelais book. The notion of carnival has had a massive impact on literary studies and cultural history. Among the historians who have been influenced are such figures as Carlo Ginzburg, Peter Burke, Stephen Greenblatt and Aron Gurevich, while works such as Allon White's and Peter Stallybrass's book *The Politics and Poetics of Transgression* (Stallybrass and White 1986) have served to bring the notion of carnival into the very centre of cultural studies. Our whole picture of early-modern culture has been transformed as forms of culture not previously considered worthy of serious attention have been subjected to scholarly analysis. Especially notable here are Ginzburg's *The Cheese and the Worms* (1992) and Greenblatt's *Renaissance Self-Fashioning* (1980), which draw upon Bakhtin, Marx and Foucault. The main criticisms of Bakhtin's work levelled in these studies pertain to the inapplicability of Bakhtin's generalisations to specific historical circumstances. This is not really surprising since, as we have seen, Bakhtin downplays the referential capacities of discourse and grants to 'symbolic forms' a questionably large degree of autonomy from the material conditions of their production. Nevertheless, the categories used to describe carnival have successfully been applied to contemporary culture, with Robert Stam's Bakhtinian reading of contemporary film in the 1989 book *Subversive Pleasures* being among the most fruitful. Interpretations and developments have varied considerably, to include Marxist, feminist and 'queer-theory' versions, but it becomes ever more apparent that these need to be better grounded in historical research than hitherto.

The influence of Bakhtin's final methodological work has been more diffuse, mainly affecting the methodology of certain areas of cultural studies, particularly since structuralism has become the target of much criticism. The 'Discursive Genres' essay has proved the most influential up to the present, perhaps thanks to the way in which it seems to form a bridge between the central work on the novel and Voloshinov's work on language in the 1920s. However, the growth of interest in these often fragmentary late works is apparent. Evidence of this is the appearance of two new anthologies of work on the relationship of Bakhtinian ideas to social theory (Bell and Gardiner 1998; Brandist and Tihanov 2000). It is in these late methodological works, however, that some of the more fundamental problems of Bakhtinian theory have become apparent. This is especially clear in the case of Bakhtin's distinction between the natural and the human sciences and the isolation of culture as a realm of freedom from nature as a realm of necessity.

Problems and tensions

After a period in which the application of Bakhtinian ideas has been so fruitful, it is hardly surprising that the flow of radically new applications of the works of the Circle has slowed to a trickle. While Bakhtin's name routinely appears in new studies, applications are already often mannered and mechanical, adding little of substance to our established knowledge. If the Bakhtinian research project is not to degenerate, the inner tensions and inadequacies of the work of the Circle need to be addressed. What is of value needs to be consolidated and elaborated, while the weaker areas need to be rethought and reworked. In what remains I shall suggest some areas in which this overhaul of Bakhtinian concepts would be advantageous and suggest some ways in which it might be carried out. It is for the reader to decide whether the 'hard core' of the Bakhtinian research programme remains intact after the 'little revolution' in its positive heuristic that I am about to propose.

While deeply sociological, the Circle's work is constructed on the basis of a philosophy that was designed to deal with forms of individual interaction with the result that when the various members of the Circle moved on to the discursive interaction of social groups, they were stretching categories not designed for such an application. This leads the effacement of institutional factors in favour of a subtle analysis of forms of discursive relations: dialogue. Dialogue, in turn, becomes a term that is given an almost impossible load to bear. We have seen that its senses include the nature of all discourse, specific types of relationship between two or several discourses and a particular type of discourse. Terms such as novelistic, monologic, or poetic also accumulated such diverse meanings. To make sense of such terminology, one needs to recognise that members of the Circle treat discursive interaction primarily as a new form of the interaction of subjects and social groups. On top of the philosophy of intersubjectivity is laid a philosophy of language and an account of cultural history. At each stage the result is an uneasy but genuine attempt at a fusion of different ideas. Although those attempts are only partially successful, the value of the works that result is not to be doubted. They have changed the way we look at many problems and opened up new perspectives.

One of the factors that is increasingly gaining recognition is the importance of the interaction between the different members of the Circle. Bakhtin began as a philosopher, but was in contact and discussions with specialists in literary theory, linguistics and other disciplines. While Bakhtin's philosophy had a considerable influence on the work of the other members of the Circle, their work also influenced Bakhtin's decisively. This is one of the reasons the work of the Circle, from the middle of the 1920s, is an ongoing attempt to unify different areas of study. It is therefore the product of a dialogic relationship, which continued even after the Circle had finally ceased to meet at the end of the 1920s.

Although Bakhtin's most important work appeared after this cessation, he had already assimilated a great deal from the Circle's meetings. The influence and expertise of Voloshinov and Medvedev in particular provided Bakhtin with new ways of approaching the relations between intersubjectivity and artistic production, and led to his most influential formulations. Nevertheless, much was lost when the Circle ceased to meet, and it has been one of the aims of this book to suggest some of the still unrealised potential of the Circle's work. Voloshinov, in particular, had limited the dependence of the Circle's ideas on German idealism, and tethered questions of meaning to the empirical psychology of the period. With this line cut, Bakhtin's grounding in idealist philosophy led him to treat culture as a domain of freedom, unaffected by material necessity. While phenomenological description of literary form and the intentions that lie behind it was still possible, Bakhtin methodologically severed his philosophy of culture from the concerns of the necessity-bound natural sciences. This, without a doubt, facilitated some bracing readings of the history of the novel and some compelling analyses of wider cultural forms, but these analyses were no longer firmly secured to the structures of the material world within which such cultural forms arise. Bakhtin's neo-Hegelian turn certainly liberated him from the static analyses of his youth, focusing his attention more closely on the trans-subjective structures which intersect in culture. However, it also allowed him more fully to move into the more restricted area of the German idealist philosophy of culture with its aim, in Windelband's famous phrase, of 'the dissolution of being into processes of consciousness' (Schuhmann and Smith 1993: 457).

To Bakhtin's credit he was never able to complete this dissolution: the given world persistently precipitated out of his intellectual solvent, leaving a rather conspicuous sediment. The given world became a sort of amorphous bearer of qualities that the mutually implicated subjectivities of the world constantly invest with meaning. In this sense, Vitalii Makhlin's characterisation of Bakhtin's philosophical programme as a 'social ontology of participation' is quite appropriate (Lähteenmäki 2001: 75). As with all such theories, however, the problem with this perspective is that it effaces the distinction between the structure of things and the structure of thought, which is an inevitable consequence of collapsing the distinction between perception and cognition. While Bakhtin's work may have been more consistent in this regard than that of Voloshinov and Medvedev, who equivocated between erasing and inking in the distinction, consistency came at a very high price.

Realist alternatives

What if the other choice had been made? Inking in the distinction between perception and cognition would have shifted the Circle into territory now occupied by the various currents of that other contemporary combination of disciplines, cognitive science. Several problems would have arisen, such as how to combine an analysis of the epistemological capacities of discourse with a theory that foregrounds the intersubjective dimension of meaning production. Bakhtin solved this problem by arguing that in and through intersubjective interaction a symbolic world of knowledge is produced, and if that world is not as we would like, this is because the structure of intersubjectivity is unethical. However, if the world is already structured before we encounter it, and we as human beings have a given range of needs and capacities, then there are given limits to the forms intersubjectivity can take at any given point, limits that we need to discover. This does not mean that all the limits are in principle untransformable, but only that as a species we cannot change the world just as we like, with only the limits of our imaginations and the a priori categories of thought to restrain us. We are embodied beings in a way more fundamental than Bakhtin was prepared to acknowledge, while the world itself is resistant to our attempts to make it just as we please.

Bakhtin's own starting point, our responsibility to act, needs to be rethought in this regard. Responsibility needs to be linked to the emergent natural and social structures within which we are embedded. As human beings we have physical structures and biological requirements, we are located within institutional structures and thus have structural capacities to act. Our actions are conditioned by external factors and are endowed with a significance that is not always immediately apparent. One does not need to abandon the notion of moral agency to acknowledge this fact (as a poststructuralist approach would suggest), but only to recognise that agency is necessarily linked to structure. Any neo-Kantian attempt to separate off agency, our morally legislative will (*der Wille*), from structure, our naturally determined will (*Willkür*), is untenable. While Bakhtin locates agency within a flow of intersubjective relations and cultural forms, his juridical model of agency abstracts it from social structure and institutions. The identity of the agent is certainly distinctive and, in Bakhtin's terms, occupies a unique place in being, but every individual human being is 'being in structure' (Norrie 2000: 199). While concretely singular, an individual is constituted and sustained socially, through his or her integration into wider social structures. Thus, while Bakhtin overcomes the Kantian model of the monadic individual by integrating personal identity into an intersubjective dynamic, he does not integrate that identity into the wider structures that constitute it. The Kantian model hypostatises one element of our being (moral agency), and vestiges of this remain in Bakhtin's formulation. Further revisions are necessary if we are not to succumb to this hypostatisation and recognise that moral agency is but an element of our being that is compounded with other elements at a 'molecular' level. Instead of the juridical model of the person we need a concretely singular agent who stands at a specific juncture of natural and social structures. Responsibility then becomes conjunctural (Norrie 1991, 2000; Kerruish 1991).

The great virtue of the approach taken by Voloshinov, however compromised and faltering his steps may have been, is that he aimed to establish a platform of empirical methodology and theoretical modelling that would be common to 'cultural studies' and 'cognitive science'.[1] He rejected the isolation of symbolic media from perceptual structures by treating them as irreducible but ontologically connected moments of every act of meaning. He was attracted to the ideas of Bühler because the latter had also tried to combine these moments in the concrete speech act without dissolving the given in the posited. In this, Voloshinov's approach was more reminiscent of the Graz School than of Bakhtin's brand of neo-Kantianism. As Albertazzi (2001: 46–7) has shown, the Graz School maintained that each representational act has three moments:

(1) The act of presentation (*Vorstellung*) with a duration shaped according to the 'consecutive order of content-features'.

(2) A transitional moment in which these content features are then mentally present (if sensorily absent) in a 'simultaneous contemporaneity' that preserves certain temporal traits such as before and after. Here there is a transition from sensory modality to cognitive modality, from what Kanisza (1979) calls 'seeing' to 'thinking', from presentation to *re*presentation (*Darstellung*).

(3) The reactivation of presentation-content by memory: 'the whole is reactualised by the *composition* and *recomposition of its parts* in an *order* which is *not* that in which it was originally constituted'.[2]

The second of these moments is the lower level of what Voloshinov and Vygotskii, probably influenced by Goldstein, called 'inner speech'. It is here that directly perceived forms gain a *symbolic* significance. The forms are previously meaningful in a direct sense, 'on the basis of their being-so (*So-sein*), they are not signs that represent a meaning'. This type of meaning corresponds to what Gibson calls 'affordances', that is, the 'opportunities for interaction that things in the environment possess relative to the sensorimotor capacities of the animal' (Varela et al. 1996: 203). In contradistinction to presentational forms, representational meaning arises in connection with the means of communication, when presented forms are objectified, transformed into mental contents and built into representative (semiotic) terms.

This type of objectification is quite different from the neo-Kantian account of the production of the object of knowledge since it does not, as Albertazzi puts it (2001: 50), 'create a world separate from the reality of transphenomenal things'.[3] Instead, the (veridical) cognitive act is a 'slicing' of the world of transphenomenal things according to a determinate level of its own 'granularity'. By this I mean that in making a veridical statement the transitive boundaries induced by human demarcation coincide with certain intransitive boundaries of the object of that statement. If, for example, I wish to delineate a group of people from a larger crowd, there are various possible transitive boundaries I can draw, but the demarcation is veridical if and only if that boundary does not cognitively bisect a person. The intransitive boundaries between people here constitute the 'granularity' of the crowd.

These ideas suggest that there is a dynamic relationship between perception and cognition, but this does not imply that meaning is something added on to directly perceived structures. The stimulus complex is already meaningful to us as organisms, it has what Neisser (1976) calls 'ecological validity', but we are further motivated in our perceptual activity by social aims. Voloshinov barely touched on the intricacies of this question, but they were taken up by Vygotskii and his collaborators A.R. Luria and A.N. Leont´ev. After Vygotskii's death in 1934, and following the increasingly narrow specialisation of experimental psychology in the Soviet Union, as elsewhere, investigation of these areas was separated from consideration of wider cultural phenomena. Nevertheless, Luria (1973) was able experimentally to examine how 'semantic priming' enhances perceptual performance. He concluded that perceptive activity

> includes the search for the most important elements of information, their comparison with each other, the creation of a hypothesis concerning the meaning of the information as a whole, and the verification of this hypothesis by comparing it with the original features of the object perceived.

Luria's argument is related to developmental psychology rather than to the wider cultural forms that occupied the Bakhtin Circle. However, it remains close to Voloshinov's ideas in that the guiding of attention is a 'social act' that

> can be interpreted as the introduction of factors which are the product, not of the biological maturing of the organism but of forms of activity created in the child during his relations with adults, into the complex regulation of this selective mental activity. (Quoted in Harré and Gillet 1994: 168–70)

Voloshinov's simultaneous orientation within nascent cognitive science and cultural studies could have led to some very interesting analyses of how changing social and cultural structures interact with voluntary perceptual orientation in approaching the *given* structures of the world. Culture would no longer be a separate domain of freedom, but would be an emergent structure that is dependent on, though irreducible to, other natural and social structures.

Exactly how the representative capacities of language relate to perceptual structures was an issue that Voloshinov and the Vygotskii Circle never systematically examined, and that Bakhtin totally ignored. It is an area that has developed in recent years within cognitive linguistics, especially in the work of Ronald Langacker and Leonard Talmy. Like Voloshinov, these thinkers draw explicitly on the figure–ground model developed within Gestalt psychology, but they develop the idea in a different direction. Talmy (1999), for example, argues that linguistic forms 'window attention' over a 'referent scene' according to a certain pattern. Language draws boundaries within which there is continuity and across which there is disjuncture. The examples these thinkers analyse show that linguistic and perceptual structures can be mapped onto one another quite closely.

Barry Smith has philosophically strengthened the realist employment of these ideas by arguing that this delineation does not need to posit some 'spurious transcendent realm' since 'an act of visual perception stands to a visual field as an act of (true) judgement stands to a state of affairs' (1999: 320). Sentences about rabbits are about rabbits not, as Bakhtin would contend, about 'conceptual rabbits' that need to be constructed by degrees.[4] Practical developments in artificial intelligence, robotics and industry further suggest that a necessarily fallible but theoretically coherent synthetic description of the 'common sense world', a 'naive physics', is at least possible. The junk-food industry has, for example, developed sophisticated devices to measure the aroma and flavours of foodstuffs and even, most intriguingly, 'mouthfeel':

> The universal TA-XT2 Texture Analyser, produced by the Texture Technologies Corporation, performs calculations based on data derived from twenty-five separate probes. It is essentially a mechanical mouth. It gauges the most important rheological properties of a food – the bounce, creep, breaking point, density, crunchiness, gumminess, lumpiness, rubberiness, springiness, slip-

periness, smoothness, softness, wetness, juiciness, spreadability, springback, and tackiness. (Schlosser 2001: 128)

From this the industry manages to construct some remarkably convincing, if nutritiously useless (even hazardous), synthetic approximations to naturally occurring eating experiences. There are clearly important lessons to be drawn from the synthetic models of the given structures of the world, for the very failure of a model illuminates something about the structures of the given world itself.[5] The same is surely true of semiotic models of the world, whether in scientific theories or in more mundane utterances.

Cognitive linguists have begun to analyse and theorise the referential capacities of utterances which the Bakhtin and Vygotskii Circles neglected, but they generally fall into the opposite error of not giving due attention to the intersubjective dimension of language use. One could imagine a constructive meeting of these ideas, with the effect that the 'windowing of attention' is linked to social activity, including analyses of the interested and indeed manipulative use of language. An ideological use of language (in the negative sense) does not need to present a false model, but only a one-sided and selective manipulation of figure and ground. A certain cognitive 'slicing' of the world in discursive acts may be designed to 'window' one aspect of reality and 'gap' another, drawing attention towards one 'granularity' of the world while distracting attention away from other, more fundamental but inconvenient facets and dimensions. Discursive encounters in dialogue are now encounters between different patterns of 'windowing', different castings of light and shade on the contours of the given world.

One of the advantages of revising Bakhtinian ideas in this way is that it allows his subtle analysis of discursive interaction to be linked to a consideration of *what* is said (or written) as well as *how* it is said. Like the implicit philosophers of discourse that he detects in 'novels of the second stylistic line', Bakhtin regards the 'direct meaning the word gives to objects' as 'the false front of the word'. What matters to Bakhtin is 'the actual, always self-interested use of this meaning and the way it is expressed by a speaker, defined by his position (profession, class etc.) and the concrete situation' (DN 401; SR 212). Unlike Bühler, who distinguished between the informational characteristics of an utterance that are independent of context or situation (*feldfremd*) and those that are derived from these factors (*feldeigen*) (1927: 183), Bakhtin considers the former to be uniformly false. Thus, the (in)adequacy of all discourses vis-à-vis the extradiscursive world is equal, and the logical propositions made by a discourse are reducible to the interests of that discourse's 'proprietor'.

The problem with this position is that the apparent adequacy of a discourse in explaining a phenomenon is one of the reasons (though by no means the only one) it can exercise authority within a society. One aspect of this adequacy is logical coherence. As Margaret Archer (1996) has shown, the logical properties of theories or beliefs affect the way they can be utilised in society: they create certain 'situational logics'. Logical properties condition the different patterns of the development of ideas in society and mould the contexts of action within the cultural sphere. These differences in situational logic mark subsequent patterns of social and cultural interaction differently, and this in turn conditions modifications of the emergent idea structure. Certain logical contradictions within a ruling belief system may constrain its ability to adapt to new developments, leading to certain strategies of containment at the level of socio-cultural relations (censorship or other strategies to marginalise competing perspectives, and so on) and/or modification of the idea structure itself. One might consider, for example, the strategies adopted by the Catholic Church when faced with Galileo's astronomical observations.[6] The strategy adopted will depend upon other crucial factors at the socio-cultural level, such as the distribution of social power, the level of opposition organisation and the like. Nevertheless, an idea structure that is currently secure both logically and empirically will create a different situational logic in relation to any pressures that might arise at the level of social consensus.

There is thus a dynamic relationship between the socio-cultural level (marked by greater or lesser consensus) and the cultural system (marked by a greater or lesser degree of logical coherence). Bakhtin conflates these levels by treating discourses exclusively as embodiments of social and cultural relations. The logical structure of a discourse and the relations between discourses are thus undoubtedly related, but one is not reducible to the other. This conflation is probably the source of Bakhtin's talk about monologic and dialogic discourses as well as monologic and dialogic relations between discourses.

Critical and political alternatives

Bakhtin's analyses of relations between discourses are some of the most interesting and fruitful features of his entire oeuvre. Especially productive are his reflections on 'authoritative' and 'internally persuasive' discourses in 'Discourse in the Novel', which we discussed in Chapter 5. Again, it is confusing that Bakhtin treats authoritarian and egalitarian relations between discourses as types of discourse, but the point made is very significant:

> The authoritative word demands that we acknowledge it and make it our own, it binds itself to us regardless of the degree it internally persuades us; we encounter it with its authority already fused to it. The authoritative word is in the distanced zone, organically connected to the hierarchical past. It is, so to speak, the word of our fathers. (SR 155; DN 342)

What is being described here is not a type of discourse, but a hierarchical relation between discourses. The authoritative word is accepted because of the subordination of the person it confronts to the bearer of the discourse. There is no organic link between the words of the bearer and the receiver, rather the authoritative perspective is imposed 'regardless of the degree it internally persuades'. The 'internally persuasive word' on the other hand,

> is tightly interwoven with 'one's own' word in the process of its affirmed assimilation ... Its creative productiveness is precisely in the fact that it awakens independent thought and independent new words, that it organises the mass of our words from within ... Moreover, it enters into an intense interaction and struggle with other internally persuasive words. Our ideological formation [*stanovlenie*] is also just such an intense struggle within us for dominance among various verbal-ideological points of view, approaches, directions, evaluations. (DN 345; SR 158)[7]

Here the receiver's world-view is 'organised ... from within', facilitating more coherent and productive independent thinking and articulation. The first passage describes a relation of subjugation of one discourse to another, the second a liberation through structuration. Bakhtin's multifaceted description and analysis of the interplay of these types of relations between discourses in cultural history is alone enough to make his work a crucial point of reference in cultural theory.

But what makes a discourse 'internally persuasive'? Why is one perspective able to gain 'supremacy' in the struggle that constitutes our 'ideological formation'? Bakhtin never really answers these questions, and he rules out the possibility that one discourse might have a greater degree of descriptive or explanatory adequacy by virtue of its relation to the (putative) extradiscursive world. Instead, Bakhtin provides a utopian model of a 'marketplace' of discourses in which discursive 'proprietors' are free to act and enter into exchange. The market provides the conditions for 'equity' (*Gerechtigkeit*) in that speakers are equal as (discursive) commodity owners and must be recognised as such. In the market no-one is supposedly forced to buy or sell, but each does so freely, the better bargain ultimately winning out. Through the unrestrained exchange of discursive 'commodities' there arises a relational logic, dialogism, which on the one hand is descriptive, but on the other is a standard of objective judgement. This becomes a sort of immanent legality of social relations, which guides ideological becoming, rather as Adam Smith's 'hidden hand' guides the development of a market economy in a progressive direction.

In this sense Ken Hirschkop's (1999) attempt to bring Bakhtin's ideas about language and culture together with those of Jürgen Habermas is not misplaced. Though no enthusiast for the market, Habermas, like members of the Bakhtin Circle, is a progressive traditional intellectual aiming to revise further an already heavily revised Marxism in the direction of a neo-Kantian metaethics. Like Bakhtin, Habermas seeks to defend the Enlightenment project, radicalised according to the development of communicative (dialogic) over instrumental (monologic) reason. Habermas, like Bakhtin, also treats society exclusively as a 'moral reality', and his 'unavoidable idealisation' that is the 'ideal speech situation' (Habermas 1976: 117, 110) certainly sounds like Bakhtin's free market of discourse.

One of the main problems with this perspective, however, is that interests and power relations do not 'pollute' discursive exchange as Habermas contends (1985: 130), any more than relations of production 'pollute' exchange relations. Whatever the relative autonomy of theoretical science from ideological bias that is guaranteed by the 'methodology of scientific research programmes', the 'better argument' is never judged against some neo-Kantian realm of 'objective validity', with acceptance being 'unforced', just as most consumer choices are not made according to an objective criterion of utility. Both Bakhtin and Habermas grant to the structures of norms and morality a questionably large degree of autonomy from the social conditions of particular forms of political rule.

One of the many reasons the market is a bad model for democratic freedom is that the consumer choices of subordinate classes reflect their economic subordination. As the system dictates that individual capitalists hold down wages as much as possible in order to compete, so workers and their families are compelled to economise in buying the goods needed to reproduce their labour power. The companies that produce these goods often concentrate on turning out inferior products which seem to satisfy workers' needs, spending vast amounts on advertising, packaging and the like to create and shape a demand for their products without any real concern for the needs of potential consumers. Nutritionally useless junk food, for example, is regularly shown to be disproportionately consumed by the working class, contributing to a considerable disparity between the life expectancies of workers and their rulers the world over (Schlosser 2001). Similarly, workers regularly vote for governments opposed to their own interests not so much because they simply accept the 'mono-logic' of their rulers and believe in the legitimacy of the status quo as because they are intellectually subordinate. This is a matter not of interests (*Willkür*) clouding reason (*Wille*), but of a fragmentation of social consciousness that prevents the development of a coherent perspective on society as a whole. The result is an inability on the part of subordinate classes to recognise and articulate their own interests, leading them to affirm those ideas that exercise social prestige.

Hirschkop (1999: 91–3) notes that Bakhtin understands interests as 'stable passions' which, if followed, lead to 'uncultured' behaviour. Such an approach hopelessly confuses interests and wants. As Giddens notes:

> Interests presume wants, but the concept of interest concerns not the wants as such, but the possible modes of their realisation in given sets of circumstances; and these can be determined as 'objectively' as anything else in social analysis ... [I]nterests imply potential courses of action, in contingent social and material circumstances. (1979: 189)

Consequently, while one might be aware of one's wants, this does not mean one is aware of one's interests, which requires an additional awareness of one's relationship to the natural and social structures that constitute one's environment. In this sense, interests are the social correlates of what Gibson called 'affordances', the perception of which might be veridical or not, but which are nevertheless objective. That ice might not, after all, be thick enough to afford safe walking; that cheeseburger might not, after all, be the best available meal; stopping immigration might not, after all, be the best way to combat the threat of unemployment. Just as the natural world 'affords' us certain things by virtue of our membership of a particular species, so we have interests by virtue of our membership of particular social groups, classes, and so on. It is just as futile for us to try veridically to perceive the social world independently of perceiving our interests as to perceive the natural world independently of what it affords us. Knowledge of the world will always be relative to our own niche within that world, and while this does not make our knowledge of the world *in itself* impossible, it does make it fallible.

As Marx showed in relation to market economics and the Soviet jurist Evgenii Pashukanis (1980) showed in relation to law, any account of social life that is exclusively extrapolated from exchange relations necessarily presents a distorted image. Responsible, rational actors, conscious of their rights and obligations as commodity exchangers, are idealised abstractions of the relationship between buyer and seller from wider social relations. In actual life each actor is tied to the other by relationships of mutual dependence (proletarian and capitalist, retailer and wholesaler, peasant and landlord, and the like). The juridical form corresponds to this isolation of sphere of exchange from relations of production. Once relations of production are given a central position it becomes clear that the social structure is based upon relations between free subjects and subjugated objects (capitalist and proletarian) rather than formally equal legal subjects. In such circumstances, the ability of the ruling discourse to play this leading role is due to the social and intellectual subordination of other perspectives.

The person who developed this idea most fully was Antonio Gramsci, whose kinship with some ideas of the Bakhtin Circle I have outlined elsewhere (Brandist 1996). For Gramsci, as for Bakhtin, a language embodies a world-view, and every national language is stratified according to the institutional structure of society. According to Gramsci, the resulting social dialects are at any moment the products of past socio-political conflicts between world-views, with elements borrowed from victorious languages that exercise prestige. This sedimentary linguistic environment constitutes 'common sense'. While 'common sense' is thus fragmentary and stratified, pulled apart by the various 'spontaneous grammars immanent in the language', every language has its own intellectual order or 'normative grammar', established through 'the reciprocal monitoring, reciprocal teaching and reciprocal "censorship" expressed in such questions as "What did you mean to say?", "What do you mean?", "Make yourself clearer", etc., and in mimicry and teasing' (Gramsci 1985: 180). While 'subaltern' discourses may be in opposition to the written 'normative grammar' of the official language, they are generally less coherent and more diffuse, allowing the alien 'official' perspective to infiltrate them. The resulting 'contradictory consciousness' renders the masses politically impotent and subject to the hegemony of ruling ideas that are verbally affirmed even if against their own interests. To oppose this, the 'normative grammar' of the masses needs to be elaborated, consolidated and centralised, overcoming all 'narrow and provincial psychology' by providing a more 'robust and homogeneous skeleton' for an 'expressive "individualism"' at a higher level' (1985: 181). For Gramsci it is the role of 'organic intellectuals' to develop Marxism to the point where it becomes such a fully elaborated 'normative grammar'. The Communist Party must play the leading role in this by 'penetrating into all the organisations in which the working masses are assembled' and 'impressing on the masses a movement in the direction desired and favoured by objective conditions' (Gramsci 1978: 368). The relationship between 'normative' and 'spontaneous' grammars is a quite different one from that between the ruling class's normativity and the subaltern spontaneity. Instead, Marxism is the 'exemplary phase' of subaltern discourses, 'the only one worthy to become, in an "organic" and "totalitarian" way,[8] the "common" language of a nation in competition with other "phases" and types or schemes that already exist' (Gramsci 1985: 181).

This strategy was certainly alien to the Bakhtin Circle. While Voloshinov and Medvedev often talked about developing Marxism into a systematic world-view that could deal with issues at a level of sophistication to rival bourgeois scholarship, they maintained an agenda more generally associated with what Gramsci termed the traditional intellectual: the elaboration and consolidation of the ideas of the new ruling class that was crystallising in the late 1920s. Both Voloshinov and Medvedev found their own niches within the new society in the years before the Stalinist 'revolution from above' tore the ground from beneath their feet. Marxism and certain other trends of intellectual endeavour were found to complement each other, and the hope was probably that Marxism could become more intellectually cultivated. To influence cultural policy was certainly the aim of *Voskresenie*, and although his attitude to Marxism was different, Bakhtin's own work of the 1920s was similarly directed toward 'enlightened' cohabitation with the new regime.[9] While in the 1930s and 1940s Bakhtin's work chimes rather more discordantly with the cultural policies of the Stalin regime, this is not due to his defection to the cause of organic intellectuals. Even when his work is most redolent with the spirit of populism Bakhtin is concerned with popular culture only to the extent that it renews literary form.

If David-Hillel Ruben is correct that the choice between materialism and idealism is a '"political" choice made on class allegiance' rather than an '"epistemological" choice made on grounds of stronger evidence or more forceful argument' (1979: 109), then the fact that Bakhtin remained wedded to idealism is explainable by his political orientation. Whatever his fellow-travelling motives might have been in the 1920s, by the time he was interviewed in 1973 he reflected on the experience of the 1917 February Revolution with an attitude little short of aristocratic disdain. While the monarchy could not be reinstated, he argued, there was no one to lead. This made inevitable the victory of 'the mass of soldiers, soldiers and peasants in soldiers' coats, for whom nothing is dear, the proletariat, that is not a historical class, it has no values … All its life it struggles only for narrow material wealth' (BDB 118). If values are really underivable from facts, as neo-Kantianism claims, and values need to be brought to the masses from without, then the idealism of the traditional intelligentsia is a logical source for them. If, however, like Gramsci, one regards the masses as able to develop their own socialist world-view through a veridical cognition of their interests, however fragmentary it might be under present conditions, then the systematisation of that perspective through the development of organic intellectuals is a more appealing prospect.

My argument, then, is that there is a 'hard core' within the Bakhtinian research programme that is in principle distinct from Bakhtin's ideological and idealist commitments. This has proved progressive and may do so in the future. But the positive heuristic needs considerable work. I take the 'hard core' to include: the relationality of all discourse; the intimate connection between forms of intersubjectivity and the forms of that relationality; the permeation of every utterance by power relations; the registration of the institutional structure of a society in its linguistic stratification; the extension of generic forms to all discourse; the ideological significance of artistic forms; the political nature of linguistic standards; the struggle of world-views in language. It is my contention that as part of a research programme these 'core' principles have a 'relative autonomy' from their idealist and ideological underpinnings and can better be advanced by means of a 'positive heuristic' based on materialist and realist principles. I have further suggested that there are aspects of the work of the Circle, particularly as found in the work of Voloshinov, that make such revisions consistent with the main thrust of Bakhtinian theory. These revisions promise to facilitate more productive problem shifts by allowing the forms of culture to be more closely related to the specific historical conditions within which they arose than the bifurcation of science that Bakhtin himself supported.

Abbreviations and References in the Text

Works that appear in published collections are followed by the abbreviation for that collection and the page spans they occupy therein. These are in parentheses.

Only two volumes of Bakhtin's complete works in Russian, numbers 2 and 5, had been published before the completion of this book. These volumes have been referred to where possible; otherwise the next most authoritative edition has been used.

AA	M.M. Bakhtin, *Art and Answerability* (trans. Vadim Liapunov), Austin: University of Texas Press, 1990.
AAn	'Art and Answerability' (**AA** 1–3).
AG	'Avtor i geroi v esteticheskoi deiatel´nosti' (**R1920G** 71–255).
AH	'Author and Hero in Aesthetic Activity' (**AA** 4–256).
AZPRZ	'Iz arkhivnykh zapisei k rabote "Problemy rechevykh zhanrov"' (**SS5** 207–86).
B	'The *Bildungsroman* and Its Significance in the History of Realism' (**SGLE** 10–59).
BDB	*Besedy V.D. Duvakina s M.M. Bakhtinym*, Moscow: Progress, 1996.
BSP	*Bakhtin School Papers* (ed. Ann Shukman), *Russian Poetics in Translation* 10, Colchester: University of Essex, 1983.
DA	'Dostoevskii i antichnost´' (**KT** 506–29).
DI	M.M. Bakhtin, *The Dialogic Imagination* (trans. Michael Holquist and Caryl Emerson), Austin: University of Texas Press, 1981.
DIR	'Dopolneniia i izmeneniia k Rable' (**SS5** 80–129).
DLDP	'Discourse in Life and Discourse in Poetry' (**BSP** 5–30).
DN	'Discourse in the Novel' (**DI** 259–422).
DUI	M.I. Kagan, 'Dva ustremlenia iskusstva', in *Filosofskie nauki* 1, 1995, 47–61.
EKK	M.I. Kagan, 'Evreistvo v krizise kul´tury', in *Minuvshee* 6, 1992, 229–36.

EN	'Epic and Novel' (**DI** 3–40).
ER	'Epos i roman' (**VLE** 447–83).
EST	M.M. Bakhtin *Estetika slovesnogo tvorchestva,* Moscow: Iskusstvo, 1979.
F	'O Flobere' (**SS5** 130–7).
FF	P.N. Medvedev, *Formalizm i formalisty,* Leningrad: Izd. Pisalelei, 1934.
FKO	*Freidizm. Kriticheskii ocherk* (**FSGN** 87–190).
FMC	V.N. Voloshinov, *Freudianism: A Marxist Critique* (trans. I.R. Titunik), London: Academic Press, 1976.
FML	P.N. Medvedev, *Formal´nyi metod v literaturovedenii,* Moscow: Labirint, 1993.
FMLS	P.N. Medvedev/M.M. Bakhtin, *The Formal Method in Literary Scholarship* (trans. Albert J. Wehrle), Baltimore: Johns Hopkins University Press, 1978.
FN	'From Notes Made in 1970–71' (**SGLE** 132–58).
FOGN	'K filosofskim osnovam gumanitarnykh nauk' (**SS5** 7–10).
FPND	'From the Prehistory of Novelistic Discourse' (**DI** 41–83).
FSGN	V.N. Voloshinov, *Filosofiia i sotsiologiia gumanitarnykh nauk,* St Petersburg: Asta Press, 1995.
FTCN	'Forms of Time and of the Chronotope in the Novel' (**DI** 84–258).
FVKhR	'Formy vremeni i khronotopa v romane' (**VLE** 234–407).
GIEN	'Gëte kak istorik estestvennykh nauk' (**ITIN** 183–201).
GK	M.I. Kagan, 'German Kogen', in *Nauchnye izvestiia* 2, Akademicheskii tsentr Narkomprosa, Moscow, 1922, 110–24.
GKE	I.I. Kanaev, *Gëte kak estestvoispytatel´,* Leningrad: Nauka, 1970.
GL	'Gëte i Linnei' (**ITIN** 202–18).
GN	'Gëte-Naturalist' (**ITIN** 140–82).
GTP	'Gruppa "tainstvennykh povestei"' (**KT** 448–63).
IO	'Iskusstvo i otvetstvennost´' (**R1920G** 7–8).
IPRS	'Iz predystorii romannogo slova' (**VLE** 408–46).
ITIN	I.I. Kanaev, *Izbrannye trudy po istorii nauki,* St. Petersburg: Aleteiia, 2000.
IVG	I.I. Kanaev, *Iogann Vol´fgang Gëte: Ocherki iz zhizni poeta-naturalista,* Leningrad: Nauka, 1961.
IZ	'Iz zapisei 1970–1971 godov' (**EST** 336–60).
KFP	'K filosofii postupka' (**R1920G** 11–68).
KP	K.K. Vaginov, *Kozlinaia pesn´,* New York: Serebraiannyi vek, 1978.

KPKD   'K pererabotke knigi o Dostoevskom' (**EST** 326–46).
KT   L.V. Pumpianskii, *Klassicheskaia traditsiia: Sobranie trudov po istorii russkoi literatury*, Moscow: Iazyki russkoi kul´tury, 2000.
L   'Lermontov' (**KT** 599–648).
LDV   'Lichnoe delo V.N. Voloshinova' in *Dialog Karnaval Khronotop* 2, 1995, 70–99.
LIZL   M.M. Bakhtin, *Lektsii po istorii zarubezhnoi literatury*, Saransk: Izd. Mordovskogo universiteta, 1999.
LS   'Literary Stylistics' (**BSP** 93–152).
LT   'The Latest Trends in Linguistic Thought in the West' (**BSP** 31–49).
LVB   'Lektsii i vystupleniia M.M. Bakhtina 1924–1925 gg. v zapisiakh L.V. Pumipanskogo', in L.A. Gogotishvili and P.S. Gurevich (eds) *Bakhtin kak filosof*, Moscow: Nauka, 1992, 221–52.
M   'K voprosam teorii romana. K voprosam teorii smekha. <O Maiakovskom>' (**SS5** 48–62).
MFIa   *Marksizm i filosofiia iazyka* (**FSGN** 216–380).
MGN   'K metodologii gumanitarnykh nauk' (**EST** 361–73).
MHS   'Toward a Methodology for the Human Sciences' (**SGLE** 159–72).
MPL   V.N. Voloshinov, *Marxism and the Philosophy of Language* (trans. Ladislav Matejka and I.R. Titunik), Cambridge, Mass.: Harvard University Press, 1973.
NT   'Noveishie techeniia lingvisticheskoi mysli na Zapade' (**FSGN** 190–215).
OK   'Opisanie konspektov, prednaznachennykh dlia ispol´zovaniia v knige "Problemy tvorchestva Dostoevskogo"' (**SS2** 654–758).
OVNM   'Otvet na vopros redaktsii *Novogo mira*' (**EST** 328–36).
PCMF   'The Problem of Content, Material and Form in Verbal Art' (**AA** 257–325).
PDP   M.M. Bakhtin, *Problems of Dostoevsky's Poetics* (trans. Caryl Emerson), Manchester: Manchester University Press, 1984.
PND   'From the Prehistory of Novelistic Discourse' (**DI** 41–83).
PPD   *Problemy poetiki Dostoevskogo* (**PTPD** 205–492).
PRZ   'Problema rechevykh zhanrov' (**SS5** 159–206).
PSG   'The Problem of Speech Genres' (**SGLE** 60–102).
PSMF   'Problema soderzhaniia materiala i formy v slovesnom khudozhestvennom tvorchestve' (**R1920G** 260–318).

PT	'Problema teksta' (**SS5** 306–26).
PTD	*Problemy tvorchestva Dostoevskogo* (**PTPD** 8–179).
PTLPHS	'The Problem of the Text in Linguistics, Philology, and the Human Sciences: An Experiment in Philosophical Analysis' (**SGLE** 103–31).
PTPD	M.M. Bakhtin, *Problemy tvorchestva/poetiki Dostoevskogo*, Kiev: Next, 1994.
PTSS	'Po tu storonu sotsial´nogo. O freidizme' (**FSGN** 25–58).
R1920G	M.M. Bakhtin, *Raboty 1920-kh godov*, Kiev: Next, 1994.
RQNM	'Response to a Question from the *Novy Mir* Editorial Staff' (**SGLE** 1–9).
RT	'Romany Turgeneva i roman *Nakanune*: istoriko-literaturnyi ocherk' (**KT** 381–402).
RV	'Roman vospitaniia i ego znachenie v istorii realizma' (**EST** 118–236).
RW	M.M. Bakhtin, *Rabelais and His World* (trans. Hélène Iswolsky), Bloomington: Indiana University Press, 1984.
S	'Satira' (**SS5** 11–35).
SGLE	M.M. Bakhtin, *Speech Genres and Other Late Essays* (trans. Vern W. McGee), Austin, University of Texas Press, 1986.
SKhR	'Stilistika khudozhestvennoi rechi', *Literaturnaia ucheba* 1(2) 48–66; 1(3) 65–87; 1(5) 43–59, 1930.
SNRG	'Sovremenniki o nauchnykh rabotakh Gёte' (**ITIN** 231–40).
SR	'Slovo v romane' (**VLE** 72–233).
SS2	M.M. Bakhtin, *Sobranie sochinenii* t.2, Moscow: Russkie slovari, 2000.
SS5	M.M. Bakhtin, *Sobranie sochinenii* t.5, Moscow: Russkie slovari, 1996.
SZSP	'Slovo v zhizni i slovo v poezii' (**FSGN** 59–86).
T	M.M. Bakhtin, *Tetralogiia,* Moscow: Labirint, 1998.
TAA	M.I. Kagan, 'Two Aspirations in Art (Form and Content: Non-Objectivity and Subject-Matter)' (trans. F. Goodwin), *Experiment* 3, 1997, 254–64.
TFR	M.M. Bakhtin, *Tvorchestvo Fransua Rable i narodnaia kul´tura srednevekov´ia i Renessansa*, Moscow: Khudozhestvennaia literatua, 1965.
TPA	M.M. Bakhtin, *Towards a Philosophy of the Act* (trans. Vadim Liapunov), Austin: University of Texas Press, 1993.
TRDB	'Toward a Reworking of the Dostoevsky Book' (**PDP** 283–304).

TT   K.K. Vaginov, *The Tower* (trans. B. Sher), 1997 <http://www.websher.net/srl/twr.html> (accessed 13 July 2001).

VDG   'Vik D'Azir i Gëte' (**ITIN** 218–30).

VLE   M.M. Bakhtin, *Voprosy literatury i estetiki*, Moscow: Khudozhestvennaia literatura, 1975.

ZAM   '1961 god. Zametki' (**SS5** 364–74).

Notes

Chapter 1

1. The distinct perspectives will be further developed in Brandist, Shepherd and Tihanov (forthcoming).
2. I am indebted to Dmitrii Iunov for this information.
3. For an assessment of the recent state of the authorship dispute see Hirschkop (1999: 126–40).
4. For a detailed account of the dissertation defence see Pan´kov (2001).
5. This irreconcilable opposition Simmel also terms the 'tragedy of culture' (Simmel 1997: 55–75).
6. It is, however, likely that the Circle had some familiarity with the work of Lask, who was known to some prominent Russian commentators at the time, such as S.A. Alekseev (Askol´dov), Bogdan Kistiakovskii and Sergius Hessen.
7. The influence of Marrism on the shape of Bakhtin's work is completely overlooked in both extant biographies (Clark and Holquist (1984a); Konkin and Konkina (1993)).

Chapter 2

1. For a detailed analysis of the importance of the culture–life opposition in Bakhtin's early work see Tihanov (2000a).
2. Chukovskii argues that Vaginov's cyclical mythology of history derives from Oswald Spengler's *Der Untergang des Abendlandes* (*The Decline of the West*, 1918–1922) (Spengler 1980). The cyclical account of history, however, dates back at least to Giambattista Vico (1668–1744).
3. This issue has more recently been raised from a very different philosophical perspective by J.J. Gibson, who argues for a realist unity of 'ecological science' and mathematical science (Gibson 1982; 1986).
4. This is also the source of the resemblances between Bakhtin's work and that of Martin Buber and Emmanuel Levinas. The latter thinkers are, however, much more deeply implicated in Jewish mysticism than Bakhtin.
5. Bakhtin's only apparent mention of Christiansen is a dismissive reference to his 'monologic aesthetics' in the Dostoevsky books (PDP 21; PTD 30; PPD 225).
6. A similar connection with regard to German literature and phenomenology was made by Oskar Walzel, in an article known to the Circle and which appeared in Russian in 1922 (Val´tsel´ 1922).
7. Bakhtin was not, however, the first to distinguish between feelings of empathy and sympathy in the context of aesthetics. The Graz School philosopher Stephan Witasek (1904) was particularly associated with this distinction in the early years of the twentieth century, and Bakhtin

197

indicates his familiarity with this source in the *Author and Hero* essay (AG 136; AH 61). On Witasek's aesthetics, including his ideas on empathy and sympathy, see Smith (1996).

8. Walzel had already drawn attention to the unstable and shifting identity of Dostoevsky's heroes and associated this with philosophical relativism as early as 1920. Bakhtin does not acknowledge this source (Val´tsel´ 1922: 52) and it is unclear whether he drew upon it.

Chapter 3

1. K.N. Kornilov (1879–1957). Director of the Moscow Institute of Experimental Psychology, in which L.S. Vygotsky and A.R. Luria, among others, began their careers.

2. On the many early Soviet attempts to combine Gestalt theory and Marxism see Scheerer (1980). Max Horkheimer also regarded Gestalt psychology and Marxism to be complementary, on which see Harrington (1996: 121–3).

3. On this see Burwick and Douglass (1992). The translated Kanaev article is published under the name of Bakhtin here (76–97).

4. Bühler called Freud a '*Stoffdenker*' or content-thinker, a thinker concerned exclusively with the content rather than the form of thinking. In addition, Freud was criticised for formulating theories without sufficient empirical evidence, explaining everything in the present in terms of the past and ignoring such matters as *Funktionslust* (pleasure in functioning) and *Schöperfreude* (joy in creativity). It is significant that Bühler was one of the most important influences on philosophers and linguists of the period as well as on psychologists. Among those systematically influenced were Roman Jakobson and the Prague School as well as the Polish phenomenologist Roman Ingarden, with whose works those of the Bakhtin Circle have often been compared.

5. It should be noted that Goldstein's perspective differed in important ways from that of the Graz and Berlin Schools. Goldstein happened to be the cousin of a philosopher who was to prove very important for Voloshinov and other members of the Circle, Ernst Cassirer. Goldstein and Cassirer were significant influences on each other, and each referred to the other in his works. Harrington (1996: 148) argues that 'intensive correspondence between the two men through the 1920s shows that not only was Goldstein writing his material with a pen dipped in the thinking of the Marburg School, but that Cassirer was granting Goldstein's brain-damaged soldiers a distinct programmatic status in his own thinking'. For more on Cassirer's influence on Goldstein see Goldstein (1948: 32). On Goldstein's influence on Cassirer see Cassirer (1933; 1957) Krois (1992: 448–52) and Itzkoff (1971). The compatibility of the ideas of Goldstein with other philosophers who influenced the Circle, such as Bergson, Cassirer and Husserl, was claimed by Schutz (1971). For a general overview of Goldstein's writings on language see Noppeney and Wallesch (2000).

6. Scheerer (1980: 127) claims to have detected the influence of Goldstein on the work of A.R. Luria written as early as 1927. It should also be noted that Goldstein (1948: 96–8) later endorsed Vygotskii's revision of his account of inner speech, which the latter criticised for being too general and inadequately related to language

7. Noppeney and Wallesch (2000) show that Goldstein introduced the Gestalt notions of figure and ground into his analyses of brain processes and incipient semantics from 1927 onward, and from 1936 was explicitly linking them to Bühler's representative function of language.

8. See, for example, Rubenstein (1944: 191) and Gurwitsch (1949). Goldstein was also an important influence on Maurice Merleau-Ponty (1962), on whose resemblances with Bakhtin see Gardiner (1998 and 2000). It is also notable that Roman Jakobson turned to the question of aphasia in the 1950s, on which see Luria (1977).

9. The notion of *refraction* will be discussed in the section on Voloshinov's *Marxism and the Philosophy of Language*, below.

10. On the notion of *reification* in the Bakhtin Circle see Tihanov (1997). The significant difference between reification and objectification should be stressed. In a classic neo-Kantian move, the former is objectification (the production of the object of cognition) according to the methods of the 'exact' sciences, while the latter is more neutral and also encompasses the 'human sciences'. Reification in the study of literature thus signifies an impermissible application of the methods of the natural sciences to material that constitutes the object domain of the human sciences.

11. In the Russian translation of Walzel's 1924 article 'Das Wesen des dichterischen Kunstwerks' (The Essence of Poetic Works of Art) (Val´tsel´ 1928a: 2–3) *Gehalt* is translated as *soderzhimyi,* meaning 'that which is contained', in contrast to the more usual *soderzhanie* (content, German: *Inhalt*) and which Zhirmunskii, the editor of the publication explicitly connected to worldview (*mirovozzrenie*). *Gestalt* is translated as *oblik,* a term which suggests both the appearance or aspect of something, and its manner or 'cast of mind' in the sense of character. A style is now defined as the appearance of an ideology (Zhirmunskii 1928).

12. The multifunctional model of the speech act is central to Bühler's 'organon model', and was later adopted and expanded upon by Roman Jakobson (Holenstein 1981) and Roman Ingarden.

13. Details of the revisions and a translation of the added chapter are provided by Kaiser (1984).

14. For a clear explication of this difference in 'realist phenomenology' see Schuhmann and Smith (1985). See also Shanon (1993) for an explication of the distinction in contemporary psychology.

15. Bakhtin only speaks of the refraction of authorial *intention* or *meaning* (*smysl*) through the voices or intentions of others.

16. The Circle had direct contact with the GAKhN debates through Matvei Kagan, who worked there at precisely this time (TAA: 254).

17. On this see Lähteenmäki (2001: 67–71).

18. On the ideas behind this see the discussion of the legal subject in Chapter 1.

Chapter 4

1. For a sustained analysis of this distinction see Tihanov (2000b: Chapter 7).
2. Spielhagen's ideas had been brought into Russian scholarship on the novel by A.N.Veselovskii as early as 1886 (Veselovskii 1939: 5ff.).
3. This is again Bakhtin's application of the Marburg School notion that jurisprudence is the 'mathematics' of the human sciences.
4. 'An utterance of another person included in the author's statement. Depending on lexico-syntactical means and properties, the transmission of *chuzhaia rech´* may be direct or indirect' (Rozental´ and Telenkova 1972: 484).
5. The notes Bakhtin took from Spitzer's book have now been published, helping us to assess the influence of Spitzer on the Dostoevsky book (OK 735–58). Spitzer, it seems was not simply a subjectivist, but an eclectic thinker who also drew upon Husserl and Freud at various points and influenced a variety of different thinkers in Russia at the time. On this see Odesskii (1988).

Chapter 5

1. Note Cassirer's use of this term, which in the translated texts quoted below appears as 'spirit': 'We should use it in a functional sense as a comprehensive name for all those functions which constitute and build up the world of human culture' (Krois 1987: 77–8).
2. Bakhtin would already have been familiar with most of the main sources of Marr's ideas on the origin of language and primitive mentality, Lévy-Bruhl, Wilhelm Wundt and Ludwig Noiré, from Cassirer (1955a). Bukharin had also cited Lévy-Bruhl, who was a student of Durkheim, as an authority on primitive mentality (Bukharin 1926: 206–7).
3. As Alpatov notes, the claims by Marr and his followers that their ideas were based on 'dialectical materialism' rested on 'unsubstantiated ascription of their own ideas to the founders of Marxism; quoting out of context; and deliberate silence about the actual views of Marx and Engels'. In actuality, Marr's linguistic ideas, including the thesis of the class character of language, significantly predated his attempts to connect his contentions to Marxism after the 1917 revolution (Alpatov 1991: 17–18; 2000: 176–7).
4. Medvedev's personal involvement with Freidenberg and Frank-Kamenetskii in 1929 was on a joint project entitled 'The Paleontology and Sociology of the Epic'.
5. This positive attitude led one French scholar of Marrism to consider Voloshinov's book to be a Marrist text. However, the Marrists generally received Voloshinov's book in a hostile fashion (Alpatov 1998: 527). Alpatov contends, reasonably, that Marr's works were simply 'taken account of' in MPL and Marrism is certainly not accorded the status of 'Marxism in linguistics' (1995: 125). Voloshinov's last work (LS; SKhR) is much more superficially Marrist, although it may be verging on parody. On this see Parrott (1984).

6. It seems that at least one footnote reference to Marr was excised from the published version of this essay by the Russian editors (Hirschkop 1999: 123n).

7. The affinity of Marr and Voloshinov was noted as early as 1987 (L'Hermitte 1987: 28), although the connection was relatively unexplored.

8. Bakhtin was certainly familiar with this text, even if only through Gustav Shpet's critical discussion, from which Bakhtin made many notes. I am indebted to Brian Poole for this information.

9. Interestingly, however, it has been claimed that some of Marr's ideas actually derived from Wundt (Thomas 1957: 113–14; Zvegintsev 1960: I, 228), while Bukharin had also cited Wundt positively on related matters (Bukharin 1926: 95, 206).

10. It should be noted that Marr too drew upon Veselovskii (Alpatov 1991: 9), making his influence in the 1930s particularly strong. On the contemporary Russian sources see Tihanov (1999: 48–50); on the older German sources see Todorov (1984: 86–91) and Poole (2001a).

11. In drawing this parallel Bakhtin may have been referring back to the Circle's earlier concerns with the 'Third Renaissance'. On this see Nikolaev (1997).

12. The cultic connotations of laughter which Bakhtin mentions probably derived from Freidenberg.

13. On the specific passages Bakhtin drew upon from these books see Poole (1998).

14. The terms of this debate may also have been influenced by the 1936 disputation between the Marrists and traditional folklorists over the alleged aristocratic roots of the epic, which even reached the pages of the government newspaper *Izvestiia*. In an interview with the outspoken Marrist I.I. Meshchaninov entitled 'Dead Theory and the Living Epic', the traditional folklorists were chastised for 'scientific conservatism' and 'literary purism', which led them to consider the epic as a popular elaboration of the literature of the dominant class (Sorlin 1990: 279).

Chapter 6

1. The notion of 'semantic clusters' based on a 'symbiosis of perceptions in the primitive mind' derives from Lévy-Bruhl (Thomas 1957: 80).

2. For more on Bakhtin's debt to Freidenberg, charitably presented as a coincidence, see Moss (1984: 150–91).

3. However, Marr himself had objected to Lévy-Bruhl's notion of 'prelogical thought' on the basis that it was an oversimplification. Marr distinguished more than one period of prelogical thought (Thomas 1957: 114).

4. It is interesting to compare Nikolai Bakhtin's characterisation of perception as the 'building' of a stable reality out of 'shapeless material'. Looking at the starry sky, a Greek of the fourth century BC. '*saw* there (and not only thought) the slow revolution of concave spheres with luminous points fixed on them'. We, however, *see* something quite different (Bachtin 1963: 102–3). Thus for both the brothers Bakhtin there

is no distinction between seeing and thinking, perception and cognition, the structures of things and the structures of thoughts.

Chapter 7

1. On the influence of Croce on the Circle's notion of discursive genres see Tihanov (2000b: 99n28). Bakhtin actually cites this very passage from Croce, without acknowledgement, in some archival notes made in preparation for this article (AZPRZ 273).
2. Marr argued that 'language acts as a drive belt [*privodnoi remen*] in the region of the superstructural categories of society' (quoted in Alpatov 1991: 35).
3. Note that the currently available translation of this passage is significantly flawed.
4. There is no evidence that Bakhtin was familiar with Reinach's work, but it is certainly possible. I examine the respective ideas of Bakhtin and Reinach in a future paper.
5. The term 'speech act' was first used by Bühler (1990) and integrated into anglophone language theory by Alan Gardiner (1932). See also Smith (1990). It is important to note, however, that the resemblances between Bakhtin's theory and that of Searle have been challenged by Linell and Marková (1993).
6. On this paradox see Tihanov (2000b: 269) and Côté (2000: 24).
7. The translation of '*prazdnik vozrozhdeniia*' as 'homecoming festival' is especially misleading given the importance of rebirth in Bakhtin's writing on carnival. On this see Shepherd (1996: 144, 157n.).

Chapter 8

1. On this in relation to Lewin, Bühler and Cassirer see Wildgen (2001).
2. Benny Shanon (1993) has recently presented a similar perspective, without reference to the Graz School or the Bakhtin Circle, but with reference to Vygotskii, as an alternative to the 'representational-computational view of mind' which dominated cognitive science until recently. The parallels between the inadequacies of representationalism and the neo-Kantian paradigm are often uncanny.
3. Bakhtin's 'superbeing' [*nadbytie*] (FN 137–8; IZ 341–2) that we discussed in the previous chapter is a classic example of the creation of such a spurious world.
4. Compare here Daubert's critique of Husserl's 'noema' theory of meaning as reported in Schuhmann and Smith (1985).
5. This is a powerful argument against the notion that a theory of the structures of common-sense experience is impossible, as advanced in different ways by Heidegger, Merleau-Ponty and Wittgenstein. In actual fact several areas of such a theory have already been developed. On this see Smith (1995).
6. Perhaps the best analysis of this in relation to scientific theories is Lakatos (1970).

7. Emerson and Holquist translate '*gospodstvo*' as 'hegemony'. Since the latter is strongly linked to the term '*gegemoniia*' in political discourse in Russia at the time, I choose the more general term 'dominance'.

8. As the editors of Gramsci (1971: 335) point out, Gramsci uses 'totalitarian' in the sense of 'simultaneously "unified" and "all absorbing"' rather than in its contemporary sense of associated with authoritarianism.

9. In this context Bakhtin's resemblances with the Eurasian movement are interesting. On this see Brandist (1995: 33–4) and Tihanov (2000c).

Bibliography

For the works of the Circle referred to in this book see 'Abbreviations and References in the Text'. The works of the Circle are still appearing in Russian and English, and are already large in number, with some materials but fragments. For the most comprehensive list of these see the primary analytical database at the Sheffield University Bakhtin Centre site on the World Wide Web at the following URL: <http://www.shef.ac.uk/uni/academic/A-C/bakh/bakhtin.html>

There are now several thousand works about the Bakhtin Circle. The most extensive bibliography of the work of and about the Circle is available on the secondary analytical database at the Sheffield University Bakhtin Centre site on the World Wide Web at the URL given above. Given the huge amount of material already available, the bibliography here refers only to works directly relevant to the current volume and concentrates on English language material. Entries marked with an asterisk include substantial bibliographies. (Most recent editions and English translations are given where available.)

Albertazzi, L. (2001) 'The Primitives of Presentation', in L. Albertazzi (ed.) (2001), 29–60.
—— (ed.) (2001) *The Dawn of Cognitive Science: Early European Contributions*, Dordrecht, Boston and London: Kluwer, 29–60.
Alpatov, V.M. (1991) *Istoriia odnogo mifa: Marr i marrizm*, Moscow: Nauka.
—— (1995) 'Kniga "Marksizm i filosofiia iazyka" i istoriia iazykoznaniia', *Voprosy iazykoznaniia* 5, 108–26.
—— (1998) 'Lingvisticheskoe soderzhanie knigi *Marksizm i filosofiia iazyka*', in T, 517–29.
—— (2000) 'What is Marxism in Linguistics?', in C. Brandist and G. Tihanov (eds) (2000).
Archer, M.S. (1996) *Culture and Agency: The Place of Culture in Social Theory*, Cambridge: Cambridge University Press.
Ash, M. (1998) *Gestalt Psychology in German Culture 1890–1967: Holism and the Quest for Objectivity*, Cambridge: Cambridge University Press.
Bachtin, N.M. (1963) *Lectures and Essays*, Birmingham: University of Birmingham.
Bauman, Z. (1993) *Postmodern Ethics*, Oxford: Blackwell.
Bazylev, V.N. and Neroznak, V.P. (2001) 'Traditsiia, mertsaiushchaia v tolshche istorii', in V.P. Neroznak (ed.) (2001) 3–20.
Belinskii, V.G. (1962a) 'Thoughts and Notes on Russian Literature', in R.E. Matlaw (ed.) (1962) 3–32.
—— (1962b) 'A Survey of Russian Literature in 1847: Part Two', in R.E. Matlaw (ed.) (1962) 33–82.
Bell, M.M. and Gardiner, M. (eds) (1998) *Bakhtin and the Human Sciences: No Last Words*, Thousand Oaks and London: Sage.

Bergson, H. (1956) 'Laughter', in W. Sypher (ed.) *Comedy*, Baltimore and London: Johns Hopkins University Press, 61–190.

Berrong, R.M. (1986) *Rabelais and Bakhtin: Popular Culture in 'Gargantua and Pantagruel'*, Lincoln: University of Nebraska Press.

Bhaskar, R. (1979) *The Possibility of Naturalism*, Brighton: Harvester Press.

Bloor, D. (1997) *Wittgenstein, Rules and Institutions*, London: Routledge.

Bottomore, T. and Goode, P. (eds) (1978) *Austro-Marxism*, Oxford: Clarendon Press.

Brachev, V.S. (2000) *Russkoe masonstvo XX veka*, St. Petersburg: Stomma.

Brandist, C. (1995) 'Politicheskoe znachenie bor´by s ideiami Sossiura v rabotakh shkoly Bakhtina', *Dialog Karnaval Khronotop* 2, 32–43.

—— (1996) 'The Official and the Popular in Gramsci and Bakhtin', *Theory, Culture and Society* 2, 13, 59–74.

—— (1997) 'Bakhtin, Cassirer and Symbolic Forms', *Radical Philosophy*, 85, 20–27.

—— (1999a), 'Bakhtin's Grand Narrative: the Significance of the Renaissance', *Dialogism* 3.

—— (1999b) 'Ethics, Politics and the Potential of Dialogism', *Historical Materialism*, 4.

—— (2000) 'Bakhtin, Marxism and Russian Populism', in C. Brandist and G. Tihanov (eds) (2000), 70–93.

—— (2001a) 'El marxismo y el nuevo "giro ético"', *Herramienta* 14, 125–39.

—— (2001b) 'The Hero at the Bar of Eternity: The Bakhtin Circle's Juridical Theory of the Novel', *Economy and Society* 30 (2), 208–28.

Brandist, C., Shepherd, D. and Tihanov, G. (eds) (forthcoming) *The Bakhtin Circle: In the Master's Absence*, Manchester: Manchester University Press.

Brandist, C. and Tihanov, G. (eds) (2000) *Materializing Bakhtin: The Bakhtin Circle and Social Theory*, Basingstoke: Macmillan.

Brentano, F. (1969) *The Origin of the Knowledge of Right and Wrong* (trans. R.M. Chisholm and E.H. Schneewind), London: Routledge and Kegan Paul.

Bruhn, J. and Lundquist, J. (eds) (2001) *The Novelness of Bakhtin: Perspectives and Possibilities*, Copenhagen: Museum Tusculanum Press.

Bühler, K. (1919) 'Kritische Musterung der Neureren Theorien des Satzes', *Indogermanisches Jahrbuch* 6, 1–20.

—— (1922) 'Vom Wesen der Syntax', in V. Klemperer, and E. Lerch (eds) (1922) *Idealistische Neuphilologie: Festschrift für Karl Vossler*, Heidelberg: Carl Winter, 54–84.

—— (1926) 'Die Krise der Psychologie', *Kant-Studien* 31, 455–526.

—— (1927) *Die Krise der Psychologie*, Jena: G. Fischer.

—— (1990) *Theory of Language: The Representational Function of Language* (trans. D.F. Goodwin), Amsterdam and Philadelphia: John Benjamins.*

Bukharin, N. (1926) *Historical Materialism: A System of Sociology*, London: Allen and Unwin.

Burckhardt, J. (1990) *The Civilization of the Renaissance in Italy* (trans. S.G.C. Middlemore), Harmondsworth: Penguin.

Burwick, F. and Douglas, P. (eds) (1992) *The Crisis in Modernism: Bergson and the Vitalist Controversy*, Cambridge: Cambridge University Press.

Cassirer, E. (1923) *Substance and Function* and *Einstein's Theory of Relativity* (trans. Swabey and Swabey), Chicago and London: Open Court.

—— (1933) 'Le Language et la Construction du monde des objets', *Journal de Psychologie normale et Pathologique*.

—— (1946) *Language and Myth* (trans. S. Langer), New York: Dover Publications.

—— (1949) '"Spirit" and "Life" in Contemporary Philosophy', in P.A. Schlipp (ed.) *The Philosophy of Ernst Cassirer*, Illinois: Evanston, 857–80.

—— (1950) *The Problem of Knowledge: Philosophy, Science and History Since Hegel* (trans. W. Woglom and C. Hendel), New Haven and London: Yale University Press.

—— (1951) *The Philosophy of the Enlightenment* (trans. F. Koelln and J.P. Pettegrove), Princeton: Princeton University Press.

—— (1953) *The Platonic Renaissance in England* (trans. J.P. Pettegrove), London: Nelson.

—— (1955a) *The Philosophy of Symbolic Forms, Vol. 1: Language* (trans. R. Manheim), New Haven and London: Yale University Press.

—— (1955b) *The Philosophy of Symbolic Forms, Vol. 2: Mythical Thought* (trans. R. Manheim), New Haven and London: Yale University Press.

—— (1957) *The Philosophy of Symbolic Forms, Vol. 3: The Phenomenology of Knowledge* (trans. R. Manheim), New Haven and London: Yale University Press.

—— (1963) *The Individual and the Cosmos in Renaissance Philosophy* (trans. M. Domandi), New York: Harper and Row.

—— (1996) *The Philosophy of Symbolic Forms, Vol. 4: The Metaphysics of Symbolic Forms* (trans Krois), New Haven and London: Yale University Press.

Catano, J.V. (1988) *Language, History, Style: Leo Spitzer and the Critical Tradition*, Routledge, London.*

Cattaruzza, S. (1996) 'Meinong and Bühler', *Axiomathes* 7 (1–2), 103–7.

Christiansen, B. (1909) *Philosophie der Kunst*, Hanau.

Chukovskii, K. (1989) 'Iz vospominanii', *Wiener Slawistischer Almanach* 24, 97–114.

Clark, K. (1995) *Petersburg, Crucible of Cultural Revolution*, Cambridge, Mass.: Harvard University Press.

Clark, K. and Holquist, M. (1984a) *Mikhail Bakhtin*, Cambridge, Mass. and London: Belknap Press.*

—— (1984b) 'The Influence of Kant in the Early Work of M.M. Bakhtin', in Joseph P. Strelka (ed.) (1984) *Literary Theory and Criticism: A Festschrift in Honor of René Wellek*, New York: Peter Lang, 299–313.

Coates, R. (1998) *Christianity in Bakhtin: God and the Exiled Author*, Cambridge: Cambridge University Press.

Cohen, H. (1871) *Kants Theorie der Erfahrung*, Zweite neubearbeitete Auflage, Berlin: Dümmler.

—— (1904) *Ethik des reinen Willens*, Berlin: Bruno Cassirer.

—— (1923) *Aesthetik des reinen Gefühls*, Berlin: Bruno Cassirer.

Côté, J.-F. (2000) 'Bakhtin's Dialogism Reconsidered through Hegel's "Monologism": the Dialectical Foundations of Aesthetics and Ideology in Contemporary Human Sciences', in C. Brandist and G. Tihanov (eds) (2000), 20–42.

Croce, B. (1978) *Aesthetic: As Science of Expression and General Linguistic* (trans. D. Ainslie), Boston: Nonpareil Books.

Crowell, S.G. (1996) 'Emil Lask: Aletheiology and Ontology', in *Kant-Studien* 87, 69–88.

Crowley, T. (2001) 'Bakhtin and the History of Language', in K. Hirschkop and D. Shepherd (eds) (2001) 177–200.

Dunlop, F. (1991) *Scheler*, London: Claridge Press.

Eagleton, T. (1990) *The Ideology of the Aesthetic*, Oxford: Blackwell.

Emerson, C. (1997) *The First Hundred Years of Mikhail Bakhtin*, Chichester, N.J.: Princeton University Press.

Erlich, V. (1969) *Russian Formalism: History-Doctrine*, The Hague: Mouton.*

Ermarth, M. (1978) *Wilhelm Dilthey: the Critique of Historical Reason*, Chicago and London: University of Chicago Press.

Ferguson, W.K. (1948) *The Renaissance in Historical Thought: Five Centuries of Interpretation*, Cambridge, Mass.: Riverside Press.

Freiberger-Sheikholeslami, E. (1982) 'Forgotten Pioneers of Soviet Semiotics', in M. Herzfeld and M. Lenhart (eds) *Semiotics 1980*, New York and London: Plenum Press, 155–65.

Freidenberg, O.M. (1991) 'The Main Goals Used in the Collective Study of the Plot of *Tristan and Iseult*', *Soviet Studies in Literature* 27 (1), 54–66.

—— (1997) *Poetika siuzheta i zhanra*, Moscow: Labirint.

Frings, M.S. (1997) *The Mind of Max Scheler*, Milwaukee: Marquette University Press.*

Gardiner, A. (1932) *The Theory of Speech and Language*, Oxford: Clarendon Press.

Gardiner, M. (1992) *The Dialogics of Critique: M.M. Bakhtin and the Theory of Ideology*, London: Routledge.*

—— (1996a) 'Alterity and Ethics: a Dialogical Perspective', *Theory, Culture and Society* 13, 2, 121–44.

—— (1996b) 'Foucault, Ethics and Dialogue,' *History of the Human Sciences* 9 (3), 27–46.

—— (1998) '"The Incomparable Monster of Solipsism": Bakhtin and Merleau-Ponty', in M.M. Bell and M. Gardiner (eds) (1998) 128–44.

—— (2000) '"A Very Understandable Horror of Dialectics": Bakhtin and Marxist Phenomenology', in C. Brandist and G. Tihanov (eds) (2000) 119–41.

Gasparov, B. (1996) 'Development or Rebuilding: Views of Academician T.D. Lysenko in the Context of the Late Avant-Garde', in J.E. Bowlt and O. Matich (eds) *Laboratory of Dreams: The Russian Avant-Garde and Cultural Experiment*, Stanford: Stanford University Press.

Gibson, J.J. (1982) 'The Problem of Event Perception', in E.J. Reed and R. Jones (eds) *Reasons for Realism: Selected Essays of James J. Gibson*, Hillsdale: Lawrence Erlbaum, 203–16.

—— (1986) *The Ecological Approach to Visual Perception*, Hillsdale: Lawrence Erlbaum.

Giddens, A. (1979) *Central Problems in Social Theory: Action, Structure and Contradiction in Social Analysis*, Berkeley, Calif.: University of California Press.

Ginzburg, C. (1992) *The Cheese and the Worms: the Cosmos of a Sixteenth-Century Miller*, London: Penguin.

Goldstein, K. (1948) *Language and Language Disturbances*, New York: Grune and Stratton.

Gramsci, A. (1971) *Selections from the Prison Notebooks* (trans. Q. Hoare and G. Nowell-Smith), London: Lawrence and Wishart.

—— (1978) *Selections from Political Writings 1921–1926*, London : Lawrence and Wishart.

—— (1985) *Selections from the Cultural Writings* (trans. W. Boelhower), London: Lawrence and Wishart.

Greenblatt, S. (1980) *Renaissance Self-Fashioning: From More to Shakespeare*, Chicago and London: University of Chicago Press.

Gurwitsch, A. (1949) 'Gelb-Goldstein's Concept of "Concrete" and "Categorial" Attitude and the Phenomenology of Ideation', *Philosophy and Phenomenological Research* 10 (2), 172–196.

Habermas, J. (1976) *Legitimation Crisis*, London: Heinemann.

—— (1985) *The Philosophical Discourse of Modernity*, Cambridge: Polity.

Harré, R. and Gillet, G. (1994) *The Discursive Mind*, London: Sage.

Harrington, A. (1996) *Reenchanted Science: Holism in German Culture from Wilhelm II to Hitler*, Princeton: Princeton University Press.

Hartmann, N. (1932) *Ethics* (3 vols, trans. Stanton Coit), London: Allen and Unwin.

Hegel, G.W.F. (1975) *Aesthetics* (trans. T.M. Knox), Oxford: Clarendon Press.

—— (1977) *Phenomenology of Spirit* (trans. A.V. Miller), Oxford: Oxford University Press.

Hendel, C. (1955) 'Introduction', in Cassirer, E. (1955a), 1–65.

Hirschkop, K. (1998) 'Bakhtin Myths, or Why We All Need Alibis', *South Atlantic Quarterly* 97 (3/4), 579–98.

—— (1999) *Mikhail Bakhtin: An Aesthetic for Democracy*, Oxford, Oxford University Press.*

Hirschkop, K. and Shepherd, D. (eds) (2001) *Bakhtin and Cultural Theory* (second edition), Manchester: Manchester University Press.*

Holenstein, E. (1981) 'On the Poetry and the Plurifunctionality of Language', in B. Smith (ed.) *Structure and Gestalt: Philosophy and Literature in Austria-Hungary and Her Successor States*, Amsterdam: John Benjamins, 1–44.

Holquist, M. (1990) *Dialogism: Bakhtin and His World*, London: Routledge.

Husserl, E. (1997) *Husserliana, Vol. 7: Thing and Space: Lectures of 1907*, Dortrecht, Boston and London: Kluwer.

Innis, R. (1988) 'The Thread of Subjectivity: Philosophical Remarks on Bühler's Language Theory', in A. Eschbach (ed.) *Karl Bühler's Theory of Language*, Amsterdam and Philadelphia: John Benjamins.

Itzkoff, S.W. (1971) *Ernst Cassirer : Scientific Knowledge and the Concept of Man*, Notre Dame, London: University of Notre Dame Press.

Ivanov, V.I. (1952) *Freedom and the Tragic Life: A Study of Dostoevsky* (trans. N. Cameron), New York: Noonday Press.

Joravsky, D. (1989) *Russian Psychology: A Critical History*, Oxford: Blackwell.*

Kagan, Iu. (1998) 'People Not of our Time', in D. Shepherd (ed.) (1998), 3–17.

Kagarlitsky, B. (1989) *The Thinking Reed: Intellectuals and the Soviet State 1917 to the Present* (trans. B. Pearce), London: Verso.

Kaiser, M. (1984) 'P.N. Medvedev's "the Collapse of Formalism"', in B.A. Stolz et al. (eds) *Language and Literary Theory*, Michigan: Ann Arbor, 405–41.

Kanisza, G. (1979) 'Two Ways of Going Beyond the Information Given', in *Organization in Vision: Essays on Gestalt Perception*, New York: Praeger, 1–24.

Kerruish, V. (1991) *Jurisprudence as Ideology*, London: Routledge.

Khoruzhii, S.S. (1994) 'Transformatsii slavianofil´skoi idei v XX veke', *Voprosy filosofii* 11, 52–6.

Kiesow, K. (1990) 'Marty on Form and Content in Language', in K. Mulligan (ed.) *Mind Meaning and Metaphysics: The Philosophy of Anton Marty*, Dordrecht: Kluwer, 51–65.

Köhnke, K.C. (1991) *The Rise of Neo-Kantianism: German Academic Philosophy Between Idealism and Positivism*, Cambridge: Cambridge University Press.

Konkin, S.S. and Konkina, L.S. (1993) *Mikhail Bakhtin, stranitsy zhizni i tvorchestva*, Saransk: Mordovskoe knizhnow izdatel´stvo.

Korsch, K. (1970) *Marxism and Philosophy*, London: New Left Books.

Krois, J. (1987) *Cassirer: Symbolic Forms and History*, New Haven and London: Yale University Press.*

—— (1992) 'Cassirer, Neo-Kantianism and Metaphysics', *Revue de Métaphysique et de Morale* 4, 437–53.

Kusch, M. (1995) *Psychologism: a Case Study in the Sociology of Philosophical Knowledge*, London: Routledge.*

Kusch, M. (1999) *Psychological Knowledge: A Social History and Philosophy*, London: Routledge.

L'Hermitte, R. (1987) *Marr, Marrisme, Marristes: une page de l'histoire de la linguistique soviétique*, Paris: Institut d'études slaves.

Lähteenmäki, M. (2001) *Dialogue, Language and Meaning: Variations on Bakhtinian Themes*, Jyväskyla: University of Jyväskyla.

Lakatos, I. (1970) 'Falsification and the Methodology of Scientific Research Programmes', in I. Lakatos and A. Musgrave (eds) (1970) *Criticism and the Growth of Knowledge*, Cambridge: Cambridge University Press, 91–197.

Linell, P. and Marková, I. (1993) 'Acts in Discourse: From Monological Speech Acts to Dialogical Inter-Acts', *Journal for the Theory of Social Behaviour* 23 (2), 173–95.

Lodge, D. (1990) *After Bakhtin: Essays on Fiction and Criticism*, London: Routledge.

Lovibond, S. (1983) *Realism and Imagination in Ethics*, Oxford: Blackwell.

Lukács, G. (1935) 'Roman kak burzhuaznaia epopeia', *Literaturnaia entsiklodediia* t. 9, Moscow: Izdatel, 795–832.

—— G. (1978) *Theory of the Novel* (trans. Bostock), London: Merlin, 1978.

Luria, A.R. (1973) *The Working Brain* (trans. B. Haigh), Harmondsworth: Penguin.

—— (1977) 'The Contribution of Linguistics to the Theory of Aphasia', in D. Armstrong and C.H. van Schooneveld (eds) *Roman Jakobson: Echoes of His Scholarship*, Lisse: Peter de Ridder Press, 237–52.

McAlister, L. (1982) *The Development of Franz Brentano's Ethics*, Amsterdam: Rodopi.

Macnamara, J. and Boudewijnse, G.-J. (1995) 'Brentano's Influence on Ehrenfels's Theory of Perceptual Gestalts', *Journal of the Theory of Social Behaviour* 24 (4), 401–18.

Marty, A. (1908) *Untersuchungen zur Grundlegung der allgemeinen Grammatik und Sprachphilosophie, Vol. 1*, Halle: Max Niemeyer.

Matejka, L. (1996) 'Deconstructing Bakhtin', in C. Mihailescu and W. Hamarneh (eds) *Fiction Updated: Theories of Fictionality, Narratology, and Poetics*, Toronto and Buffalo: University of Toronto Press, 257–266.

Matlaw, R. (ed.) (1962) *Belinsky, Chernyshevsky and Dobrolyubov: Selected Criticism*, New York: Dutton.

Medvedev, Iu.P. (1998) 'Na puti k sozdaniiu sotsiologicheskoi poetiki', *Dialog Karnaval Khronotop* 2, 5–57.

Merleau-Ponty, M. (1962) *Phenomenology of Perception* (trans. C. Smith), London: Routledge.

Mihailovic, A. (1997) *Corporeal Words: Mikhail Bakhtin's Theology of Discourse*, Evanston: Northwestern University Press.

Mikheeva, L. (1978) *Pamiati I.I. Sollertinskogo*, Leningrad: Sovetskii kompozitor.

Misch, G. (1950) *A History of Autobiography in Antiquity* (2 vols, trans. E.W. Dickes), London: Routledge and Kegan Paul.

Moretti, F. (1987) *The Way of the World: The Bildungsroman in European Culture*, London: Verso.

—— (1996) *Modern Epic: The World-System from Goethe to García Márquez*, London: Verso.

Morson, G.S. and Emerson, C. (1990) *Mikhail Bakhtin: Creation of a Prosaics*, Stanford: Stanford University Press.*

Morson, G.S. and Emerson, C. (eds) (1989) *Rethinking Bakhtin: Extensions and Challenges*, Evanston: Northwestern University Press.

Moses, S. and Wiedebach, H. (eds) (1997) *Hermann Cohen's Philosophy of Religion*, Hildesheim: George Olms.

Moss, K. (1984) 'Olga Mikhailovna Freidenberg: Soviet Mythologist in a Soviet Context' (unpublished PhD dissertation, Cornell University).

—— (1994) 'Byla li Ol'ga Freidenburg marristkoi?', *Voprosy iazykoznaniia* 5, 1994, 98–106.

—— (1997) 'Introduction', in Olga Freidenberg, *Image and Concept: Mythopoetic Roots of Literature*, Amsterdam: Harwood Academic Publishers, 1–29.

Motzkin, G. (1989) 'Emil Lask and the Crisis of Neo-Kantianism: the Rediscovery of the Primordial World', *Revue de Métaphysique et de Morale* 94 (2), 171–90.

Munk, R. (1997) 'The Self and the Other in Cohen's Ethics and Works on Religion', in S. Moses and H. Wiedebach (eds) (1997) 161–81.

Muratov, A.B. (1996) *Fenomenologicheskaia estetika nachala XX veka i teoriia slovesnosti (B.M. Engel'gardt)*, St Petersburg: Izd. S-Peterburgskogo universiteta.

Murphy, G. and Kovach, J.K. (1994) *Historical Introduction to Modern Psychology*, Henley on Thames: Routledge and Kegan Paul.

Natorp, P. (1903) *Platos Ideenlehre: eine Einführung in den Idealismus*, Leipzig: Dürr'schen.

—— (1908) *Religion innerhalb der Grenzen der Humanität*, Tubingen: Mohr.

—— (1974) *Sozialpädagogik: Theorie der Willenserziehung auf der Grundlage der Gemeins*, Paderborn: Ferdinand Schöningh.

—— (1995) 'Sotsial'nyi idealizm' (trans. M.I. Kagan), *Dialog Karnaval Khronotop* 1, 55–126.

Neisser, U. (1976) *Cognition and Reality: Principles and Implications of Cognitive Psychology*, New York: W.H. Freeman.

Neroznak, V.P. (ed.) (2001) *Sumerki lingvistiki: Iz istorii otchestvennogo iazykoznaniia*, Moscow: Academia.

Nikolaev, N.I. (1997) 'Sud´ba idei Tret´ego Vozrozhdeniia', *MOYSEION: Professoru Aleksandru Iosifovichu Zaitsevu ko dniu semidesiatiletiia*, St Petersburg, 343–50.

Noppeney, U. and Wallesch, C.-W. (2000) 'Language and Cognition: Kurt Goldstein's Theory of Semantics', *Brain and Cognition* 44, 367–86.

Norrie, A.W. (1991) *Law, Ideology, and Punishment: Retrieval and Critique of the Liberal Ideal of Criminal Justice*, Dordrecht and London: Kluwer.

—— (2000) *Punishment, Responsibility, and Justice: A Relational Critique*, Oxford: Oxford University Press.

Oakes, G. (1980) 'Introduction', in Georg Simmel, *Essays on Interpretation in Social Science* (trans. Oakes), Manchester: Manchester University Press, 3–94.

Odesskii, M.P. (1988) 'K voprosu o literaturovedcheskom metode L. Shpitsera', in V.V. Kuskova and L.V. Zlatoustova (eds) *Teoriia i praktika v literaturovedcheskikh i literaturovedcheskikh issledovanii*, Moscow: MGU, 54–60.

Orr, J. and Iordan, I. (1970) *An Introduction to Romance Linguistics: Its Schools and Scholars*, Oxford: Blackwell.

Osovskii, O.E. (2000) '"Iz sovetskikh rabot bol´shuiu tsennost´ imeet kniga O. Freidenberg": Bakhtinskie marginalii na stranitsakh *Poetiki siuzheta i zhanra*', in V.L. Makhlin (ed.) *Bakhtinskii sbornik IV*, Saransk: MGPI, 128–34.

Pan´kov, N. '"Everything else depends on how this business turns out …": Mikhail Bakhtin's Dissertation Defence as Real Event, as High Drama and as Academic Comedy', in K. Hirschkop and D. Shepherd (eds) (2001), 26–61.

Parrott, R. (1984) '(Re)Capitulation, Parody, or Polemic?', in B.A. Stolz et al. (eds) *Language and Literary Theory*, Michigan: Ann Arbor, 463–88.

Pashukanis, E. (1980) 'The General Theory of Law and Marxism', in *Selected Works on Marxism and Law*, London: Academic Press, 40–131.

Perlina, N. (1988) 'A Dialogue on the Dialogue: The Baxtin-Vinogradov Exchange (1924–65)', *Slavic and East European Journal* 32, 526–41.

—— (1989) 'Funny Things Are Happening on the Way to the Bakhtin Forum', *Kennan Institute Occasional Papers* 231, 3–27.

—— (1991) 'Ol´ga Freidenberg on Myth, Folklore, and Literature', *Slavic Review* 50 (2), 371–84.

Petitot, J. et al. (eds) (1999) *Naturalizing Phenomenology: Issues in Contemporary Phenomenology and Cognitive Science*, Stanford: Stanford University Press.

Peursen, C.A. van, (1977) 'The Horizon', in F.A. Elliston and P. McCormick (eds) *Husserl: Expositions and Appraisals*, Notre Dame and London: University of Notre Dame Press.

Poleva, N.S. (2000) 'Vnutrenniaia forma khudozhestvennogo proizvedeniia kak predmet nauchnogo issledovaniia', in T.D. Martsinkovskaia (ed.) *Gustav Gustavovich Shpet: Arkhivnye materialy, vospominaniia, stat´i*, Moscow: Smysl, 304–19.

Poma, A. (1997a) *The Critical Philosophy of Hermann Cohen*, Albany: State University of New York Press.*

―― (1997b) 'Humour in Religion: Peace and Contentment', in S. Moses and H. Wiedebach (eds) (1997), 183–204.

Poole, B. (1995) 'Nazad k Kaganu', in *Dialog Karnaval Khronotop* 1, 38–48.

―― (1998) 'Bakhtin and Cassirer: The Philosophical Origins of Bakhtin's Carnival Messianism', *South Atlantic Quarterly* 97(3/4), 537–78.

―― (2001a) 'Objective Narrative Theory: The Influence of Spielhagen's "Aristotelian" Theory of "Narrative Objectivity" on Bakhtin's Study of Dostoevsky', in J. Bruhn and J. Lundquist (eds) *The Novelness of Bakhtin: Perspectives and Possibilities*, Copengagen: Museum Tusculanum Press.

―― (2001b) 'From Phenomenology to Dialogue: Max Scheler's Phenomenological Tradition and Mikhail Bakhtin's Development from *Towards a Philosophy of the Act* to his Study of Dostoevsky', in K. Hirschkop and D. Shepherd (eds) (2001), 109–35.

Raeff, M. (1966) *Origins of the Russian Intelligentsia: The Eighteenth-Century Nobility*, New York and London: Harcourt Brace.

Reinach, A. (1969) 'Concerning Phenomenology' (trans. D. Willard), *The Personalist* 50(2), 194–221.

―― (1983) 'The A Priori Foundations of Civil Law' (trans. J.F. Crosby), *Aletheia* 3, 1–142.

Rose, G. (1981) *Hegel Contra Sociology*, London: Athlone.

―― (1984) *Dialectic of Nihilism: Post-Structuralism and Law*, Oxford: Blackwell.

―― (1993) *Judaism and Modernity*, Oxford: Blackwell.*

Roy, J.-M. et al. (2000) 'Beyond the Gap: An Introduction to Naturalizing Phenomenology', in J. Petitot et al. (eds) (1999) 1–82.

Rozental´, D.E. and Telenkova, M.A. (1972) *Spravochnik lingvisticheskikh terminov*, Moscow: Prosveshchenie.

Ruben, D.-H. (1979) *Marxism and Materialism: a Study in Marxist Theory of Knowledge*, Brighton: Harvester Press.

Rubenstein, S. (1944) 'Soviet Psychology in Wartime', *Philosophy and Phenomenological Research* 5(2), 181–198.

Rudova, L. (1996) 'Bergsonism in Russia: The Case of Bakhtin', *Neophilologus* 80, 175–88.

Saltzman, J.D. (1981) *Paul Natorp's Philosophy of Religion Within the Marburg Neo-Kantian Tradition*, New York: Georg Olms Verlag Hildesheim.*

Scheerer, E. (1980) 'Gestalt psychology in the Soviet Union: (I) The period of enthusiasm', *Psychological Research* 41 (2-sup-3), 113–32.

Scheler, M. (1954) *The Nature of Sympathy* (trans. Peter Heath), London: Routledge and Kegan Paul.

―― (1973) *Formalism in Ethics and Non-formal Ethics of Values: A new Attempt Toward the Foundation of an Ethical Personalism* (trans. Manfred S. Frings and Roger L. Funk), Evanston: Northwestern University Press.

Schlipp, P.A. (ed.) (1949) *The Philosophy of Ernst Cassirer*, Evanston: Library of Living Philosophers.

Schlosser, E. (2001) *Fast Food Nation: What the All-American Meal is Doing to the World*, London: Penguin.

Schnädelbach, H. (1984) *Philosophy in Germany 1831–1933* (trans. E. Matthews), Cambridge: Cambridge University Press.

Schuhmann, K. and Smith, B. (1985) 'Against Idealism: Johannes Daubert vs. Husserl's *Ideas I*', *Review of Metaphysics* 39, 768–93.

—— (1993) 'Two Idealisms: Lask and Husserl', *Kant-Studien* 83, 448–66

Schutz, A. (1971) 'Language, Language Disturbances, and the Texture of Consciousness', in *Collected Papers, Vol. 1*, The Hague: Nijhoff, 260–86.

Searle, J.R. (1969) *Speech Acts: An Essay in the Philosophy of Language*, Cambridge: Cambridge University Press.

Shanon, B. (1993) *The Representational and the Presentational: An Essay on Cognition and the Study of Mind*, New York: Harvester Wheatsheaf.

Shepherd, D. (ed.) (1993) *Bakhtin: Carnival and Other Subjects*, Amsterdam: Rodopi.

—— (1996) '"Communicating with Other World": Contrasting Views of Carnival in Recent Russian and Western Work on Bakhtin', *Bakhtin Newsletter* 5 (special issue *Bakhtin Around the World*, ed. S. Lee and C. Thomson), 143–60.

—— (ed.) (1998) *The Contexts of Bakhtin*, Amsterdam: Harwood Academic Press.

Shor, R.O. (2001) 'Krizis sovremennoi lingvistiki', in V.P. Neroznak (ed.) (2001), 41–65.

Shpet, G. (1989) 'Vvedenie v etnicheskuiu psikhologiiu', in *Sochineniia*, Moscow: Pravda, 475–574.

—— (1991) *Appearance and Sense: Phenomenology as the Fundamental Science and its Problems* (trans. Thomas Nemeth), Dordrecht, Boston and London: Kluwer Academic Publishers.

—— (1996) *Vnutrenniaia forma slova*, in *Psikhologiia sotsialnogo bytiia*, Moscow-Voronezh: Institut prakticheskoi psikhologii, 49–260.

Simmel, G. (1971) 'The Transcendent Character of Life', in G. Simmel, *On Individuality and Social Forms* (ed. D.N. Levine), Chicago and London: University of Chicago Press, 353–74.

—— (1997) 'The Concept and Tragedy of Culture', in D. Frisby and M. Featherstone (eds), *Simmel on Culture*, London: Sage, 55–75.

Skorik, N.Ja. (1952) 'Teoriia stadial´nosti i inkorporatsiia v paleoaziatskikh iazykakh', *Protiv* 2, 136–56.

Slezkine, Y. (1991) 'The Fall of Soviet Ethnography, 1928–38', *Current Anthropology* 32(4), 476–84.

—— (1996) 'N. Ia. Marr and the National Origins of Soviet Ethnogenics', *Slavic Review* 55(4), 826–62.

Smith, B. (ed) (1988) *Foundations of Gestalt Theory*, Munich: Philosophia.*

—— (1990) 'Towards a History of Speech Act Theory', in A. Burckhardt (ed.) *Speech Acts, Meaning and Intentions: Critical Approaches to the Philosophy of John R. Searle*, Berlin and New York: de Gruyter, 29–61.

—— (1995) 'The Structures of the Common-Sense World', *Acta Philosophica Fennica* 58, 290–317.

—— (1996) 'Pleasure and its Modifications: Stephan Witasek and the Aesthetics of the Grazer Schule', *Axiomathes* 7(1–2), 203–32.

—— (1999) 'Truth and the Visual Field', in J. Petitot et al. (eds) (1999), 317–29.

Smith, B and Smith, D.W. (1995) *The Cambridge Companion to Husserl*, Cambridge: Cambridge University Press.*

Sorlin, I. (1990) 'Aux Origines de l'étude typologique et historique du folklore: L'institut de linguistique de N. Ja. Marr et le jeune Propp', *Cahiers du Monde Russe et Soviétique* 31(2–3), 275–84.

Spengler, O. (1980) *The Decline of the West* (trans. C.F. Atkinson), London: Allen and Unwin.

Spiegelberg, H. (1982) *The Phenomenological Movement: a Historical Introduction* (third edition), The Hague and London: Nijhoff.

Spielhagen, F. (1883) *Beiträge*, Leipzig: L. Staackmann.

—— (1898) *Neue Beiträge zur Theorie und Technik der Epik und Dramatik*, Leipzig: L. Staackmann.

Spitzer, L. (1922) *Italianische Umgangssprache*, Bonn and Leipzig: Kurt Schroeder.

—— (1948) *Linguistics and Literary History: Essays in Stylistics*, Princeton: Princeton University Press.

Stallybrass, P. and White, A. (1986) *The Politics and Poetics of Transgression*, London: Methuen.

Stam, R. (1989) *Subversive Pleasures: Bakhtin, Cultural Criticism, and Film*, Baltimore and London: Johns Hopkins University Press.

Stikkers, K. (1980) 'Introduction', in Max Scheler, *Problems of a Sociology of Knowledge* (trans. M. Frings), London: Routledge and Kegan Paul, 1–30.

Stucchi, N. (1996) 'Seeing and Thinking: Vittorio Benussi and the Graz School', *Axiomathes* 7(1–2), 137–72.

Talmy, L. (1999) 'The Windowing of Attention in Language', in M. Shibatani and S.A. Thompson (eds) (1999) *Grammatical Constructions: Their Form and Meaning*, Oxford: Oxford University Press, 235–87.

Terras, V. (1974) *Belinskij and Russian Literary Criticism: The Heritage of Organic Aesthetics*, Madison: University of Wisconsin Press.

Thomas, L.L. (1957) *The Linguistic Theories of N. Ja. Marr*, Berkeley: University of California Press.

Tihanov, G. (1997) 'Reification and Dialogue: Aspects of the Theory of Culture and Society in Bakhtin and Lukács', in Miha Javorkin et al. (eds), *Bakhtin and the Humanities*, Ljubljana: University of Ljubljana, 73–93.

—— (1998a) 'Voloshinov, Ideology and Language: The Birth of Marxist Sociology from the Spirit of *Lebensphilosophie*', *South Atlantic Quarterly* 97(3/4), 599–621.

—— (1998b) 'The Ideology of *Bildung*: Lukács and Bakhtin as Readers of Goethe', in *Oxford German Studies* 27, 102–40.

—— (1999) 'Bakhtin's Essays on the Novel (1935–41): A Study of their Intellectual Background and Innovativeness', in *Dialogism* 1, 30–56.

—— (2000a), 'Culture, Form, Life: the Early Lukács and the Early Bakhtin', in C. Brandist and G. Tihanov (eds) (2000), 43–69.

—— (2000b) *The Master and the Slave: Lukács, Bakhtin and the Ideas of their Time*, Oxford: Oxford University Press.*

—— (2000c) 'Cultural Emancipation and the Novelistic: Trubetskoy, Savitsky, Bakhtin', *Bucknell Review* 43(2), 47–67.

—— (2001) 'Bakhtin, Joyce and Carnival: Towards the Synthesis of Epic and Novel in Rabelais', *Paragraph* 24(1), 66–83.

Todorov, T. (1984) *Mikhail Bakhtin: the Dialogical Principle* (trans. Wlad Godzich), Minneapolis: University of Minnesota Press.

Toporkov, A.L. (1997) *Teoriia mifa v russkoi filologicheskoi nauke XIX veka*, Moscow: Inarik.

Ukhtomskii, A.A. (2000) 'O khronotope', in *Dominanta dushi*, Rybinsk: Rybinskoe podvor´e, 77–80.

Ushakov, D.N. (2001) 'Kratkii ocherk deiatel´nosti lingvisticheskoi sektsii nauchno-issledovatel´skogo instituta iazyka i literatury', in V.P. Neroznak (ed.) (2001) 71–7.

Val´tsel´, O. (1922) *Impressionizm i ekspressionizm v sovremennoi Germanii (1890–1920)* (trans. Kotelnikov), St Petersburg: Academia.

—— (1923) *Problema formy v poezii* (trans. M.L. Gurfinkel´), St Petersburg: Academia.

—— (1928a) 'Sushchnost´ poeticheskogo proizvedeniia' (trans. M.L. Trotskaia), in V. Zhirmunskii (ed.) *Problemy literaturnoi formy*, Leningrad: Academia, 1–35.

—— (1928b) 'Khudozhestvennaia forma v proizvedeniiakh Gete i nemetskikh romantikov' (trans. M.L. Trotskaia), in V. Zhirmunskii (ed.) *Problemy literaturnoi formy*, Leningrad: Academia, 105–134.

van der Veer, R. and Valsiner, J. (1991) *Understanding Vygotsky: A Quest for Synthesis*, Oxford: Blackwell.

Varela, F.J. et al. (1996) *The Embodied Mind: Cognitive Science and Human Experience*, Cambridge, Mass.: MIT Press.

Vasil´ev, N.L. (1995) 'V.N. Voloshinov: biograficheskii ocherk', in FSGN 5–22.

—— (1998) 'K istorii knigi *Marksizm i filosofiia iazyka*', in T 530–41.

Venturi, F. (1960) *Roots of Revolution: Populist and Socialist Movements in Nineteenth-Century Russia* (trans. F. Haskell), Chicago: University of Chicago Press.

Veselovskii, A.N. (1939) 'Istoriia ili teoriia romana?', *Izbrannye stat´i*, Leningrad: Khudozhestvennaia literatura.

—— (1940) *Istoricheskaia poetika*, Leningrad: Khudozhestvennaia literatura.

Vinogradov, V.V. (1951) 'Nasushchnye zadachi sovetskogo literaturovedeniia', in *Voprosy literaturovedeniia v svete trudov I.V. Stalina po iazykoznaniiu*, Moscow: Izd. Akademii nauk SSSR.

—— (1959) *O iazyke khudozhestvennoi literatury*, Moscow: GIKhL.

Vossler, K. (1932) *The Spirit of Language in Civilization* (trans. O. Oester), London: Kegan Paul.

Vygotsky, L.S. (1997) 'Consciousness as a Problem for the Psychology of Behavior', in *Collected Works, Vol. 3* (trans. van der Veer), New York and London: Plenum Press, 63–81.

Walicki, A. (1969) *The Controversy over Capitalism: Studies in the Social Philosophy of the Russian Populists*, Oxford: Oxford University Press.

Walzel, O. (1926) *Das Wortkunstwerk: Mittel seiner Erforschung*, Leipzig: Quelle and Meyer. (See also Val´tsel´)

Wildgen, W. (2001) 'Kurt Lewin and the Rise of "Cognitive Sciences" in Germany: Cassirer, Bühler, Reichenbach', in L. Albertazzi (ed.) (2001), 299–332.

Willey, T. (1978) *Back to Kant: The Revival of Kantianism in German Social and Historical Thought, 1860–1914*, Detroit: Wayne State University Press.*

Windholz, G. (1984) 'Pavlov and the demise of the influence of Gestalt psychology in the Soviet Union', *Psychological Research* 46(3), 187–206.

Witasek, S. (1904) *Grundzüge der allgemeinen Ästhetik*, Leipzig: Barth.

Wittgenstein, L. (1997) *Philosophical Investigations*, Oxford: Blackwell.

Worringer, W. (1953) *Abstraction and Empathy: a Contribution to the Psychology of Style* (trans. Michael Bullock), London: Routledge.

Wundt, W. (1907–8) *Ethics* (3 vols, trans. M.F. Washburn), London: Swan Sonnenschein.

Zelinskii, F.F. (1995) *Iz zhizni idei*, Moscow: Ladomir.

Zhirmunskii, V.M. (1927) 'Noveishie techeniia istoriko-literaturnoi mysli v Germanii', *Poetika: Sbornik statei*, Leningrad: Academia, 5–28.

—— (ed.) (1928) *Problemy literaturnoi formy: sbornik statei*, Leningrad: Academia.

Zvegintsev, V.A. (1960) *Istoriia iazykoznaniia XIX i XX vekov v ocherkakh i izvlecheniiakh* (2 vols), Moscow: Gos. uchebno-pedagogicheskoe izd.

Zweigert, K. and Kötz, H. (1987) *Introduction to Comparative Law* (trans. T. Weir), Oxford: Clarendon Press.

Index

DATE DUE